SO-CEW-530

BELOIT COLLEGE LIBRARIES

Purchased with funds provided
under Title II, of The Higher
Educational Act of 1965

Presidential Responsiveness and Public Policy-making

Presidential Responsiveness and Public Policy-making

The Public and the Policies That Presidents Choose

Jeffrey E. Cohen

Ann Arbor
THE UNIVERSITY OF MICHIGAN PRESS

Copyright © by the University of Michigan 1997
All rights reserved
Published in the United States of America by
The University of Michigan Press
Manufactured in the United States of America
⊗ Printed on acid-free paper

2000   1999   1998   1997   4   3   2   1

No part of this publication may be reproduced, stored in a retrieval system, or transmitted in any form or by any means, electronic, mechanical, or otherwise, without the written permission of the publisher.

A CIP catalog record for this book is available from the British Library

Library of Congress Cataloging-in-Publication Data

Cohen, Jeffrey E.
    Presidential responsiveness and public policy-making : the public
and the policies that presidents choose / Jeffrey E. Cohen.
        p.   cm.
    Includes bibliographical references (p.) and index.
    ISBN 0-472-10812-3 (acid-free paper)
    1. Presidents—United States.   2. Political leadership—United
States.   3. Political planning—United States.   4. Public opinion—
United States.   I. Title.
JK516.C53   1997
324.6'3'0973—dc21   97-4690
                                                                    CIP

To George Grassmuck and the late Barbara Hinckley

Contents

Figures

Tables

Acknowledgments

I have incurred a large number of debts in writing this book. First, I want to thank several friends and colleagues who read major portions of the manuscript in its various stages of development. Because of their good thoughts they probably won't be able to recognize the manuscript that they read in this book. Elaine Sharpe, a colleague of mine at the University of Kansas, read most of the manuscript and made many helpful comments. Paul Quirk, University of Illinois, read the entire manuscript, again posing important issues to me. My department chair, Ron Francisco, provided a wonderful work atmosphere and much cheerleading and encouragement.

The reviewers associated with the University of Michigan Press also deserve some thanks. Paul Brace, of Rice University, went above and beyond the call of reviewer duty in his helpfulness, meticulousness, and overall encouragement. I also owe the staff at the University of Michigan Press. Malcolm Litchfield initiated Michigan's interest in my book. When he left to go to Princeton University Press, in the middle of the reviewing process, my heart sank. But his successor, Charles Myers, ably picked up where Malcolm left off and saw the book through to its publication. Both deserve more than I can say here.

Also, I want to acknowledge the *American Journal of Political Science,* which is published by the University of Wisconsin Press, for allowing me to use some material that appeared in my article published in that journal, "Presidential Rhetoric and the Public Agenda," 39 (February): 87–107.

Many others, too many to mention, have heard me talk about this project and provided words of advice and useful comments. They include especially David Nice of Washington State University, Bryan Jones of the University of Washington, and Jim Kuklinski of the University of Illinois. They probably don't know how helpful they have been.

This book is dedicated to two political scientists who have profoundly affected me, my career, and my research: George Grassmuck and Barbara Hinckley. George offered me much support while I did my graduate work at Michigan, too many years ago now to recall. He is totally generous in spirit and a whole generation of presidency scholars were nurtured under his wing at Michigan. I hope that I can thank him for all of us, too. Barbara's work greatly inspired mine, and her passing has left a void, not only among presidency scholars but in the political science community in general. Through no obligation other than collegiality, she made herself and her time available to me when I was then a green assistant professor. She provided me with a model of how senior people should behave. I thank both George and Barbara. I am richer for knowing both of them.

Introduction

Modern presidents face not only high but contradictory expectations. The contradiction between providing active policy leadership for the mass public while also being responsive to its policy preferences strikes at the core of the modern presidency. This book is about how presidents manage these conflicting expectations. Can presidents satisfactorily lead but also follow? Can they be both in front of the public on policy matters while also being responsive to or following it on policy issues? Can presidents do both simultaneously? If they can't, under what conditions will presidents act as leaders, offering policies to deal with pressing problems, and under what conditions will they follow public dictates and merely attempt to implement the public's wishes about public policies? What cost do these contradictory expectations have on the office, the governability of the nation, the linkage between the people and the president, and public attitudes about government in the United States?

In the pages to follow I detail the nature of this contradiction. I will argue that though presidents want the freedom to lead as they see fit, especially to carry out their program and preferred policies, their need for public support constrains them. Presidents must show some level of responsiveness to the public to garner the support necessary to get their policies implemented.

The dual expectation for presidential policy leadership and responsiveness provides often contradictory incentives and constraints on the president. The fact that the public may withdraw its support for the president, either expressed in public opinion surveys and/or the voting booth, leads presidents to consider public opinion. Furthermore, as responsiveness to the public may enable presidents to better mobilize public support for other political uses, such as persuading members of Congress to accept their policy directions, presidents have a reason, an incentive, to be responsive to public opinion. This punishment/reward relationship may condition presidential behavior to *at least consider* the public when developing policy.

But the leadership expectation pulls the president in an opposite direction. To lead the public, he must stake a position and attempt to move the public in the direction that he wants to head. To provide policy leadership, presidents cannot wait for public opinion to form. In some instances, it may not form beyond the level of complaint and concern.

Moreover, the public holds the president responsible for the policies that he implemented. Effective policies once implemented have a way of building public support for the president. Although responsiveness to the public may build short-term public support, that support may erode quite quickly if the policies that result from that responsiveness are ineffective or defective. And the public will rarely blame itself for ill-conceived policies. Thus, the president has a strong incentive to produce policies that will prove effective, not only to help shape the character of government and the nation as he desires, but also to lay a foundation for public support into the future. And this future support is likely to be more stable than short-term support generated through responsiveness because it is built on the actual performance of public policies. From this, a president's reputation as a leader will emerge; such reputations are quite resistant to revision.

To ensure such effective policies, presidents aim to control the policy-making process, from the determination of agenda priorities to the substance of the policies to the implementation process. This control need undercuts any responsiveness tendency, except when the public and the president find themselves in agreement. Such agreement is not always present, which leads the president to manufacture agreement by mobilizing the public behind his alternatives—an act of leadership, not responsiveness.

Thus, the president is presented with a classic quandary. He must be responsive to the public. This is something that the public expects, but it also has short-term benefits in terms of public support. But the president is also expected to lead, and other factors, like long-term support and the quality of public policy, drive the president to control the policy-making process. This naturally creates a barrier to short-term responsiveness to the public.

This book is about how presidents manage these contradictory expectations. My basic argument, which flows from the calculations of costs and benefits associated with both responsiveness and leadership, is that presidents will be responsive when such behavior does not constrain their ability to control the policy-making process. Primarily, presidents will demonstrate their responsiveness symbolically. Political symbolism is found in all actions and decisions, but the mix of symbolism and substance varies. The more heavily that mix leans toward pure symbolism, the more responsive the president is expected to be.

Once policy decisions turn more substantive, the benefits to be derived from leadership and policy control enter into the president's calculus. Responsiveness pressures and incentives are still present, but the costs of responsiveness are also now felt. Consequently, the degree of presidential responsiveness to public opinion declines from that witnessed for actions and decisions that are mostly symbolic and relatively void of substantive implication.

The Plan of the Book

The first chapter details the argument just presented. It considers the growth of responsiveness pressures; reviews the literature on presidential responsiveness, which is quite limited; and offers reasons why high levels of presidential responsiveness to the public in the policy-making process are not to be expected.

The next six chapters (2 through 7) provide an empirical examination. These chapters are built around the stages of the policy process, from agenda setting to policy legitimation. The model outlined in the previous section hypothesizes a rhythm to presidential responsiveness, with greater levels of responsiveness when presidential actions and decisions are symbolic as opposed to substantive.

To make this empirical assessment, I develop quantitative indicators of four presidential policy activities. The four indicators are problem identification in agenda setting, position taking in agenda setting, policy formulation, and position taking on roll calls before Congress. These data are collected for the Eisenhower through Bush (1989) years. I also present a series of case studies to provide context, nuance, and richness to the otherwise stark quantitative assessments. The integration of the various types of evidence hopefully strengthens the argument and bridges the gap between the abstraction of quantification and the reality of actual cases.

Chapter 2 looks at presidential problem identification, a mostly symbolic policy activity. Chapter 3 discusses the substantive content of presidential rhetoric about policy areas. Chapters 4 and 5 look at presidential policy formulation. In particular, I develop an indicator called presidential policy liberalism and assess how responsive the president is to public opinion. The several indicators vary in their symbolic-substantive mix. In chapter 6 I create and assess a parallel indicator for roll calls, presidential roll call liberalism. Chapters 7 and 8 change the level of analysis, presenting eight case studies of important presidential decisions. Chapter 9 provides a summary of the findings and puts them into a broader perspective. In that chapter I address the question, What are the implications of substantive policy nonresponsiveness for the most majoritarian, and most important, institution of the modern American polity?

CHAPTER 1

Public Expectations of the President and Presidential Policy-making Behavior

Americans have high expectations of their presidents. Although true, this observation is based more on impressionistic evidence than empirical observation (but see Edwards 1983; Herzik and Dodson 1982; Wayne 1982). We do not know very much about the content of these expectations and whether they change over time. Nor do we know if all Americans hold each expectation or if the "expectation set" varies across individuals.[1] And we only possess a vague notion of how these expectations are set.

Several generalizations about expectations are nevertheless possible. Most scholarship asserts that public expectations of the president are demanding for both personal behavior and policy performance. Policy performance is especially critical for the long-run public evaluation of the administration, in that the public assigns policy responsibility to the president and holds him accountable for policy performance. Thus, if a president's policies do not work or if they produce more harm than good, the president will become the focus of public blame. Meeting this expectation, then, becomes a paramount goal of presidents.

Contradictory Expectations: Leadership and Followership

Not only are public expectations of the president demanding, they are also contradictory. Just as the public expects the president to lead, it also expects presidents to be responsive to the public. Edwards states the problem quite well:

> We expect the president to be a leader, an independent figure who speaks out and takes stands on the issues even if his views are unpopular. . . . In sharp contrast to our expectations for presidential leadership is our expectation that the chief executive be responsive to public opinion and that he be constrained by majority rule as represented in Congress. . . . The contradictory expectations of leadership versus responsiveness place the

president in a no-win situation. If he attempts to lead, he may be criticized for losing contact with his constituents and being unrepresentative. Conversely, if he tries to reflect the views of the populace, he may be reproached for failing to lead and for not solving the country's problems. (1983, 196–97)

Cronin makes a similar point in his discussion of presidential paradoxes.

> we expect our presidents to provide bold, innovative leadership and at the same time respond faithfully to public opinion majorities. . . . Put simply, we want our presidents to offer leadership, to be architects of the future and providers of visions, plans, and goals, and at the same time we want them to stay in close touch with the sentiments of the people. . . . Presidents can get caught whether they are coming or going. We want them to be both *leaders* of the country and *representatives* of the people. We want them to be decisive and rely mainly on their own judgement; yet we want them to be responsive to public opinion, especially to the "common sense" of our own opinion. (1980, 8–9)

Rockman (1984) also notices this problem but stresses the costs of leadership when responsiveness is absent. As he writes,

> we need to accept that leadership, while a critical element of governing, is but one side of the constitutional equation. For every request for leadership and direction, there is, after all, implicitly a request not to be led. While we want government to promote effective responses to problems, we also want it to be responsive to our concerns. (1984, 4; also see 29–31)

This conflict between responsiveness and leadership is rooted, in part, in the design of the institution. The presidency has a dual nature. On the one hand, it is the institution that was given the responsibility for carrying out the nation's policies. This is evident in the Constitution, which states that the "executive Power shall be vested in a President" (Article II, Section 1) and that "he shall take Care that the Laws be faithfully executed" (Article II, Section 4). But the presidency also has a public nature.

Its single occupancy, its visibility, and the electoral and political process by which people become president embed the office in public and popular politics. This public side of the office, in which public pressures for responsiveness bear on the occupant, have intensified over the years. The democratization of the nomination and election process, the development of communications systems that directly link the president to the mass public, and the rise of public opinion polling are several reasons for the increase in public pressure that the president be responsive.

At the same time, however, the policy responsibility of the presidency has also grown. Government is bigger, and the president plays a more active part in directing the nation's policies, from the halls of Congress in the legislative process to the rooms of the bureaucracy in the implementation process. Pressures to respond but also to provide policy leadership have grown with the development of the presidency into the office we now recognize. The tension between leading the public versus following it has consequently deepened.

This conflict between leadership and responsiveness creates a major problem for the president. To carry out those policies that will meet the performance test, presidents seek to control all aspects of the policy-making process, from the timing of initiatives to their content to the agency assigned to execute them. Only by controlling the flow of the policy-making process can presidents ensure that their policies will work as intended and that the several policies that comprise the president's program will not work at cross-purposes. Too much responsiveness may undermine this presidential objective.

But to hold such sway over the policy process requires presidential influence and power. In the modern age, public prestige and popularity are among the most important resources that a president can possess if he wants to influence the policy-making process (Kernell 1993). Thus, the president's problem is that to lead he needs public support, but to get that public support he must produce effective policies that address the major concerns of the public. This creates a vicious cycle for the president.

Being responsive to the public enables the president to reap the public reward for his policy achievements. And responsiveness to the public has another payoff. It sets the conditions by which the president can mobilize public support. Only a president who has forged strong ties to the public can rally public support behind his policy alternatives when needed. A president who seems aloof from the public, even if he can construct policy options that promote the public interest, will not be seen as a "man of the people." Consequently, he will not be able to exploit public support when trying to influence the policy-making community. Responsiveness provides an important foundation upon which to build popularity and public prestige. Nonresponsiveness, the arrogance of leadership, the isolation of the president—whatever term one wishes to employ—create a barrier that impedes the president's ability to gather public support when he needs it.

Thus, the elements of responsiveness—public support, leadership and control, and policy effectiveness—are all intertwined and interrelated. The difficulty for the president is that it is not always possible to both lead and follow, to offer policy directions, while also responding to public concerns. The president's success hinges on his ability to maneuver between the calls for responsiveness and leadership.

How do presidents manage these conflicting expectations? Do they cede their policy leadership and blindly follow the public or do they maintain their leadership responsibility? Moreover, what are the political consequences of pursuing either path? These are the questions that I address in this book.

In the next section, I detail the development of public pressures on the president. These pressures push the president in the direction of responsiveness. After my discussion of presidential responsiveness, I discuss the barriers to responsiveness. These barriers are rooted in both the cost of following the public when making public policy and the expectation for policy leadership. Presidential goals other than public support enter the picture here.

From these two discussions, I develop the model suggested in the introduction, that presidential responsiveness is highest when nonsubstantive policy decisions are being made but wanes as policy decisions and actions become more substantive. I discuss this in the context of stages of the policy-making process, which serves as the structure for the analysis that follows. I also review the empirical literature on presidential responsiveness to public opinion. That literature is quite limited and rarely focuses on policy-making activities. Moreover, findings display both responsiveness and resistance to public pressures. Dealing with these disparate findings is another task of this book. The chapter ends with a note on detecting presidential responsiveness to public opinion.

Increasing Public Pressures on the President

The presidency was never meant to be immune to public pressures, but as it has developed it has probably become less resistant to the public than the founders intended. The constitutional design of the office gives us a sense of the early linkage between the president and the public. First, making the executive unitary, rather than plural, has an impact on the presidential-public tie. The public has an easier time focusing on a single executive than a plural one. This also makes it easier for a single executive to gain the attention of the public than could either a plural executive or the legislature. The structural property will always advantage the executive over the legislature in gaining public attention and support.

Second, the election of the president through the electoral college, while now considered an indirect and less populist method of selection than direct election, was a considerable concession to those who argued for direct popular election of the president at the Constitutional Convention in Philadelphia. The other alternative was election by Congress, which would have limited the independence of the executive and undermined the aims of the separations of powers.

Direct election, however, was also considered impractical, given the size of the nation and the difficulty of communication. These factors, it was felt, would undermine the ability of the public to make an informed choice (Slonim 1989). The electoral college became a compromise that preserved the balance that had been struck between the large and small states and the northern and southern states in creating a bicameral legislature. But it also denied the Congress the ability to control the presidency by naming its occupant, and it made the executive office look toward the people as the basis of selection. In this sense, a connection, however tenuous by modern standards, between the president and the public was forged right from the start.

The president was also viewed by many at the Convention as the "guardian" of the people (Slonim 1989, 40), a guardian against legislative tyranny, again a separation-of-powers notion. The "great and wealthy" were thought to be the ones who would populate the legislature. To balance this tendency of an oligarchy from controlling government, a countervailing force was needed from someone who would look toward a larger interest (Slonim 1989, 40–41). Thus, some populist seeds were planted into the foundation of the presidency to help provide this balance.

These "populist" tendencies are observable during the tenure of the first incumbent, George Washington, who also expanded the populist base of the presidency. First, he helped to solidify the constitutional barriers between the executive and the legislature along several fronts, such as treaty negotiation. This forced him to look outward from Congress for support and political resources. Further, he insisted that "constitutional government needed order as well as liberty" (Phelps 1989, 279), directing state militia into the war against the six Indian nations. He took similar actions to subdue the Whiskey Rebellion. These actions helped the independence of the *national* executive, pointing the executive in the direction of being accountable and "responsive to the people of the United States, not to the several states" (Phelps 1989, 279) or the Congress. Lastly, Washington's request for political and policy advice from Chief Justice John Marshall was rebuffed, with Marshall pointing to the separation of powers as the rationale for the rebuff. With the two other branches effectively separated from the presidency, and with a national perspective of the office and its duties, Washington naturally turned to the people.

Washington's need for public support was not for narrow policy goals but to provide a bulwark for the institution. Thus he aimed to lead the public by word and deed, becoming a symbol of the "nation," focusing the young republic's national aspirations and meaning on the chief executive's office. He restrained his personal behavior while in office, stepping down voluntarily after the end of his second term. He rarely entered directly into political fights and debates, leaving his cabinet secretaries, especially Alexander Hamilton, that task. In his farewell address, he famously cautioned against the "mischiefs of faction" that divide the people, reinforcing the national and popular message of the presidency. These actions helped create standards of service to the nation rather than personal aggrandizement, a standard to which all his successors would be judged. By becoming a national symbol, he was forging links between the presidency and the people.

Over time, by design, response to crisis, and technological innovation, the popular ties of the presidency were strengthened. These themes seem so powerful that some have now come to call the office a plebiscitary presidency (Lowi 1985). In the next two sections I detail these developments, giving special attention to electoral and technological reform and change, a well-known story, but one crucial to the argument being offered here.

Election Reforms

Changes in the election process were instrumental in strengthening the link between president and the public. The first important change came with the expansion of the franchise in the 1820s. Votes became the basis of political power, as politicians who could deliver voters on election day replaced the aristocracy of notables that had run the government since the revolutionary period. Political debate and division were no longer an elite affair; the era of good feelings, of one-party dominance was over. New politicians, like Henry Clay, Martin Van Buren, John Calhoun, and especially Andrew Jackson, would use their ability to rouse the mass public to support their positions. Parties, party competition, and political machines all resulted.

This altered the relationship between the president and the mass public. The president was no longer only the symbol of rectitude who led the public by example, as had Washington. The president was now one of the people, and he aimed to use their support to build his party and promote his policies. The public had become a participant in political debate, with the power to determine who would win the debate.

Presidential ties to the public were built around the party apparatus and the political machine. Holding the machine together were the twin pillars of votes and spoils. Presidents and their parties needed votes. Responsiveness pressures on the president increased as a result; patronage was one indication of the growing responsiveness of the office. The democratization of the franchise showed the president that he needed the people.

Still, mediating institutions existed that attenuated these public pressures. Presidents could hide behind their party banners, and nomination was not entirely a public affair. The rise of the Progressives around the turn of the twentieth century hacked away at some of these mediating institutions, helping to more directly link the president and the public. The most important of these changes involved the nomination process.

The primary, an innovation that aborted in the early part of the twentieth century, after spreading quite quickly, became the dominant force of nomination politics in the 1970s. This had important consequences for the president-public relationship in a number of ways. First, the importance of party leaders and organizations to the presidential candidate waned. Those old-line, traditional partisans had little to offer candidates seeking the nomination and the office. The parties could not ensure votes to a favored candidate.

As a consequence, presidential candidates had to construct their own campaign organizations from the ground up, without the long-standing state and local party cells that for so long had structured who won the nomination. Presidential candidates were now left to their own devices to win the nomination, with less aid from party leaders. This process, in turn, nationalized the presidential perspective toward politics. No longer having to build a winning coalition out of diverse and entrenched state and local party organizations, those seeking the presidency would look toward building a national constituency, one that traversed state boundaries. In effect, these new presidential hopefuls were to look even more to national public opinion than the leaders of the party boss age, and they would begin doing so before they assumed office. They would do so in the process of trying to attain the office.

Once in office, and despite the electoral college mechanism that still existed, presidents would be more beholden to the public for their office than ever before. Popularity got them the nomination, and popularity won them the office. Old institutions that had once helped, primarily the party, were moribund.

Election financing reforms introduced in the 1970s reinforced this trend. Acceptance of federal money for the general election prohibited acceptance of private money, rendering the candidate independent of money sources at this stage of the contest. The provisions during the primaries for matching money, with their focus on small donations across many states, reduced the impact of special, moneyed interests on presidential candidates. Few candidates could collect so much private money that they would eschew the matching grants. But matching money was dependent on popularity. This accented the importance of popularity to presidents in this era. The public held the keys not only to votes, but also to money, at least for this highest office.

Changing Technology

The political reforms and changes I just noted were not the only forces tightening the relationship between the president and the public. Changes in the technology of communication and of measuring the public pulse also had a role in increasing public pressures on the president.

The development of mass media was critical. Mass communications were always important to American politics and debate, and as they increased their ability to build a mass audience their importance rose. Throughout the nineteenth century, the press was both mass based and highly partisan. Newspapers and magazines served largely as party organs and through this mediation helped link the president to the mass public.

But it was the development of electronic communications, radio and television primarily, that provided the president with an unmediated avenue to the public. Through these media, the president could speak directly to the public, circumventing the parties and journalists in the process. This tightened the bond between the president and the public, providing the president with a near monopoly in his ability to rally the public (Miroff 1982). No one else had such easy access to these media. The president was usually able to preempt the entertainment fare on the media to give speeches. Some of these even became public occasions, most notably FDR's fireside chats, which set the standard for future electronic communications to the mass public.

But this access to the public did not come without binds onto the president from the mass public. Expectations about presidential responsibility heightened. The public began to look to the president for guidance, comfort, and leadership whenever a problem or crisis arose. Demands that the president speak out on all matters public began to form and mount. This presidential resource also became a presidential burden and responsibility to carry.

Technological innovations for reaching the mass audience have continued to develop. President Clinton has wired the White House into the new channel, the Internet, for instance, a medium even less confining than mass television, where private, but regulated, networks must grant presidential access. Access to the president and from the president to the audience through the Internet and related systems may be more direct and malleable to presidential needs than traditional broadcast television. Moreover, these new technologies hold out the promise of more interactive communications between the president and the public (Arterton 1987). (And the Clinton administration has pursued policies to develop these types of technologies for the future, perhaps looking at the potential political payoff, as well as the hoped for economic benefits that might result.)

Another technological development is equally as profound, the rise of public opinion polling. Early in the polling era, politicians were quite suspicious of this new "science." The embarrassments of the *Literary Digest* magazine poll in 1932, which predicted Landon's victory over FDR, and Truman's unexpected upset over Dewey in 1948 undermined the credibility of these early polls (Erikson and Tedin 1995, 8–11).

But presidential candidates found polls useful for framing their campaigns and providing information about the public. Polls began to be used by presidential candidates in their campaigns in the 1950s and 1960s and helped them structure their election strategies. John Kennedy seems the innovator here (Jacobs and Shapiro 1994, 528).

Moreover, by Kennedy's term pollsters had become a White House fixture. Kennedy relied on pollster Louis Harris, who provided strategic advice on civil rights and foreign policy based on his polling operation (Reeves 1993, 364–65). Johnson was quite well aware of the use of polls and is said to have carried his latest popularity reading around with him in his pocket (Altschuler 1990). Nixon specially commissioned a series of polls during 1971 and 1972, which highlighted to him how the public was responding to his economic policies and may have been important in his decision to impose wage and price controls (see more on this point in chap. 7; also Jacobs and Shapiro 1995a).

Our latest two presidents have also relied heavily upon polls, spending large sums of money on polling operations. Reportedly, Bush spent $216,000 in 1989 and 1990 on pubic opinion polls, while Clinton massively outspent him with nearly $2 million on polls in 1993, the first year of his presidency (Edwards 1995, 234).

Bush was keenly sensitive to poll results, and pollster Robert Teeter was a major adviser. Duffy and Goodgame (1992) argue that often Bush would rely on polls to tell him how to sit on a policy. For instance, he shifted his position on drugs, from one that emphasized reducing demand to one that would strongly crack down on drugs, because polls indicated that the public supported the tougher policy course (p. 104). Generally, Bush thought that he stayed "in touch with the concerns of average Americans . . . because he reads the polls" (Duffy and Goodgame 1992, 225). His reality about Americans and public opinion was constructed on polls, indicating his heavy reliance on them for information on the public, from a person who interacted so seldomly and superficially with average Americans. He was amazed at one point to discover supermarket price scanners, though they had been in operation for years. It would not be surprising to find such a president responding to public opinion, at least as expressed in polls.

Clinton also integrated polls into his policy decision-making apparatus. Stanley Greenberg was his prime pollster. More than mere polls were used in gauging public reactions to Clinton. Greenberg set up a dial meter with some of the viewers of Clinton's economic message of February 1993, where he outlined his economic policy. The meter recorded reactions every two seconds, allowing the administration to appraise how people reacted to particular sentences and phrases. The administration would employ those most popular themes later on when trying to get Congress to pass the program (Woodward 1994, 151–52).

Public opinion polls have become ingrained into the culture of politics in

Washington and around the nation. They are more frequent and are referred to by partisans in almost all policy debates. Most important for the president is that the ups and downs in presidential popularity are followed closely and are used to assess the performance of the president on a continual and seemingly ceaseless basis. Small movements in popularity are tracked, even though they may be a function of sampling and other types of error associated with survey instruments, and thus do not represent true change. In a sense, the polls have become a running barometer of the presidency, almost a running referendum or interelection "election." Knowing that they are used this way heightens presidential sensitivity to poll results and anticipations of public reactions to presidential actions.

Whether by design or accident, taking advantage of technological changes or being swept along by them, public pressure on the president has intensified. This creates incentives for presidents to attend to public opinion, with the concern that the public might withhold its support if the president is viewed as being out of touch with the public. Moreover, as public support has become a singular political resource for the president, lack of public support may have strong implications for the president's bargaining situation with others in Washington as well as his ability to accomplish his policy and political aims. As Clinton pollster Stanley Greenberg admitted, "We need popular support to keep pressure on Congress to vote for change" (Edwards 1995, 235).

The president needs the public, thus the incentive to be responsive to it. Through responsiveness, the president can sell the public the notion that he speaks in the public's interest. This provides the basis or reservoir of potential support that the president can mobilize when he needs an activated and aroused public. If he appears unresponsive to the public, out of touch with it, the foundation for such mobilization might not exist, and his attempts to galvanize the public behind his policies might fail. For short-term instrumental reasons, the president is likely to be responsive to public opinion. But there are barriers to such unbridled responsiveness, a point I will address in the next section.

Barriers to Presidential Responsiveness to Public Opinion

The idea that public pressures on presidents lead them to become responsive to the public is predicated on the assumptions that the public holds a resource important to the president. That resource is public support, which the president wants to acquire so he may convert it into other uses, for instance, moving Congress to support his policies. If responsiveness to the public is one route to the acquisition of public support, then presidents, by this view, will be responsive to public opinion.

But presidential motivations and goals are more complex than this simple public support acquisition model. Presidents have other goals that may conflict, not with the need for public support, but with the responsiveness route to acquiring it. Importantly for my present purposes, presidents are dearly concerned with the conduct of public policy (Light 1982). There are many sources of this alternative goal. Presidents may have a view of the world and aim to shape the nation to conform as closely as possible to that view, using the office of the presidency for that purpose. Similarly, presidential concern with public policy may derive from a goal to make a mark on history, to leave a legacy. With only a short tenure in the national executive allowed because of the two-term limitation, and with no other comparable political office to seek after the presidency, presidents naturally look toward loftier goals, like history and accomplishment.

But presidents may also be concerned with the conduct and performance of public policy because of its implications for public support. Implementing policies that solve problems, that are viewed as successful, that leave the nation better off than it was prior to the president's taking office can build public support behind the president. Policy effectiveness and accomplishment can help build a president's reputation, and such repute can effectively build public support for the president.

This type of public support is likely to be realized in the future or the long term, unlike support that comes from responding to the public, which is realized in the short run. The problem for the president is that short-run responsiveness may undercut the goal of implementing desired policies and may undermine the ability to implement effective policies. Thus, there are costs to responsiveness.

The cost of short-term presidential responsiveness to public opinion is that presidents must cede some control over the substance of public policy to the public. This may mean that the policies that result may be less effective than they could have been had the president controlled their construction. Later I will discuss why this is the case. And less effective policies limit the ability of presidents to build their reputation, which limits the ability to build longer-term public support. Ineffective policies may actually destroy any chance for the president to acquire such long-term support.

Moreover, short-term responsiveness may interfere with the president's other goals, such as implementing his policy vision and securing his historic reputation and legacy. Thus, while short-term benefits may accrue to presidents who are responsive to the public, there are also costs, in terms of potential future public support and control over public policy. The presidential calculus becomes one of weighing the benefits and costs of responsiveness and policy leadership.

As long as responsiveness does not affect the substance of policy-making, presidents are likely to be quite responsive to the public. But once actions become more substantively oriented, the costs of responsiveness and the benefits of policy leadership enter into the president's calculus. We then expect levels of responsiveness to decline.

In the remainder of this section, I discuss the costs of responsiveness and the benefits to be derived from policy leadership. Here policy leadership means that the president chooses a policy direction and attempts to gather public support for that alternative. The expectation for policy leadership and the responsibility that presidents feel for public policy are closely linked. This expectation leads presidents to feel responsible, and this responsibility motivates presidents to take on leadership. First I begin with a review of the development of the policy responsibility expectation.

The Development of Policy Responsibility in the Presidency

The presidency as initially designed was not given much policy responsibility. As conceptualized by the founders, the presidency was to be a clerkship except during times of emergency, like war. Ironically, the acquisition of policy responsibility in the presidency developed hand in hand with the strengthening of ties between the mass public and the president, even though, as I argue, these two expectations are in tension and are often contradictory.

The story of increasing presidential responsibilities for the conduct of public policy is well known, and I will not review it completely here (see Greenstein 1988; Burke 1992; McDonald 1994). The foundation for this expectation is the president's constitutional duty to faithfully execute the laws. From this base, the expectation that the president would be responsible for the conduct of public policy grew. This growth was closely associated with the growth of the national government, a process that began at the turn of the twentieth century (Skowronek 1982). This process accelerated with the New Deal and the administration of Franklin Roosevelt. In part impelled by the crisis of the Great Depression, public eyes began to focus on the presidency, a process that Roosevelt encouraged. Administrative responsibility and capacity centralized in the White House in this process.

But the development of the expectation of policy responsibility is not solely a function of the Roosevelt years, no matter the importance of those years to this development. Policy responsibility was being reposited in the presidency before the Depression, and after the Roosevelt years more policy responsibility accreted to the president. We see an early transfer of such responsibility through the creation of an executive budget in the early 1920s. The president was held responsible for preparing a budget to be submitted to Congress. Staff assistance was provided to the president in this task with the establishment of the Bureau of the Budget (BOB). Other laws would follow that placed policy responsibility on the president. Among the most notable are the Full Employment Act of 1946 and the Full Employment and Balanced Growth Act of 1978, also known as the Humphrey-Hawkins Act. Numerous other examples exist.

Another indication of the growing policy responsibility of the president is the accumulation of staff support to help the president carry out these duties. The creation of the Executive Office of the President (EOP) in 1939 is a landmark in providing the president with staff assistance. Later on, specific policy advisers were attached to this office and the presidency, most notably the Council of Economic Advisers (CEA) and the National Security Adviser.

The process of placing greater and greater policy responsibility on the president can be seen through the development of the Bureau of the Budget, later the Office of Management and Budget (OMB). This agency has turned into a central staff agency for the president, with wide-ranging policy control and coordination responsibilities.

Originally a unit of the Treasury Department, BOB was transferred to EOP, and in time has risen to cabinet-level status. This relocation led to BOB/OMB's acquisition of policy control, as opposed to only accounting-budgeting functions. In the late 1940s, legislative clearance duties began, whereby BOB would rule on whether to allow legislation originating in the bureaucracy to be transmitted to Congress. The test was to be whether the legislation was consistent with the president's program. In the 1980s, OMB took on regulatory rule review functions that would determine if the bureaucracy would be allowed to implement regulations based on certain criteria. During the Reagan and Bush years a cost/benefit standard was used. Policy-making and bureaucratic decision making were being centralized in this most important of presidential agencies, increasing the president's control over what government does and making him responsible for the actions and decisions of government.

The president also began to make policy outside of the normal legislative processes. McDonald (1994, 294–97) documents presidential intercession into industrial disputes dating back as early as Theodore Roosevelt, as well as such extranormal procedures as making proclamations, issuing executive orders, and calling events national emergencies. Each device allowed the president to make policy outside of the legislative process, independent of congressional action.

Although we can document these additional responsibilities in more detail, the important point is that, whether forced upon the president by

Congress or actively sought by the president, the political culture surrounding the presidency altered. No longer the clerk, presidential "stewardship" became institutionalized. The public would come to look for presidential policy leadership; presidents who refused to take such leadership would be criticized as not "acting presidential." Even Congress looked to the president for policy leadership.

An instructive example of this new political culture dates to the early Eisenhower administration. By the early 1950s, the nation had come to expect that the president would submit a program to Congress. This would serve as a blueprint for congressional legislative action. In his first year in office, 1953, Eisenhower failed to provide Congress with a program. He wanted to steer the nation back to a less expansive and active view of government and the presidency. He was roundly criticized, however, and returned to the practice of submitting a program during the remainder of his time in office (Neustadt 1955). Not only was the president given formal responsibility for public policy through statutes and legal requirements, but he was given informal responsibility through this agenda-setting activity and expectation.

Similarly, no matter how hard George Bush tried to scale back these public expectations, he seemed unable to convince the public to accept a smaller presidency (Jones 1991). This gap between what he offered to the public in terms of policy leadership and public expectations is arguably one element of his electoral defeat in 1992. Bill Clinton offered the public the traditional policy leadership to which it had grown accustomed and preferred. A political culture highly expectant of presidential policy leadership developed, and it was an expectation highly resistant to modification.

Policy responsibility leads presidents to become policy-making leaders, and the public expectation of presidential leadership increases the weight of policy responsibility that the president feels. This weight of responsibility sometimes leads presidents in directions contrary to public desires on specific policy issues. Ironically, while the weightiness of this policy responsibility is in part a function of changes in public expectations, it may also lead the president in a policy direction to which the public might be opposed. It helps create the tension between being responsive to public preferences and also providing the public with policy leadership.

The Costs of Responsiveness and the Weight of Policy Leadership

Presidents seem quite conscious of their policy responsibility and the tension between this and responsiveness to the public. For example, Truman seemed quite disdainful of using public opinion and poll results to guide his decision making and policy choices. In a private memo written to himself near the end of his term, when his polls were among the lowest he had ever received, he wrote, "I wonder how far Moses would have gone if he'd taken a poll in Egypt? . . . What would Jesus Christ have preached if he'd taken a poll in Israel? . . . It isn't polls or public opinion of the moment that counts. It's right and wrong" (cited in McCullough 1992, 914–15).

Similarly, Lyndon Johnson, a president seemingly more concerned with his popularity than Truman, was also conscious of the costs of blindly following public opinion. He carried poll results around with him, ready to show them to anyone who questioned him or his presidency. Yet he was not a slave to public opinion polls. He felt that his support would dwindle; each action he took would cost him public support. For Johnson, public support was instrumental to getting things done, but getting things done that would be remembered, his legacy, was what really counted. "Speculating in 1967 that his grandchildren would be proud of what he had done for blacks and what he had done 'to see it through in Vietnam,' Johnson calculated that 'the Negro cost me 15 points in the polls and Vietnam cost me 20' " (Skowronek 1993, 340).

The weight of policy leadership and responsibility on the president means that presidential responsiveness to the public will sometimes be costly to the president. This cost derives from the fact that the public not only judges the president on his responsiveness to the public but also on how well government and its policies are functioning. To ensure that policies operate effectively, perhaps with an eye on enhancing his long-term or future reputation, as well as accomplishing such goals as leaving a legacy and making a mark on history, presidents strive to control as much of the policy-making process as possible. One cost of responsiveness is that it may cede some policy control to the public. This may undermine policy effectiveness, future public support, and these other presidential goals. Being responsive to the public may require that the president adopt policy directions that he does not want to take.

The Costs of Following

Following the public may cede policy control to the public, but the president will still be held responsible for the execution and performance of that policy. This may result in poorly conceived policy that ultimately falls short of expectations. The president, will, however, have to pay the price of the failed policy in terms of diminished reputation and prestige. His effectiveness and influence in other policy realms and at later dates may suffer, he may not be reelected, and lastly history may view him as a failure.

Policy costs may also be incurred if a president only follows but does not lead. Policies may not be coordinated and the expertise that government has to offer may not be used. Policy complications and second order consequences may not be considered, and policy-making may become solely reactive, as new problems are not dealt with until they are large enough to capture the public's limited attention. Less foresight and more crisis control may characterize policy-making when the president follows without providing leadership.

Henry Kissinger pessimistically assessed the impact of too much responsiveness on the quality of public policy:

> as the pressures of the electoral process have increased, governments have become more and more tactically oriented. The more tactically oriented they are, the more short-term their policies. The more short-term their policies, the less successful they are. So we have the paradox that governments following public opinion polls begin to look more and more incompetent. As they look incompetent, confidence in government begins to disintegrate. (quoted in Kernell 1993, 190)

Sources of Policy Conflict between Presidents and the Public

Exacerbating the tension between leadership and responsiveness is that the president and the public may disagree over which public policy course to take. Several structural factors may lead to presidential-public conflict over policy. Thus, the potential for policy conflict is always present. It is not likely to be a random or rare occurrence. These factors include different time perspectives on the part of the president and the public and multiple presidential constituencies.

Different Time Perspectives.   The time perspectives of the public and the president may differ, causing conflict over preferred policy actions. Generally, the public's time perspective is quite short, and it wants to realize policy benefits quite swiftly. A Tory member of parliament has this to say about the problems of democracy and policy-making; it is also pertinent to the American case: "I think the weakness in a democracy really is that you get a mass of people who really take a short-term view of what their immediate benefits are, as opposed to the person who thinks and takes a long-term view for the sake of the country, and I think that's always a weakness in a democracy" (quoted from Putnam 1973, 166). This has important consequences for policy choice: the public will rarely tolerate sacrifice for long, even if will mean long-term benefits, but it will usually opt for immediate benefits, even if the result is future pain. A consumption rather than an investment mentality better characterizes the public mind on most matters of policy most of the time.

The president's time perspective is more complex. On the one hand, the electoral clock imposes a short-term calculation on presidential policy choice. But this effect is really presidential responsiveness to public demands, and by the second term (if there is one) the electoral imperative is all but gone.[2] The policy performance test and the desire to build a lasting and effective policy legacy for the nation, which may translate into a historical reputation as a great president, may motivate the president to also consider the long term. For instance, the passage of his economic policy required that President Clinton convince the public that a lasting solution to the nation's economic problems would require long-term diligence and perhaps sustained periods of sacrifice. Again, Clinton fought against the tide of public opinion with his support for the North American Free Trade Agreement (NAFTA). Clinton is not the only president to take such highly publicized and unpopular positions. During the depths of the 1982 recession, Reagan repeatedly appealed to the public to give his economic policies more time to take effect, to, in his words, "stay the course" (Ingold and Windt 1984).

Moreover, not all policy problems are amenable to short-term solutions. This may also motivate presidents to consider the long term when building a policy response to a problem. Furthermore, short-term solutions may do more harm than good. Although presidents are not immune to short-term pressures, other factors may lead them to consider the long term. Inasmuch as presidents do consider the long term, presidential and public choice about preferred policy courses may diverge.

Multiple Competing Presidential Constituencies. Another important source of policy conflict between the president and the public is that the president does not always define the relevant policy constituency as being the whole nation on each policy problem that he faces. Many have noted that only the president has the incentive to represent the nation as a whole, being elected by a national constituency. It does not follow that the president has to respond to a national constituency just because he is the only politician with a national electoral constituency. It only means that no one else has the incentive to even attend to a national constituency.

Presidents have considerable latitude in how they define the relevant constituency for each policy problem that arises. This even applies to cases when presidents view the relevant constituency as the nation at large. On these macro issues, presidents can define the national constituency as the aggregation of the mass of individual members. In doing so, presidents may look to the average citizen or to majority opinion. Poll results give a portrait of a national constituency defined this way. Yet presidents may also define the national constituency as the agglomeration of interest groups, much in the spirit of Mueller's (1970) idea of a coalition of minorities and other pluralist and group interpretations of American politics. Aggregating across individuals does not always lead to the same policy option as aggregating across groups.

Policy conflict between the president and the mass public may also arise when a competing, less inclusive interest is able to tug the president away from the mass public. Neustadt (1990, 8) raises the issue of competing constituencies, suggesting that presidents have five constituencies to consider: executive officialdom, Congress, his partisans, other nations, and the citizenry at large. A further complication is the fact that none of these presidential constituencies is identical to the president's electorate. Greenstein (1974) makes a similar point when he writes of the role conflict between being leader and symbol of the nation versus being a party leader. Kallenbach (1975) notes that the constitutional framework places dual, often conflicting, constituencies—the whole people and the party (or faction that put him into office)—onto the president.

Fenno's (1978) notion of congressional constituencies provides a useful framework for understanding the multiple, competitive nature of the president's constituencies. Fenno (1978, 1) suggests that members of Congress view their constituencies as a nest of concentric circles. The representative's constituency successively narrows from the geographic constituency to the member's reelection constituency to the member's primary constituency to the personal constituency, which is composed of the member's close friends and advisers.

This notion of successively narrowing constituencies arranged in a nested, concentric circle is also useful for organizing thinking about the president's constituencies. The president's array of constituencies begins with the entire nation. It proceeds to their general election supporters, then their primary election supporters, and ends with their intimates and advisers. This grouping differs from Neustadt, who views the term *constituency* in broader and looser terms.

The important point, however, is that presidents have several different ways of defining the relevant constituency of the moment. It need not be the nation, defined as majority opinion. Whenever one of these alternatives replaces the majority opinion definition, policy conflict between public opinion and the president may result, as presidents follow a policy course that differs from that which public opinion prefers.

Summary and Problem

At some basic level, the president must show his responsiveness to the public. Through such demonstration the president can build popular support, which is an important political resource. But he is still held responsible for public policy and will aim to control the policy-making process to ensure the policy results he wants. Additionally, the motivation to develop a historical reputation impels the president to retain control over the direction and performance of public policy.

The president needs to prove his responsiveness because he needs the public and the power that public support provides him. But he must also lead, especially with the aim of controlling public policy. If the president and the public's ideas about public policy alternatives converge, the president can solve this dilemma. Following his own best judgment will result in the same policy choice as following public dictates. But two factors may lead to divergence between the president and public opinion: the differing time horizons of the president and the public and competing presidential constituencies. The structural nature of these two factors means that presidents will frequently find themselves in conflict with the mass public over policy choice.

Presidents are faced with a management problem. They require public support. Public support can be converted into political influence. To acquire that public support, a president must connect with the public, convincing it that he stands for them, that he has their best interests in mind. One way of making this connection is to be responsive to public concerns about public policy. But presidents also know they will be judged on the performance of the policies that they implement. Their future reputations and historical legacies are rooted in this performance but so is long-term public support. The support that presidents acquire through responsiveness may be eroded if those resulting policies fail. Presidents will be blamed for these performance failures, and linking the president to performance failure may make it difficult, if not impossible, for him to mobilize public support. Thus, to ensure that implemented policies are effective and not failures, presidents attempt to control the policy-making process. This may result in presidents being less responsive to the public.

But presidents may be highly responsive to the public in policy-making activities that are not substantive and that have few implications for his control of the policy-making process. In other words, presidents may be symbolically responsive to the public. On substantive decisions in the policy-making process, the concern for policy control emerges, attenuating the level of presidential responsiveness to the public: presidents will be more symbolically responsive than substantively responsive to the public.

Presidential Responsiveness to Public Opinion: A Review of the Findings

No single literature looks directly at presidential responsiveness to public opinion, but several studies report findings relevant to the issue. The results of these studies are scattered and divergent. Some find presidents responsive to public opinion, while others find presidents resistant to the public or nonresponsive. In general, these studies seem to suggest that presidential responsiveness is more pronounced for public relations behavior, a type of nonsubstantive and symbolic behavior, while substantive policy-making behavior seems less responsive to public opinion. This is consistent with the theme offered in this study. Still, some studies suggest presidential responsiveness for some substantive policy activities.

Symbolic and Public Relations Activities of Presidents

Early research by Ragsdale finds that movement in presidential popularity leads presidents to make speeches: "The greater the change in presidential popularity, the greater the likelihood of presidential speechmaking" (1984, 976). Thus, presidents seem to try both to capitalize on upward movement in their popularity and to stem the tide of declining popularity by making speeches. Brace and Hinckley (1992, 1993) modify the Ragsdale finding. Drops in public approval are associated with increases in presidential speech-making, but only during first terms, and the effect is marginal. Several studies have found another type of responsiveness in presidential speechmaking—presidents seem to tailor their message to the audience they are addressing (Miller and Sigelman 1978; Goggin 1984), and the Goggin study finds that Reagan was somewhat more likely to moderate his speeches when his popularity was lower.

Hager and Sullivan (1994) combine several types of presidential activities into an index, including minor speeches, head-of-state activities, and political speeches. They find that declines in approval stimulate these types of activities (1,097). But unlike Ragsdale and Brace and Hinckley, they find no impact of approval shift on major speeches. It is noteworthy that Hager and Sullivan use annual aggregations of activities, while the Ragsdale and Brace and Hinckley studies disaggregate into monthly units. This may account for the different results.

Presidential trips to other nations and around the United States seem responsive to shifts in public approval, but the pattern is complex (Brace and Hinckley 1992, 1993). During first terms, declines in presidential approval lead them to travel to foreign nations more frequently, perhaps in an attempt to reverse the decline in their support. But increases in support during the second term lead presidents to travel around the United States more frequently.

Another public activity, holding press conferences, shows no relationship to shifts in approval (Lammers 1979; Hager and Sullivan 1994). Rather, press conference activity has declined steadily from the 1930s to the present. The lack of presidential control in press conferences, especially in comparison to other public activities, seems to account for this decline (Mannheim 1979).

Substantive Policy Activities

Each of the activities just described is primarily a public relations activity. Policy information may be conveyed by them, but they are not policy decisions in themselves. A smaller literature has looked at presidential responsiveness in making policy decisions. Again a mixed picture emerges.

One important set of policy decisions concerns foreign affairs. Ostrom and Job (1986) have found that the presidential commitment of troops is very sensitive to presidential approval. The higher the president's approval rating, the less likely the use of force because "the president will be concerned with the possibility that the use of force, if unsuccessful, could reduce his personal resources" (Ostrom and Job, 557). The popularity variable was the strongest in the Ostrom-Job model.

Their results, however, have been challenged, most notably by Brace and Hinckley (1992). Approval has no impact on the use of force. Moreover, public approval has little impact on any type of foreign policy activity, including foreign policy actions that do not involve troops, major foreign policy speeches, messages to Congress, and treaties. Only during the first term is a direct response noted: declines in popularity are associated with treaty activity. Still, Brace and Hinckley note a possible indirect connection. Conditions that erode popularity, such as a poor economy, often stimulate presidential foreign policy activity. Presidents may be using these activities "preemptively, to forestall a drop in the polls" (Brace and Hinckley 1992, 99).

On the domestic front, the evidence is scantier. Brace and Hinckley (1992) indicate that presidents are more likely to take positions on legislation before Congress when their popularity is higher, but this seems more a function of presidents using their public support to move Congress. It does not indicate that the president is taking more stands on issues popular or unpopular, important or unimportant, to the public.

In a series of interviews with White House staffers, Light (1982) suggests that issues get onto the president's agenda when there is great public concern, when the issue is "hot" (92–93). He does not indicate, however, if the president subsequently takes positions on those issues consistent with public preferences. Moreover, such insider accounts may be subject to rationalization effects. We require other types of evidence, such as the matching of public preferences with presidential decisions, to sort out these possibilities.

Jacobs and Shapiro (1995b) have made an initial attempt to do this. They find that during the first year of the Clinton administration, the president seemed quite responsive to the public on many domestic issues but not on foreign policy ones. There are limitations of this study, however. Only one year of a single administration was used. Moreover, that year was the first year of a new administration. Many of the positions that Clinton took originated with the election campaign, when we might expect public pressures on the president to be at their highest. As an administration ages and new issues arise, perhaps through nonelectoral processes, ties between the president and the public might weaken. Also, the Jacobs and Shapiro study did not control for other factors that might determine presidential positions. Their findings may be spurious.

Lastly, in an intriguing report, Stimson, MacKuen, and Erikson (1995) find a relationship between the public mood and overall presidential policy positions on roll call voting and cases before the Supreme Court. This result, while highly suggestive, does not represent a full range of ways and types of presidential policy-making activities and decisions.

Reviewing these studies suggests that presidents may be responsive to the public, but responsiveness seems clearer in publicity activities that are not primarily decision-making venues. These activities are designed more to attract the public's attention and gather support for the president. Some of these activities are highly symbolic. But responsiveness seems less evident when presidents are making policy-relevant decisions, though some support exists for presidential responsiveness to public opinion in these situations.

Moreover, this literature is not directly aimed at the question of presidential responsiveness to public opinion. Other questions motivated these studies; presidential responsiveness is but one subquestion raised in them. Nor do these studies, taken as a group, present systematic evidence of presidential responsiveness across the full range of the policy-making process. The policy-making process entails decisions from agenda setting through to implementation. A broader analysis of presidential responsiveness to public opinion would investigate the question across many of the decision points of the policy-making process. That is my intention in this study.

Presidential Responsiveness and the Policy-making Process

The president's quandary is to show the public that he is responsive to it without relinquishing his ability to control the substance and tempo of public policy-making. My basic proposition is that presidents will display greater responsiveness to the public in ways and at times that do not cost them substantive control over public policy. When substantive policy decisions are being made, presidential responsiveness will decline.

Symbolic responsiveness is one way that a president can be responsive to the public without ceding policy direction, control, and other substantive matters. The process of identifying problems, an initial phase of the agenda-setting process, affords an opportunity to engage in symbolic responsiveness. Presidents may respond to public concerns about problems symbolically without restricting later choices over policy timing, substance, and implementation.

Symbolic responsiveness does not entail loss of substantive policy discretion for presidents. The easiest symbolic response is for presidents to sympathize with people's concerns. George Bush did not seem to understand the importance of this symbolic response. Although the economy was eroding, he was criticized for attending more to international than domestic economic problems. Later in his administration, when the economy bottomed into a recessionary trough, Bush avoided offering symbolic assurance to the economically distressed. Instead, he exhorted that if the federal government did nothing, the economy would right itself in due course. The Bush administration even suggested that recessions were good for the economy, as they wiped out inefficiencies. Such a statement did little to comfort the unemployed or those worried about their future job prospects. Bush's ineptitude in symbolically responding to concerns about the economy eventually alienated the public. All that was required of Bush would have been to affirm that the economy was a major concern and that he had a program that would lead to economic recovery. This would have created the symbolic connection to the public without restricting his choice over policy details.

This suggests a major hypothesis. Presidents will be symbolically responsive to the public when doing so does not constrain substantive choices about policies; however, responsiveness to the public declines as decisions become more substantive. To test these hypotheses, I develop several indicators of presidential policy activity across four stages of the policy-making process: problem identification in agenda setting, position taking in agenda setting, policy formulation, and position taking on roll calls before Congress.

The policy approach also allows this study to take part in a wider theory-building effort on the presidency. Two recent reviews have suggested that a policy focus should serve as an overall research strategy in theory building on the presidency. Paul Quirk, for instance, argues that "the central issue [in studying the presidency] is obviously how presidents make policy decisions" (1991, 39), and he suggests "that the field should have a more definite agenda, which should focus mainly on the president's role in policy formation" (38).

Paul Light (1993) makes an even stronger case that policy should be the primary dependent variable governing presidency studies. To Light, "policy is one of the most important products of the presidency. . . . policy is the stuff of which a president's place in history is made, the end result against which to assess an administration's impact" (161). A policy focus offers five ways to test the validity of theories about the presidency, according to Light. Policy "provides a baseline against which to assess competing explanations of presidential behavior.. . . . Second, policy acts as a visible expression of a president's ideology and world view, and therefore, serves as a way to tackle a systematic study of the impact of personal belief systems in shaping outcomes. . . . Third, policy offers a reasonable tack for studying the role of process and the rule of law. . . . Fourth, policy creates a method for testing the market values of the essential resources of the presidency. . . . Fifth, policy exists as an independent variable in its own right" (162–64).

Policy Activities and the Process View of Policy-making

The four presidential policy activities studied in the chapters that follow (problem identification in agenda setting, position taking in agenda setting, policy formulation, and policy legitimation) relate to different stages of the policy process. Using such activities and presenting them in "sequential" order does not mean that I subscribe to a process or stages view of policy-making. The stages metaphor, however, provides a useful way to organize policy activities.

The stages or process approach asserts that policies must pass through several stages. There exists no clear demarcation of the stages, or the boundaries between stages, but a general ordering is usually employed. During the agenda-setting stage, problems are converted into issues, and issues are prioritized. During the next stage, policy proposals are formulated. Policies that pass through these two gates arrive at the third stage, that of policy legitimation. In this stage, authoritative decision makers decide to implement a policy. Appended to this stage are decisions about the scope, timing, duration, and budget of a policy and its programs. Then the policy is implemented—the fourth major stage. A policy may reach the next stage, policy evaluation, which may send the policy back to earlier stages, as it is redesigned, expanded, contracted, or terminated.

Several criticisms have been leveled against the stages approach to the policy-making process. First, the sequence implies a linear order to policy-making that resembles the rational decision-making paradigm. The policy-making process is messier and more chaotic than the sequential process portrays. Decisions at any stage of the process can feed back to earlier stages, creating loops and policy deadends. Moreover, if one views policy-making from a garbage-can perspective (Cohen, March, and Olsen 1972; Kingdon 1984), then the neat structure of the process model unravels. Solutions chase problems, reversing the temporal, and supposedly causal, sequence between formulation and agenda setting. As Heclo (1974, 307) so aptly advises, "salami slicing" the policy process into stages that occur in regular order and rhythm distorts the complexities and interconnections among the stages of the policy-making process.

The sequential process approach has also been criticized as not being a theory. Sabatier (1991) is a forceful critic who asserts that the process model "is not really a causal theory . . . it divides the policy process into several stages . . . and discusses some of the things going on in each stage, but contains no coherent assumptions about what forces are driving the process from stage to stage and very few falsifiable hypotheses" (267). Additionally, the stages approach has not been able to specify how decisions at one stage affect decisions at later stages.

My use of policy activities that derive from the stages model is not meant to imply that I am going to use that approach in this study. I assume no temporal ordering of the four presidential policy activities. In fact, several of the activities are derived from the same presidential document, the State of the Union Address, implying a potential simultaneity across policy activities.

Still, the process heuristic is useful for organizing a complex phenomenon, policy-making, and its terminology may be called upon from time to time. Lastly, I will draw upon the conceptual work of process theoreticians to give meaning to the policy activities and help us link the logic of the hypothesis being tested here.

Summary

The theory proposed here hypothesizes that presidents will be responsive to the public if such responsiveness does not curtail their control or discretion over the substantive aspects of policy-making. Thus, responsiveness will occur on policy activities that are mostly symbolic in nature. Problem identification fits this description well when it is void of substantive content and information. In contrast, the desire to retain policy control and discretion will reduce presidential responsiveness to the public on policy activities that are more substantively important. Discussing policies substantively, formulating policy proposals, and taking positions on roll calls are examples of activities with a strong substantive component. For each of these activities, we should witness less systematic presidential responsiveness to the public than for the more symbolic activities of agenda setting and other activities with a strong symbolic element.

A Note on Responsiveness

How will I detect how responsive a president is to the public? Achen's (1978) methodological work on representation is an important guide to the analysis that follows here. He argues that three characteristics exhaust the statistical description of representation. They are proximity, centrism, and responsiveness. Proximity measures the nearness of the representative to his or her constituents. Centrism measures the difference between the representative's proximity and the variance of opinion of the constituency and indicates how well the representative minimizes his or her distance from the mean constituency opinion.

To estimate proximity and centrism requires information on the dispersion of constituency opinion. I do not have such data. At best, I have means or proportions of nationally aggregated opinions on policies, which I relate to the president's policy behaviors. For instance, as I detail more fully in subsequent chapters, I use data on the percentage of people who view the economy as a problem. I also have an indicator of the direction of public preferences, that is, the relative liberalism or conservatism of the mass public (Stimson 1991).

These aggregate data can be used to describe the responsiveness of the president. Achen conceptualizes responsiveness in a regression-style framework:

$$r = a + Bu + e,$$

where r is here the president's observed behavior, a is the intercept, B is the regression coefficient, u the mean constituency opinion, and e an error term. A perfectly "unbiased" system would have an $a = 0$ and a $B = 1$. In such a case, the president would be no more nor less "liberal" than public opinion, and each one-unit change in public opinion "liberalness" would result in a comparable change in the president's liberalness.

The intercept tells us about the president's behavior when opinion is at the neutral, 0 point. To discern the responsiveness of the president, we must also look at the regression coefficient, which tells us how sluggishly, proportionately, or rapidly the president responds to changes in constituent opinion. When analyzing the results reported in the following chapters, I will pay close attention to the magnitude and direction of the B coefficient. A large, statistically significant, and positive B is required to show presidential responsiveness to public opinion. An insignificant and small B indicates no responsiveness. A negative and significant B indicates counterresponsiveness. The requirement that the B be significant and positive provides a strong test of the responsiveness tendencies of presidents, given that they can be both non-responsive and counterresponsive.

Lastly, Achen's study was developed to deal with mass survey data and congressional roll call data in a static design. Static designs impute the causal relationship between variables. Since my data are constructed across a time series (1953–89), I will be able to make firmer causal statements about the impact of public opinion on presidential behavior. This is done through the proper specification of leads and lags in the sequencing of public opinion and presidential behavior. These data also allow us to estimate presidential leadership of public opinion, depending on the temporal ordering of presidential behavior and public opinion.

CHAPTER 2

Presidential Leadership, Responsiveness, and the Agenda-setting Process: The President's Most Important Problem

In this chapter I look at presidential leadership and responsiveness to public opinion in the agenda-setting process. Agenda setting is often considered the initial stage of the policy-making process. During the agenda-setting process, problems are identified, converted into issues, and issues are prioritized.

Before a problem will become an issue, it must meet two tests. First, it must be considered a social or public problem, not a private one. Often problems that are widespread, affecting large numbers of people, can attain issue status (Walker 1977), but the problem must also be thought amenable to human control before it will be thought of as an issue (Stone 1988). Second, the problem must be considered within the legitimate scope of government. Even widespread problems that have a public or social cast may not attain issue status if government activity concerning the problem is not considered legitimate. For example, income support for the unemployed was not considered a legitimate federal government activity in the United States until the 1930s. Before then, the private sector and charitable organizations were supposed to take care of this problem.

Once a problem has attained issue status, it competes with other issues for government attention and resources. The active agenda consists of those issues to which decisions makers are applying resources. Not all issues reach the active agenda. Many sink down the priority list, to be stayed for future action or until decision makers identify resources to apply to the issue. These issues occupy what we may call the inactive agenda.

Two factors structure the ability of an issue to attain a high enough priority rating to get onto the active agenda. The first, the limited attention span of decision makers and the public, means that issues are dealt with serially, a few at a time (Baumgartner and Jones 1993). The second, budgetary and personnel resource constraints, limits the number of issues that the government can address formally. Health care reform and comprehensive health coverage in the United States have been kept off the active agenda because of budgetary constraint, even though they have been on the inactive agenda since passage of Medicare in the 1960s.

There are many different active and inactive agendas. Cobb and Elder (1972) distinguish between the systemic and the governmental agenda. The systemic agenda refers to those issues that people are talking and thinking about. The governmental agenda are those issues that government and its officials are talking and thinking about. There are as many governmental agendas as there are authoritative decision-making bodies. We may refer to the agendas of the different agencies of government (e.g., Congress, President, Courts, etc.) as institutional agendas.

The president plays a critical role in shaping the systemic agenda by affecting problem identification and issue prioritization in the mass public. He speaks from a national platform with a national perspective. As the economy has nationalized and people's lives have become more intertwined and interdependent, many problems are now national in scope. No other politician, except perhaps for those with presidential ambitions (Aldrich 1993), has the same incentives to seek out national problems or to see problems from a national perspective (Wilson 1908; Huntington 1973). Thus, the president's opinions about problems and issues are more likely to resonate with the public than the opinions of leaders voicing a more local outlook.

Second, transforming the media into a national system increasingly exposes the public to a homogenized, national view of problems and issues. Moreover, the media's lopsided attention to the president gives him unparalleled access to the public (Kernell 1993), and the individual nature of the office makes it psychologically and informationally more accessible to the public than the more complex, impersonal, and often byzantine Congress. Lastly, the continuing expansion of the office that began with Franklin Roosevelt's administration has concentrated public expectations about government and public policy on the president. The public has come to believe, consequently, that the president possesses the institutional resources to handle big problems. Thus, the president has come to, in Miroff's (1982) words, "monopolize the public space." When problems arise, the public looks to the president for leadership in deciding whether to consider a problem an issue and whether to consider it a high-priority issue.

These reasons underscore why we should expect presidential leadership of the public-systemic agenda. Presidents also have incentives to be responsive to the public in setting their own institutional agendas. The idea presented in this study suggests that presidents will be responsive to the public if such responsiveness does not undercut their ability to control and direct the path and substance of public policies. Presidents need to control public policies because they feel that they are held accountable for the performance of government. Only by controlling public policy can presidents ensure that they will realize the kind of performance that they seek.

During the problem definition stage presidents have an opportunity to respond to the public symbolically without constraining later substantively relevant decisions. Symbolic responsiveness entails that the president express his empathy and concern to the public about its worries, along with an air of confidence that the president is competent to deal with their worries. Thus, the president can say, "Yes, I agree that the economy is a problem" or "Yes, crime is terrorizing the nation" without having to commit to a specific policy course.

Presidents can garner public good will if the empathic message is communicated deftly. Although he does not have to commit to a policy action, he must convince the public that he cares about its problems. He must not, as George Bush did during the recession that plagued the second half of his administration, give the impression that the public's concerns were not very important to him. In contrast, FDR's fireside chats were not heavily laden with policy content. They were more notable for their ability to inspire confidence in the public about the president and whatever he decided to do. Often merely expressing concern for the public's worries is enough to calm public fears (Edelman 1964). By being receptive to the public's concerns and appearing willing and able to take action if needed, the president can retain control over later substantive policy decisions.

Moreover, capitalizing on public concern may help lay the foundations for later presidential policy initiatives on that issue. For example, President Clinton made health care reform one of his top administration priorities. The issue caught the attention of Clinton and other national political leaders after the 1990 midterm elections. Harrison Wofford, the Democratic senatorial candidate in Pennsylvania, discovered that health care worries were important to many voters in that state. He made that issue the centerpiece of his campaign. In so doing, he turned a faltering campaign into one that took him to the Senate. National surveys soon discovered that health care was among the most important problems on the public's mind. From this foundation, Clinton put health care reform onto his agenda, offering promises of reform during his presidential election bid. Once in office and after the top priority, the economy, had a policy in place, Clinton devoted his energies to health care, offering a major reform proposal to Congress. Noticing public concern was critical in paving the way for Clinton's health care reform effort, and for putting it on his agenda, though Congress ultimately refused to enact his massive reform proposal.

Problem identification is ideally suited to symbolic politics in other respects. Presidents who fail to communicate empathy may not receive public credit for resolving problems, even if they were responsible for constructing effective policy solutions. Presidents must publicize their efforts if they are to be able to claim policy credit (Mayhew 1973). Effective empathic communication during the process of issue identification is an important foundation for later credit claiming. Ironically, publicity without activity may also generate public credit. This may be the heart of what we mean by image management.

In this chapter, I look at the process of problem identification. An indicator of presidential problems is constructed by analyzing the content of the president's State of the Union Addresses from 1953 through 1989. Before turning to those data, I raise the question, Can we meaningfully detect presidential policy choice from presidential speeches, like the State of the Union Addresses?

Presidential Rhetoric and Public Policy

There are several contrasting views of presidential speech, from one extreme that views such speech as merely symbolic and, thus, void of policy content to another that views policy-making as a core aspect of presidential speech making.

The work of Hinckley (1990) and Hart (1987) focuses on the symbolic aspects of presidential rhetoric. Hinckley's study is an ambitious examination of symbolism in the rhetoric of modern presidents. According to Hinckley, presidential speech contains little policy content and rarely mentions the process by which policy is made. Other constitutional actors fail to appear in presidential oratory, and political conflict is downplayed. The president stands alone, without competitors, in an ahistorical and personal presentation.

The work of Ceaser (1985) and Tulis (1987; also Ceaser et al. 1981) on the "rhetorical" presidency also focuses on symbolism, linking it to presidential policy goals. Their argument is not that presidential speech is filled with specific references and explanations of policy options. Rather, presidents use speech to mobilize the public behind their policy efforts. In this way, speaking and governing have merged. But although speech has taken on this instrumental policy cast, other time-honored uses of presidential speech, for instance, educating the public about constitutional processes and the meaning of citizenship, have fallen into disuse.

Several other scholars see even more specific policy attributes in presidential speech, especially in the State of the Union Addresses. Light (1982) argues that the State of the Union Address is an important indicator of the nature and direction of the president's program. In a more recent essay (1993), he shows how the president's policy agenda has changed from one offering long-term policy solutions to one with a shorter time perspective. Again he uses the State of the Union Address as the database.

In an early and detailed effort, Kessel (1974, 1977) detects policy in State of the Union Addresses. He finds a temporal rhythm that emphasizes some policy areas at different time points across the presidential term. Thus, foreign policy increases in presidential attention until the fourth year of the term, when attention drops off. In contrast, social benefits policy peaks during the fourth year, while civil rights policy attention peaks during the first year of the term. Economic policy is a constant theme across all presidential addresses. Kessel suggests a policy cycle from these major addresses.[1]

Can we reconcile the symbolic approach to studying presidential speech (e. g., Hinckley 1990) with those scholars who find more policy content in presidential rhetoric? Hinckley, in fact, presents evidence that policy concerns do invade presidential speeches. She cites (on pp. 72–73) a study by Ragsdale.[2] Ragsdale distinguishes among three types of presidential statements (sentences) found in major addresses: policy actions (both promises and achievements), policy discussions (descriptions of national facts, situations, and backgrounds), and nonpolicy remarks. The first category accounts for 24 percent of statements from Truman to Carter (1949–79), the second 62 percent, and nonpolicy remarks but 14 percent. Consistent with Hinckley's portrayal is that these policy remarks were highly general. Many were merely promises of performance and/or self-congratulations for policy achievements.

Where Hinckley (1990, 73) suggests that presidents avoid politics and policy in their statements, I contend that presidents use "policy symbols" in their public discourse to rouse public support. Some of those symbols relate to policy intentions and leanings. What presidents avoid is the conflict associated with making public policy. By playing down political conflict, presidents may help foster a sense of consensus about those policy directions. Presidents may be trying to create bandwagons, rallying the public behind their policy efforts.

Still, Hinckley is correct that presidential rhetoric does not present very detailed discussions of issues or policy development. It is symbolic. But symbols can be potent political forces (Edelman 1964; Elder and Cobb 1983). They may also convey much important political information, for instance, about presidential policy emphases and directions. Symbols may help the public structure political messages and give meaning to them. In this sense, party may be an important symbol, as the huge literature on party identification argues. Knowing that one politician uses a symbol favorably, while another does not, helps the public see the sides to the debate. Linking symbols together also helps the public structure politics. Different combinations of symbols may convey different meanings, altering the basis of political debate (Baumgartner and Jones 1993). For example, linking health care reform with deficit containment raises a different debate than linking it to issues of fairness and equity.

The view taken here is that although symbols lack detail, they are not void of politically relevant content. Moreover, policies can themselves become symbols. Mentioning (or not mentioning) civil rights in a major address may have important symbolic implications. Kennedy hardly mentioned civil rights in his inaugural address, an indication that civil rights would not be a high priority in his administration. Civil rights advocates rebuked him for this slight. Still, his early actions as president reinforced the message of the inaugural that civil rights was not as important as good relations with Southern Democrats in Congress (Giglio 1991, 161–62).

The distinction between symbol and substance is often too starkly drawn in the literature (see Kemp 1981; Marshall 1993). All politics has symbolic as well as substantive implications. The relationship between symbolism and substance is more complex than the standard approach, which sees a tradeoff between them. They may be reinforcing. Lyndon Johnson's Great Society integrated liberal symbolism and policy substance. "Reaganomics" did the same two decades later but with a conservative cast. Symbolism and substance may also seem in conflict. George Bush's "kinder and gentler" theme seemed to be contradicted by his handling of the economy or civil rights (Shull 1993). Lastly, some politics may be purely symbolic, without any substantive policy referent. But whenever a substantive policy is the object of discussion or action, there also exists a corresponding symbolism, whether reinforcing or conflicting. Noting the symbolic aspects of policies helps integrate the symbolic theme of Hinckley's work with the more substantively focused work of Light and Kessel. This is the orientation that I take later in this chapter when I use State of the Union Address to elicit both the symbolic and the substantive aspects of these speeches.

A second perspective suggests that the State of the Union Address, a major data source used in this study, is a good location for learning about presidential policy choice. As Walcott and Hult (1995) argue, the process of speech writing in the White House is a policy-making process. "[W]riting can be the occasion for discovering and crystallizing policy content. When presidents must speak, they need to have something to say. If policy is unclear in advance of a speech, it often must be clarified in the writing process" (212). Furthermore, writing is an occasion where presidential advisers, speech writers, allies, and advocates, in various combinations, would come together in various formats and settings. Although sometimes interacting collegially, other times adversarially or competitively, the speech-writing process helps clarify a president's policies. "The need to state policy often amounted to a mandate that policy be established, or at least clarified" (Hult and Walcott 1995, 220).

The State of the Union Address is viewed by those who worked on it as especially important in this regard. It shares with only the budget and economic messages the characteristic of being annual, of having a forced deadline. The public and governmental anticipation of the speech heightens its importance. People wait for the State of the Union Address to see what the president will say about a topic, speculating about his offerings. Some people make judgments about the president based upon a comparison of what they hoped to see in the message and what finally emerged. Some will be disappointed, others elated.

Further, the process of writing the State of the Union Address is now highly institutionalized, a process begun in Franklin Roosevelt's term. By Truman's time, the process would include inputs from the Bureau of the Budget (now Office of Management and Budget) and the major cabinet departments about what to contain in the message. The number of others who would be asked for input, plus the scope of their suggestions, would be elaborated upon, becoming more comprehensive as the process developed to its now very formal and institutionalized pattern (Walcott and Hult 1995, 216–19, passim).

Light's (1982) study of the agenda-building process in the White House also suggests the importance of the State of the Union Address as a location for presidential policies and priorities. His interviews indicate that the Washington community views the Address "as the vehicle for the President's agenda. . . . [T]he President's top priorities will always appear in the message at some point during the term" (6).

Furthermore, the Address is a scarce resource. It is given but once a year and is somewhat constrained in length because of the format of its presentation. Thus, a considerable "battle" among policy advocates, presidential advisers, and issues occurs to influence and secure placement on the Address. Light's interviews suggest that the State of the Union Address is the "central battleground" for setting presidential priorities (1982, 160), a view reiterated by Kessel (1974). As Kessel notes about the process of getting onto the State of the Union Address, "Favorable mention of a policy gives visibility to it and confers presidential backing to the enterprise at one and the same time. Since there are obvious limits to the number of policies that can be thus favored, very real contests take place over control of this scarce resource" (1974, 11). Thus, this second perspective suggests that the State of the Union Address is a good location for studying presidential policies.

But there is one major drawback to sole reliance of the State of the Union Address for this purpose. Much policy-making happens between Addresses. Sole reliance on the State of the Union Address presents slices of presidential policy choice set out across time. It thus does not have the seamless quality that the actual process has. Resources necessitate some compromises in data collection. Also, as I detail later, the State of the Union Address presents some important comparabilities in building quantitative indicators of presidential policy choice over time.

Problem Definition: The President's
Most Important Problem

In the next section I present data series on presidential policy problems. The series is based on a content analysis of presidential State of the Union Addresses from 1953 through 1989. I call this series the president's "Most Important Problems," arguing that it is analogous in some respects to the Gallup public opinion series of the same name. I assess the impact that the president's most important problem has on the public's most important problem in order to estimate presidential leadership effects. Presidential responsiveness is determined by assessing how much impact the public's most important problem has on the president's most important problem.

To construct the indicators of presidential problem emphasis, I count the number of sentences in the president's State of the Union Address that refer to economic policy, foreign policy, civil rights, and domestic policy. Then I divide each by the total number of sentences that referred to any policy area.[3]

Economic policy constitutes all references to economic policy and problems, such as budgets, budget deficits, overall spending levels, inflation, unemployment, regulation in general (not directed at specific industries), taxes, and monetary issues. Foreign policy includes all references to relations with other nations, the United Nations, and other international organizations; foreign aid; military and defense issues, including the Korean and Vietnam Wars. Civil rights refers to issues relating to minority groups. The domestic policy designation is an agglomeration of all remaining domestic policy areas, including agriculture, social welfare, government management and administration, natural resources, the environment, energy, and science and technology.

It was not possible to disaggregate the domestic policy area into its constituent parts for several reasons. Most of the subareas, like energy, the environment, or crime, appear sporadically in the president's message. Sometimes they do not even make it into the president's message. Moreover, they tend not to have a direct Gallup public opinion counterpart and thus are not as easily amenable to the analysis as I describe in the next section. Either one would have to restrict the analysis to only those case where both the president and the public mentioned one of these policy areas or include the missing data as zeros in the data series. The first option would produce data series with too few cases for reliable statistical analysis. The second option would involve correlating data series with many zeros, which raises an important interpretation problem. It is difficult to talk of the president or the public influencing each other when both are silent or unconcerned about a policy area.

Both sentences that stake out a presidential position as well as those that do not are included in the problem totals. Concern here is with problem identification, not solutions. Mentioning an area without offering a solution or program is relevant to problem identification. The resulting percentages can be taken as the proportion of the policy component of each Address that these three policy areas command. Here I assume that presidents give greater space to those policy areas that are more important to them.

The coding weighs sentences equally. This assumes that each policy area's probability of being mentioned in a sentence is directly proportional to its importance to the president. Thus, those policy areas of greater importance have a greater probability of being mentioned. Aggregating across sentences gives us a fair representation of the president's own ordering. The major problem with this assumption is that the president might assign different weights to different sentences. For instance, early sentences might be more important because they help set the stage for what follows. Conversely, latter sentences might be more important because of the drama of concluding the Address. Furthermore, presidents may differ in how they weigh different sentences. Some may prefer early sentences, some later ones. Still, the equal weighing procedure leads to patterns across presidents that seem reasonable, and my analysis throughout this book is able to account for these patterns in ways that make theoretical sense and have considerable explanatory power.

Moreover, when people listen to the president's Address, they are likely to note that the president spent more time talking about one policy area instead of another. Across the population, it is not likely that each person will see early or late sentences as being more or less important than other sentences. But most people generally will be able to discern which policies were discussed most frequently by the president. It does not require sophisticated conceptual ability to note that the president spoke about foreign affairs or the economy a lot but did not talk about civil rights. Thus, the quantity of presidential attention to a policy area may leave an impression in the mass public of what is important to the president irrespective of placement in the speech. The public may then take this as a cue or direction from the president about the importance of a policy area or problem. From such an impression, the public may judge how responsive the president was in the Address to its policy and problem concerns. Thus, this quantitative measure of presidential attention is useful for this analysis.

Presidential Responsiveness and Policy Type

In the discussion to follow, it will become useful to distinguish between two types of policies: those that are permanently on the agenda or required (Kessel 1974 uses the term *imperative)*, and those that are discretionary (Walker 1977).[4] In terms of agenda priority, the required areas consistently gain access to the agenda. Discretionary areas compete for the remainder of the agenda space. Foreign affairs and the economy are often cited as required agenda items; all others, including civil rights, are relegated to discretionary status (on civil rights as a discretionary policy for presidents, see Shull 1993, 5–6; also see Cronin 1980, 144–53, for a general overview). This distinction will become important because presidents should be more responsive to the public for required than for discretionary policies.

Presidential responsiveness to the public's problem agenda is rooted in public expectations of the president and a reward (punishment) system that provides incentives for the president to try to fulfill public expectations. The public has many types of expectations of the president; many are contradictory (Cronin 1980; Edwards 1983). Of concern here is the responsibility that the public places on the president for the conduct of public policy and the state of the nation. The public grades the president on the performance of his policies and whether that state of the nation is improving or not. Thus, the public has high expectations for the president with regard to public policy.

The president responds to this expectation because the public can reward or punish him. The public holds resources of dear meaning to presidents: popularity and votes. Presidents believe that a strong popular base is important to the attainment of important goals, including reelection and influencing other political elites, like members of Congress, to support his policies. The public can punish the president by not voting for him and withdrawing popular support, or it can reward him with votes and expressions of popular support. Thus, presidents have a strong incentive to deliver or attempt to live up to the public's policy expectations.

Not all policies, however, are as consequential as others in evoking public concerns and presidential responsiveness to those concerns. Some policies have clear, significant, and constant electoral and popularity implications; others do not. Those that do we may call required policies, those that do not are discretionary policies. The difference between required and discretionary policies is that required ones always reach the top of the public's policy agenda, and they affect large numbers of people in significant ways. Discretionary policies or issues are less able to hold public concern and attention for long periods of time. They have to fight or compete with other problems for public attention, and required policy problems may readily push the discretionary ones from the agenda.

Presidents are more likely to respond to public concerns for required than discretionary policy problems. Presidents know that they will always have to answer for required problems. The large number of people who watch the president on these matters creates strong electoral and/or popularity consequences for the president. The electoral and popularity implications of discretionary problems are not so consequential. Even when many people are concerned about a discretionary problem, it may be easily pushed off the agenda. It may be delayed for another time or displaced by more "pressing" problems.

More likely, intensity of concern for any discretionary problems is not very strong or widespread. Thus, presidents can escape from discretionary problems sometimes, but they can rarely escape from public concern with required problems.

Two policy areas are commonly considered to be required concerns for presidents, the health of the economy and matters of war and peace (Kessel 1974; Cronin 1980). Except during periods of intense, widespread concern, all other policy problems are discretionary. That is, under some conditions, but for limited duration, a discretionary problem may be regarded as a required one. Jimmy Carter professed a desire to elevate the place of civil rights on the nation's agenda, but the energy crisis and the economic dislocations that it caused forced him to attend less to civil rights than he had hoped. This example illustrates the discretionary nature of civil rights, and the ease with which even major discretionary problems may be pushed from the agenda.

Patterns in Presidential Problem Attention

Table 2.1 presents descriptive statistics of the president's most important problems across the four policy areas, while figures 2.1 through 2.4 present plots of the series. Although required agenda areas usually attain agenda status, they do so with varying emphasis. Similarly, although discretionary areas may have to fight for agenda status, at times those areas may be quite important to the nation and thus may receive considerable presidential attention and emphasis.

Foreign affairs and the economy always reach the agenda. The only exception relates to Nixon's Addresses of 1969 and 1971.[5] Looking at the minimum column in table 2.1, we see that civil rights sometimes fails to reach the agenda, as the discretionary model suggests. Domestic policy, as measured here, always reaches the agenda but in quite variable amounts. Had I presented the domestic policy data by their components, one would notice that most of the components will fail to make it to the president's Address on several or more occasions, as the discretionary model suggests.

Excluding those two Nixon Addresses that underplayed foreign affairs,

TABLE 2.1.   Descriptive Statistics for Presidential Economic, Foreign, and Civil Rights Policy Emphases (in percentages)

Policy	Minimum	Maximum	Mean	SD
Economic	4.73	62.56	26.30	12.52
Foreign	10.90	85.98	40.74	18.37
Civil Rights	0.00	18.18	6.00	4.66
Domestic policy	4.21	59.70	27.48	12.84

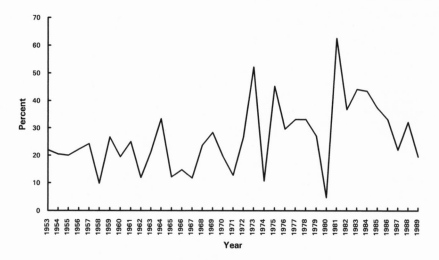

Fig. 2.1.   The percentage of sentences in the president's State of the Union Address referring to economic policy, 1953–89. (Data compiled by the author from presidential State of the Union addresses.)

foreign policy always occupies at least 10 percent of the president's attention, and on the average accounts for 40 percent of the problem agenda. (These percentages are based on the number of sentences mentioning a policy area.) Economic policy is not quite so dominant but still never fails to occupy at least 5 percent of the space on the Address and on average occupies one-

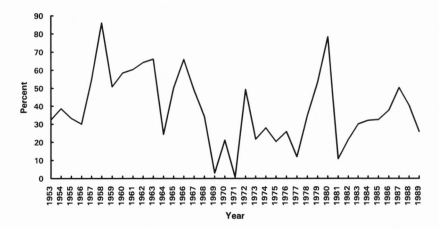

Fig. 2.2.   The percentage of sentences in the president's State of the Union Address referring to international affairs, 1953–89. (Data compiled by the author from presidential State of the Union addresses.)

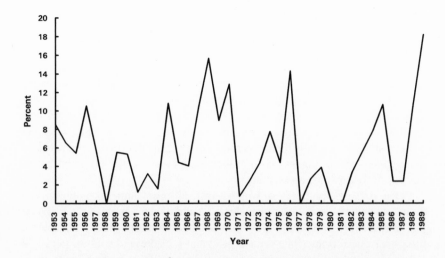

Fig. 2.3. The percentage of sentences in the president's State of the Union Address referring to civil rights, 1953–89. (Data compiled by the author from presidential State of the Union addresses.)

quarter of it. Sometimes economics or foreign policy are so important that they dominate the agenda. For instance, six times foreign policy held 60 percent or more of the space on the president's Address (1958, 1961, 1962, 1963, 1966, 1980), while the economy held over one-half of the agenda twice (1973, 1981). Together, foreign policy and the economy account for nearly two-thirds of the president's State of the Union Address. Other policy areas must compete for the remaining space.

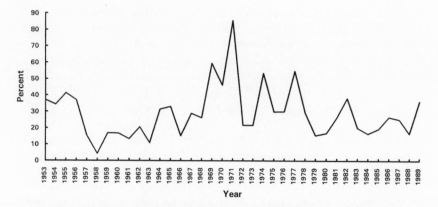

Fig. 2.4. The percentage of sentences in the president's State of the Union Address referring to domestic policy, 1953–89. (Data compiled by the author from presidential State of the Union addresses.)

Three times civil rights occupied a significant portion of the agenda (1968, 1976, 1989), but it never received more than 20 percent of any one Address. Occasionally it fails even to attain agenda status, but it never stays off the agenda for long. Over time it has evolved and expanded, intertwining with other issue areas (e.g., poverty, social welfare, and government power: see Carmines and Stimson 1989). Like foreign policy and the economy, civil rights holds a special place in the American agenda. It is an undercurrent problem in American politics, and while it may be pushed off the agenda, it is never lost. Thus, there is a persistence to civil rights that many other discretionary areas do not possess. Still, it is a less powerful attention grabber than matters of war, peace, and the economy.

The domestic policy area, which covers all other domestic policies, as a group always makes it to the president's agenda with a frequency similar to that noticed for economic policy.[6] On average, domestic policy occupies a little over one-fourth of the typical president's Address. At times, domestic policy overall can occupy a large part of the agenda, topping 50 percent in 1969, 1974, 1977, and 40 percent in 1955 and 1970.

Presidential Responsiveness to Public Opinion

The theory proposed here suggests that presidents should be responsive to public opinion during the problem identification process. They can be responsive because responsiveness does not constrain later substantive decisions about public policies. Light (1982) finds some empirical support for this in his study of the presidential agenda-setting process. Twenty-seven percent of the staffers who served from Kennedy through Carter identified public opinion as a source of issue ideas (86), but public opinion only matters when, according to a Ford staffer, "an issue gets hot" (93), that is, when public intensity over the issue grows. The percentage of the public citing an issue as the most important problem is one indicator of such intensity.

We can formalize this line of reasoning with the following equation:

President's Most Important Problem$_t$ = a + b(Public's Most Important Problem$_{t-1}$) + c(Other Factors) + error.

where a, b, and c are parameter estimates and e denotes the error term. The subscripts suggest temporal ordering and indicate in the model that the president responds to prior (or already existing) public opinion. If the president is being responsive to the public, then b should be positive and greater than zero by a statistically significant amount. If b does not differ from zero, the president is not being responsive, while a negative b indicates counterresponsiveness. The model suggests that everything else being equal, presidents will emphasize the policy areas that the public thinks most important. The equation leaves open the possibility that other factors may also affect the emphasis of presidential problems. These other factors include the type of policy, objective conditions, and cycles of attention, and in some cases competition between policy areas for attention.

Policy Type

The distinction between discretionary and required policy areas may affect the degree of presidential responsiveness to public opinion. Required policies (Kessel 1974) persist on the agenda, though they may rise and fall in relative importance. Most important, required areas may push discretionary areas off the agenda.

Required policy areas persist because they are always on the public's mind. By definition, they are of concern to large numbers of people, having profound implications for the everyday lives of people. Few events are more personally disruptive than being sent off to war or losing one's job. Moreover, the public places responsibility for these macro-required policies on the president. The combination of widespread concern, profound impact, and responsibility sensitizes presidents to the political implications of these required policy areas. As public concern over a required policy area mounts, presidential attention should increase accordingly.

In contrast, discretionary areas should not create such a strong presidential response to public opinion. Even when most of the public thinks the area is important, public attention can be diverted away from discretionary areas. For instance, presidents may ask the public to wait until required problems are resolved before attending to discretionary items.

Objective Conditions

Objective conditions may also affect presidential responsiveness to public opinion. When objective conditions show a deteriorating state of affairs, presidents may be unable to avoid attending to them. The public expects presidents to solve problems, and deterioration in objective indicators signals problems to the president and the public. Given his access to information about objective conditions, it is quite likely that the president will recognize the state of objective factors before the public does.

Deterioration in conditions associated with required areas may have more impact on the president than discretionary policy areas. As I noted earlier, the president has stronger incentives to do something about required policy areas than discretionary ones. Thus, when the international situation is hot, especially when a war is in progress or imminent, presidents should be expected to turn their attention in that direction. Similarly, when indicators suggest a declining economy, presidents will shift attention there.

Deterioration in required policy areas may divert presidential attention away from discretionary areas. Economic decline and an unstable international environment may deflect presidential attention from, for instance, civil rights policy and overall domestic policy. Problems in required policy areas may push discretionary issues off the agenda. As an example of this effect, President Carter said early in his term that he would boost attention to civil rights. He did not, however, anticipate the impact of the energy crisis on the economy and the public's mind. Attention to civil rights dissipated as Carter turned his attention to dealing with energy and the economy. Similarly, the Gulf War diverted Bush's and the public's attention from the stumbling economy. Bush's success in handling the Gulf crisis as well as the short, swift U.S. victory with very modest casualties catapulted Bush's popularity rating to among the highest ever recorded. Once, however, the Gulf crisis subsided, the economy resumed its place as the object of most public concern, and Bush's ratings took a steep dive.

Cycles of Attention

Scholars have often noted a cyclical pattern to the attention the public pays to issues. Downs (1972) writes of an issue attention cycle in which public attention peaks during the dramatic phase of policy concern, only to rapidly recede as it turns to other problems. Kingdon (1984) and Stimson (1991) discuss the public mood, suggesting that public opinion is more amenable to certain types of policies during some times rather than others. Cycles affecting the presidency have also been discussed (Cronin 1980; Kessel; 1974; Light 1982).

Perhaps the most important cycle for present purposes relates to the election process. Elections turn the attention of politicians toward public concerns (Kuklinski 1978). During election years and campaign periods, politicians, to get (re)elected, cater to public opinion. Thus, presidential sensitivity to public concerns should peak during the year they are up for reelection. As the pressures of election recede, presidential attention will shift away from those types of issues that gather votes and toward policies that presidents find ever intrusive, like international affairs (Kessel 1974; Cronin 1980). Thus, Kessel (1974) finds that presidential attention to foreign affairs builds across the term until the fourth year, a reelection year, when presidential attention to it drops precipitously.

Except during times of war and international crisis, voters find domestic matters more compelling. Foreign affairs often seem distant. It is also hard for presidents to build election constituencies around foreign affairs, except during times of war and international crisis. Bush's inability to maintain the support that he generated from the Persian Gulf War for the 1992 reelection campaign strongly illustrates the point. Domestic policies are more likely sources of distributive benefits that politicians, even presidents (Kessel 1974; Tufte 1978), find so alluring in attracting voters and building electoral coalitions.

Thus, a cycle of attention to foreign and domestic affairs characterizes the presidency. Elections heighten the importance of domestic policies. Foreign matters usually are more important to the presidents, especially in the nuclear age. Moreover, most presidents seem more interested in foreign policy, either from natural inclination or because they feel less constrained in directing policy in that realm. Of Presidents Eisenhower through Bush, perhaps only Johnson, and maybe Reagan, did not prefer foreign policy.[7] But even Johnson, the most domestically oriented president, found that foreign policy, especially the Vietnam War, consumed most of his time and energy. As these election pressures ebb, foreign policy surges onto the president's agenda.

Hypotheses and Data

The discussion in the previous section suggests that presidential policy attention will be a function of public concern, policy type, objective conditions, competition across policies, and election cycles. In this section I present more specific hypotheses, derived from that discussion. I also discuss the data used to measure each variable.

Foreign Policy

Foreign policy is a required policy area. As a required policy area, we expect to find that when the public is concerned about foreign policy, presidential attention to foreign policy should increase. Public concern with foreign policy is measured as the percentage of people who cite foreign affairs as the most important problem in the latest Gallup poll *preceding* the State of the Union Address. We can determine causality unambiguously because the Address is delivered after the public opinion reading. Presidential attention to foreign policy should also increase when the nation is at war. A dummy variable (1 = war, 0 = no war) is used to measure war. Two major wars occurred during this period, Korea and Vietnam.

Foreign policy also has to compete with the other required area, economic policy, for the president's attention. Thus, when either inflation and/or unemployment is high, presidential attention to foreign policy should ebb. Inflation and unemployment are measured at the levels they held during the month of the Address. The election cycle should also affect attention to foreign policy (Kessel 1974). During the fourth year of the president's term, attention to foreign policy should decrease. I follow Brace and Hinckley's (1992, 1993) lead and measure cyclical effects by including a dummy variable for each of the four years that make up a president's term. Specifically, I use a dummy variable to indicate year two, three, and four of the president's term. The intercept captures the effect for the first year.[8]

Economic Policy

Like foreign policy, presidential attention to economic policy should increase with increased public concern about the economy. Public concern over the economy is measured as the percentage who cite the economy as the most important problem in the latest Gallup survey preceding the Address. Attention to economic policy is also expected to increase when inflation and/or unemployment is high. Kessel (1974) did not find any cycle associated with presidential attention to economic policy, arguing instead that it is a constant concern. Cronin (1980) suggests that presidential concern with the economy peaks during the middle years of the term, as election and inaugural years divert attention to coalition building. I enter separate time point dummy variables to capture this effect. Lastly, the competition among policy areas for agenda placement leads to the expectation that when the nation is at war, attention to the economy will decline.

Civil Rights

Unlike the other two policy areas, civil rights is a discretionary policy area. Thus, we expect only modest presidential responsiveness to the public when public concern about civil rights is strong. Public concern with civil rights is measured as the percentage offering civil rights as the most important problem in the latest Gallup poll preceding the State of the Union Address. As a discretionary area, public concern with required policy areas may also push the president away from attending to civil rights. Thus, when the public is highly concerned about either the economy or foreign policy, presidential attention to civil rights policy should fall.

Deteriorating objective conditions in the economy and the international scene should also direct the president away from a discretionary area like civil rights. Thus, during wars and periods of either high unemployment and/or inflation, we expect presidential attention to civil rights to dip. The election cycle strongly affects attention to discretionary areas. We should, consequently, expect increases in attention to civil rights during the first and fourth years of the president's term. Time point dummies are used to capture this hypothesized cycle.

Domestic Policy

Domestic policy, like civil rights policy, is conceptualized here as a discretionary policy area. Thus, we expect presidential attention to the required policy areas to push domestic policy from the agenda. Similarly, we expect objective conditions associated with the economy and war to divert presidential attention from domestic issues. Like civil rights, domestic policy may rise and fall on the president's agenda with the electoral cycle. Specifically, we might find a rise in attention to domestic policy during the fourth (election or reelection) year of a president's term, as presidents and parties make appeals to interest groups to secure their votes in the upcoming election.

Lastly, as the discretionary model suggests, we expect only modest presidential responsiveness to public concern over domestic policy. To measure public concern with domestic policy, I aggregate the percentage from the Gallup Most Important Problem series citing social control, government, and miscellaneous. Greater comparability between policy area referents for public opinion and the president exist for the other three policy areas than in the case of domestic policy. The lack of good fit between the measure of domestic policy from the president's Address and the Gallup series may weaken any possible presidential responsiveness to public opinion for this policy area. Thus, finding no relationship may be a result of the fact that presidents truly are not responsive, or it may be due to measurement error.

Analysis

Table 2.2 presents results of regressing presidential attention to each of the four policy areas on public opinion, objective conditions, and yearly cycles. When equations exhibited first order autocorrelation, I employed an AR1 estimation procedure as a correction. This is noted on the table. Lagrange multiplier tests, reported on the table, also indicate the absence of any remaining autocorrelation.[9]

My central hypothesis is that presidents will be responsive to public opinion in the problem identification process. Such responsiveness is more symbolic than substantive and thus costs presidents very little in terms of later control over substantive policy decisions. This responsive reaction will be stronger for required policies than for discretionary ones. The results in table 2.2 strongly support these expectations.

Inspection of the slope coefficients (*b*) justifies this interpretation. Presidential attention to foreign and economic policy moves in tandem with the public's concern, but presidents exhibit no corresponding response for civil rights or domestic policy. Of the policy areas, the most proportionate effect is

TABLE 2.2.   Determinants of the President's Most Important Problem, 1953–89

	b	SE	t
Economic policy			
Constant	19.65	2.56	7.67
Year 2	−6.25	3.90	−1.60
Year 3	−7.76	3.82	−2.03
Public opinion	.24	.06	3.89
Reagan	9.27	3.28	2.83
R^2/Adj. R^2	.56	.50	
Rho (AR1)	−.38		
Lagrange multiplier	2.31		
International relations			
Constant	30.04	6.41	4.69
Year 1	−11.93	5.83	−2.04
Public Opinion	.45	.17	2.68
R^2/Adj. R^2	.35	.30	
Rho (AR1)	.26		
Lagrange multiplier	.44		
Civil rights			
Constant	12.61	2.96	4.26
Year 4	3.90	1.37	2.85
Unemployment	−.88	.40	−2.02
Pres. - IR	−.08	.03	−2.56
Public Opinion	.04	.07	.53
R^2/Adj. R^2	.41	.33	
DW d (OLS)	1.93		
Lagrange multiplier	.13		
Domestic policy			
Constant	82.47	3.50	23.56
Year 4	−3.53	1.34	−2.63
Pres. - Economics	−.82	.06	−13.47
Pres. - IR	−.83	.04	−19.89
Public opinion	.05	.05	.96
R^2/Adj. R^2	.95	.94	
DW d (OLS)	2.13		
Lagrange multiplier	.56		

found for foreign policy. Each 1 percent increase in public concern to foreign affairs leads to a corresponding .45 percent increase in presidential attention. Presidential responsiveness to public concern over the economy is more sluggish. Each 1 percent increase leads to only a .24 percent presidential response. Both coefficients are statistically significant at the .01 level or better. In contrast, we see no significant presidential responsiveness to public opinion for civil rights. The slope is a paltry .04, meaning that each 1 percent change in public concern over civil rights moves presidents only .04 percent. More-over, that coefficient is not statistically significant ($t = .53$). A similar story is told for domestic policy. The *b* suggests that each 1 percent increase in public attention to domestic policy moves the president a slight .05 percent, an amount that is not statistically significant. These results are consistent with expectations flowing from the distinction between discretionary and required policy.

In general, most of the other hypotheses concerning presidential attention to the policy areas are also supported. For instance, when presidential concern with required policy areas increases, attention to civil rights and domestic policy dips, as hypothesized. Each 1 percent increase in presidential attention to foreign policy reduces presidential attention to civil rights by about .08 percent. Presidential attention to economic policy, however, does not affect attention to civil rights.

Domestic policy is even more strongly affected by presidential attention to required policy areas. A 1 percent increase in presidential attention to economic and foreign policy decreases presidential attention to domestic policy by .82 and .83 percent, respectively. These effects are very strong and highly significant, with massive *t* values in the 13 to 20 range. One can almost suggest that domestic policy overall is entirely dependent on presidential attention to the required policy areas of economic and foreign policy. Only if there is any agenda room left over will presidents attend to domestic policy. This is in contrast to civil rights, which, while affected by presidential atten-tion to foreign affairs, was only marginally affected, though with statistical significance. In fact, the only other variable to affect domestic policy is the fourth year of the presidential term, and contrary to expectations the sign is negative, suggesting reductions in attention during the last year in office, when increases were anticipated. Finally, the simple equation of presidential atten-tion to economic and foreign policy and year four almost entirely accounts for presidential attention to domestic policy, with about 95 percent of the variance explained.

Objective conditions sometimes affect presidential attention. Unemploy-ment reduces presidential attention to civil rights. Each 1 percent increase in unemployment reduces relative presidential attentiveness to civil rights by nearly .9 percent. Objective factors do not affect foreign and economic policy perhaps because public opinion is mediating the impact of objective condi-tions. Thus, objective conditions stimulate public concern, and presidents respond, not to the conditions themselves, but to public concern. I provide some support for this notion in the next section, when I consider the determi-nants of public concern and the ability of presidents to lead public opinion. And objective conditions seem to have no impact on domestic policy because that policy area seems almost totally determined by presidential attention to economic and foreign policy, as I noted earlier.

Lastly, some cyclical effects exist. During the first year in office, presidential attention to foreign policy wanes. (In the results presented in table 2.2 I inserted a dummy variable for year one, instead of using the intercept, to ease reading results.) The effect is quite large. Presidential concern with foreign policy during the initial year in office dips nearly 12 percent, but I do not find the fourth year dip that Kessel (1974) noted. Kessel's analysis focused on the period 1946 to 1969. My period begins in 1953 and traces through to 1989. In the post-Vietnam period, foreign policy lost its bipartisan character. Often bitter partisan divisions over foreign policy issues were raised during the post-Vietnam era. This transformation of the foreign policy debate may have made it more useful as an election campaign theme then previously. Moreover, in this era of economic distress, presidents may be more likely to achieve significant success in foreign policy. Presidents may thus be tempted to use those achievements in election campaigns.

Economic policy also shows a cycle, but a complicated one. Again, no fourth-year cycle is found, but presidential attentiveness to the economy peaks during the first year in office. The effect, almost 20 percent, is opposite in direction to that found for foreign policy. And during the second and third year of the term, presidential attention to economic policy dips about 6 to 8 percent for each year. Presidents may be especially attentive to economic policy during the first year of each new term. They may feel this way because of the importance of the economy to making and breaking administrations and the fact that so many new administrations ride into office on the economic failure of their predecessor. This has especially been the case during the post-Kessel (post-1969) years because of the poor performance of the economy during those two decades. Presidents use the first message to indicate how their policies will differ from the previous, failed administration. If the president is a second-term incumbent or intraparty successor, there is an incentive to emphasize the previous term's economic success in the first-year message. This change may help explain why my results differ from Kessel's.

Civil rights displays classic distributive politics and election-year dynamics. Presidents pay more attention to civil rights during the fourth year in office, a 4 percent increase.[10] They may be using civil rights rhetoric to attract voters. But civil rights does not persist on the agenda during the postelection victory consolidation of the first year. This may indicate the relative ease with which discretionary policy areas are pushed from the agenda, a theme that we noticed before. And as I noted earlier, domestic policy suffers from a decline in attention during the fourth year in office.

Lastly, one presidential dummy was significant. Attention to economic policy increased while Reagan was president. The effect was quite large, over 9 percent. This result attests clearly to the often remarked importance of economic policy to the Reagan administration, including his redirection of U. S. economic policy away from government involvement and more toward allowing market solutions to problems. For civil rights policy, I found that all presidential dummies, using Bush as the criterion case, had impact. Each was positive in sign, but as these dummies did not affect the other variables of more substantive interest and complicated the analysis of the time point dummies, they were not presented. All that resulted was a increase of the R^2, as expected in such situations.[11]

Presidential Leadership of Public Opinion

The theory being tested here does not speak directly to the issue of presidential leadership of public opinion. The president's ability to lead public opinion, however, has implications for presidential responsiveness to public opinion. If the president can lead public opinion, especially with symbolic and nonsubstantive argument and rhetoric, he may be better able to control substantive aspects of the policy-making process. That is, by being able to mobilize the public behind his policy directions in the substantive stages of the policy-making process, he may be less inclined or motivated to follow public opinion. Their acceptance of his substantive policy leadership may create the impression that the president and the public are on the same wavelength concerning public policy. Consequently, charges of presidential nonresponsiveness to public opinion may be less likely to arise. Inability to lead public opinion may force presidents to consider public opinion in the substantive aspects of policy-making, thereby ceding to the public some measure of presidential control and discretion over the substantive issues of policy-making. Presidents may have to be responsive to public opinion throughout the policy-making process if they are not able to lead the public. In this section, I look at the ability of the president to lead public opinion in the problem identification process.

A large literature exists on the president's ability to lead public opinion. Past research tends to fall into two sets. The first looks at the ability of presidents to manipulate their popularity rating through political drama, like making speeches and traveling to other nations. The early rounds of that research (MacKuen 1983; Ragsdale 1984, 1987) suggested that presidents can boost their popularity through such activities but that those boosts were very short lived (MacKuen 1983). More recent efforts have revised thinking about presidential ability to manipulate their popularity (Brace and Hinckley 1993; Ostrom and Simon 1985, 1988, 1989; Simon and Ostrom 1985, 1988, 1989).

The situation is now more complex, with major speeches boosting popularity, foreign trips having no impact, and domestic trips hurting popularity, according to Brace and Hinckley (1992, 56–7).

The second research set looks at the president's ability to lead public opinion on specific policies, to gather support for his policy initiatives. These studies do not find universal presidential leadership capacity. Presidents are only able to lead public opinion on specific policies when the president is popular (Edwards 1983; Kernell 1993; Mondak 1993; Page and Shapiro 1984, 1985, 1987, 1989, 1992; Rosen 1973; Sigelman 1980; Thomas and Bass 1982; Thomas and Sigelman 1985). Unpopular presidents possess little influence and may repel public opinion (Sigelman and Sigelman 1981).

Together, these two literature streams suggest severe limitations on presidential leadership of public opinion, but they do not exhaust its avenues. Presidents can influence the public agenda. Perhaps only popular presidents can get the public to support a policy direction on a specific policy, and popular presidents need not travel or speak because their popularity is already high. But the public may respond less discriminatingly when presidents identify a problem as something that government should take action on.

A modest literature suggests this presidential agenda-setting impact. Behr and Iyengar (1985) demonstrate that when presidents give major speeches dedicated to a policy problem, the public responds (also Iyengar and Kinder 1987, 31). The effect under investigation here is subtler. Does presidential emphasis of a policy area in a general, multipurpose speech influence public concern over that and other policy areas?

Presidents and Public Opinion

Presidential ability to influence the public's policy agenda is a function of his resources and the public's receptivity to his influence attempts. Some presidential resources are constants across presidents. They tend to be associated with the office rather than individual occupants. For instance, all presidents have easy access to the mass public. The office is highly prestigious, and the glow of prestige shines on all its occupants. No other politician or office is accorded such a role; none can compete effectively with the president in terms of prestige, status, media access, public attention, interest, and so on.

Other presidential resources are more variable. They may include experience and preparation for the job, ability to articulate their positions, and possession of other political skills. Perhaps the most important variable resource is popularity. Popularity is an important political currency in Washington (Light 1982, 25–28) and may enhance the president's credibility with the public, thereby increasing his ability to influence public opinion.

Public receptivity is also important in understanding the president's ability to influence the mass public. On one level, the public is highly receptive to presidents. People are predisposed to accept presidential leadership on public policies; the public has a demand or appetite for presidential leadership. They often await presidential leadership on an issue, and criticize presidents who fail to enter policy debate and discussion. The public has no such comparable demand for leadership from any other quarter. Moreover, the public seems psychologically reliant on the president (Greenstein 1974). This may heighten their receptivity to presidential leadership, especially in crisis or stressful situations (Edelman 1964, 1974).

But barriers to public receptivity also exist. Politics is rarely an overriding or daily concern of most people. Private and personal concerns constrain the role and place of politics and policy in people's lives. Presidents must overcome this barrier to gain the mass public's attention.

The president may also have to compete with other factors that may influence the public's thinking about politics and policy. Although other politicians might not be strong competitors in this regard, preexisting attitudes, the mass media, and real-life experiences may effectively compete with the president for influence over public opinion. For example, those with preexisting attitudes may be hard to budge, while those without preexisting attitudes may be uninterested in politics. Consequently, both may be somewhat immune to the president's message, requiring extra presidential effort to get his message across.[12]

Similarly, the mass media may present information or news that undercuts the president's aims, emphasizing different issues or putting a "spin" on stories that differs from the president's spin.[13] Lastly, real-life experiences may profoundly affect people and how they think about policies and political issues (Mayer 1993). If the president's "reality" does not accord well with people's "experienced realities," the public may not be highly receptive to presidential attempts to influence them. Thus, presidential leadership of the public's agenda is not guaranteed, but the president possesses resources and opportunities to influence public opinion.

Hypotheses and Data

Our central hypothesis is that public concern with a policy area increases as presidential emphasis with the policy area increases. The president, however, is not the sole determinant of public attention, as other factors may also affect public concern. Past research has found that objective conditions affect public assessments of the importance of a policy area (Behr and Iyengar 1985; Iyengar and Kinder 1987; MacKuen 1981). Following from this research, wars should boost public concern about foreign affairs, and high inflation and unemployment should heighten public concern over the economy.

Limitations in the number of issues that the average person can attend to at any one time should result in competition among issues for public attention. Thus, when attention is directed to one issue, attention to other issues should wane. In this competition, required issues hold advantages over discretionary issue areas for public attention. Hence, not only may wars increase attention to foreign policy, but wars should divert attention from concerns about the economy, domestic issues in general, and civil rights. Similarly, a poorly performing economy will push foreign affairs, domestic concerns, and civil rights off the public's agenda, but attention to civil rights and/or domestic issues should have little impact on attention to the economy or foreign policy. I measure public concern with Gallup's Most Important Problem question in the first poll taken after the State of the Union Address. (My last analysis used the last reading prior to the presidential Address.) Other variables are operationalized as they were earlier.[14] I also add into each equation public concern with that policy area prior to the president's Address. This controls for the possibility that the president's message merely mediates prior public opinion because of presidential responsiveness to the public, as I noted earlier.

Analysis

Table 2.3 presents regression results of the impact of presidential attention and objective conditions on the public's most important problem. The hypotheses developed earlier are supported strongly. Presidential attention and objective conditions significantly affect public concern across all policy areas. The estimations proved to be very powerful, with nearly 90 percent of the variance explained for economic policy and 81 percent for foreign, civil rights, and domestic policy.

As hypothesized, presidents strongly influence public concern for each of the four policy areas. Specifically, each 1 percent increase in presidential attention leads to about a .4 percent increase in public attention to economic policy, .2 percent to foreign policy, .5 percent to civil rights policy, and .2 percent to domestic policy. Each of these is statistically significant.

Objective factors also affect public attentiveness. When the economy is souring, attention to it increases, though unemployment seems to have the stronger pull on the public than inflation. War, however, has little impact on public concern with foreign policy and international affairs.

Objective factor tradeoffs are also apparent. War does not seem to divert attention from either the economy, domestic policy, or civil rights, and nor does a poorly performing economy divert attention from foreign affairs. But unemployment, and not inflation, deflects attention from civil rights, and neither war nor the economy affects public attention to domestic policy.

By far the most important factor in determining public attention is prior

TABLE 2.3. Determinants of the Public's Most Important Problem, 1953–89

Policy Area	b	SE	t
Economic policy			
Constant	−28.84	8.64	−2.88
Inflation	.34	.62	.56
Unemployment	5.98	1.69	3.53
War	2.43	4.09	.59
President's economic mentions	.40	.11	3.71
Public opinion $_{(t-1)}$	.29	.15	1.99
R^2/Adj. R^2/equation type	.88	.85	AR1
Rho	.28		
Lagrange multiplier	1.20		
Foreign policy			
Constant	14.66	13.44	1.09
Inflation	.003	.71	.004
Unemployment	−1.81	1.43	−1.26
War	4.40	4.29	1.02
President's foreign policy mentions	.21	.10	2.13
Public opinion $_{(t-1)}$	.52	.16	3.18
R^2/Adj. R^2/equation type	.81	.77	OLS
Lagrange multiplier	1.72		
Civil rights policy			
Constant	5.18	3.24	1.60
Inflation	−.03	.17	−.18
Unemployment	−.88	.46	−1.92
War	.26	1.50	.17
President's civil rights policy mentions	.50	.16	3.04
Public opinion	.57	.07	7.67
R^2/Adj. R^2/equation type	.81	.78	AR1
Rho	−.31		
Lagrange multiplier	1.20		
Domestic policy			
Constant	−6.22	6.66	−.93
Inflation	.39	.51	.76
Unemployment	.55	.98	.56
War	−2.98	3.82	−.78
Pres. domestic policy mentions	.20	.11	1.91
Public opinion $_{(t-1)}$	.92	.16	5.93
R^2/Adj. R^2/equation type	.81	.77	OLS
DW h	.67		
Lagrange multiplier	.95		

public attention.[15] In each case, prior public attention strongly affects public attention after the president's Address. The lack of an impact from objective factors may be in part due to this variable, which is capturing some of those impacts. Removing prior public attention increases the impact of several of the objective conditions across the policy areas. That presidential influence persists in the face of this strong control attests to the ability of the president to influence and lead public opinion, at least with regard to the public's agenda.

Popularity and Decay Effects

The analysis in the previous section on presidential leadership of public opinion raises at least two other questions that the present design can address. First, are popular presidents more "persuasive" than unpopular presidents? Second, how long do the leadership effects persist?

Popularity Effects

The literature on presidential leadership of public opinion reviewed earlier indicates that popular presidents can influence public opinion (Edwards 1983; Kernell 1993; Mondak 1993; Page and Shapiro 1984, 1985, 1987, 1989, 1992; Rosen 1973; Sigelman 1980; Thomas and Bass 1982; Thomas and Sigelman 1985), but unpopular presidents either do not affect public opinion or may actually repel public opinion (Sigelman and Sigelman 1981).

I created a weighted emphasis variable by multiplying each presidential policy emphasis variable by the president's popularity level from the last Gallup poll preceding the presidential Address. The resulting variables were very strongly correlated with the original presidential emphasis variables. The two economic policy variables correlated at .89, while the correlation for the foreign policy, civil rights, and domestic policy areas were .92, .94, and .88, respectively. With such high correlations, disentangling the separate effects of the two variables may not be possible. Still, one may compare the R^2s of the equations with and without the weighted variable, while retaining the un-weighted presidential emphasis variable, to estimate whether the weighted variable adds to the equation's explained variance.

Table 2.4 presents the relevant statistics. It shows the results of equations with either the unweighted or weighted presidential emphasis variables and equations including both. Statistics on the other control variables, objective conditions and prior public opinion, are not included in the presentation. They are hardly affected by inclusion of the weighted emphasis variable, but they are retained in the equation as controls.

The results indicate no effect of presidential popularity on public concern with the economy. The equation that only includes the weighted emphasis

TABLE 2.4. Presidential Popularity, the President's Most Important Problem, and Public Opinion, 1953–89

Policy Area	Equations	b	SE	t	R^2	Adj.R^2
Economic policy	1. Pres. Ec. (unweighted)	.40	.11	3.71	.88	.85
	2. Pres. Ec. (weighted)	.51	.19	2.71	.86	.83
	3. Pres. Ec. (unweighted)	.80	.35	2.25	.88	.85
	+ Pres. Ec. (weighted)	−.64	.56	−1.16		
Foreign policy	1. Pres. IR. (unweighted)	.20	.08	2.48	.81	.78
	2. Pres. IR (weighted)	.47	.16	2.90	.83	.79
	3. Pres. IR. (unweighted)	−.08	.22	−.36	.83	.79
	+ Pres. IR. (weighted)	.58	.37	1.58		
Civil rights policy	1. Pres. CR. (unweighted)	.50	.16	3.04	.81	.78
	2. Pres. CR (weighted)	1.01	.32	3.21	.82	.78
	3. Pres. CR. (unweighted)	.12	.45	.26	.82	.78
	+ Pres. CR. (weighted)	.81	.87	.93		
Domestic policy	1. Pres. DP. (unweighted)	.20	.11	1.91	.81	.77
	2. Pres. DP. (weighted)	.0005	.002	.27	.78	.74
	3. Pres. DP. (unweighted)	.84	.19	4.48	.88	.85
	+ Pres. DP. (weighted)	−.01	.003	−3.81		

Note: All equations control for war, inflation, unemployment, and prior public opinion. See text for details.

variable performs a tad poorer than the unweighted economic policy emphasis variable. Moreover, including both in the equation shows that the original, unweighted variable attains statistical significance, while the weighted variable is not only statistically insignificant, but its sign points in the wrong direction. Lastly, the R^2s of the equation that has only the unweighted variable and the one that has both are identical. Adding presidential economic policy emphasis weighted by presidential popularity does not affect the president's ability to influence public opinion over this policy area.

Popularity seems more important for foreign policy, though. Comparison of results of the equations with either the unweighted or weighted foreign policy emphasis variables reveals that the weighted variable is more potent. First, the b for the weighted variable is more than twice that for the unweighted version (.20 to .47). Also, the R^2 for the equation with the weighted variable is somewhat stronger (.83 to .81), but an F test ($F = .63$, see endnote 11) does not find the difference to be statistically significant. Turning to the equation that includes both variables shows again that the weighted variable performs better than the unweighted version. In this equation, the unweighted variable fails to reach statistical significance, and its sign points in the wrong direction. In contrast, the weighted variable has the correct sign, though it barely fails to reach statistical significance at the .10 level. Multicollinearity between the two variables accounts for this failure. Lastly, the R^2 slightly surpasses that for the unweighted variable equation, but again that difference is not statistically significant. Though arguable, these results suggest that presidential emphasis on foreign policy, weighted by popularity, has stronger, although modest, effects than unweighted presidential emphasis to that policy area.

The civil rights policy area repeats the findings for the foreign policy area. There is some indication that civil rights policy emphasis weighted by presidential popularity more strongly affects public opinion than unweighted policy emphasis. First, comparison of the b for the two equations that include either the unweighted or weighted variable shows that presidential emphasis weighted by popularity has about twice the impact of the unweighted variable (1.01 to .50), though little improvement is noted for the R^2. When both are entered into the equation, neither reaches statistical significance, presumably because of their high intercorrelation, but again the weighted variable seems the stronger of the two ($b = .87$ versus $b = .12$).

The most complicated results come from the domestic policy area. By itself, the weighted presidential mentions variable has little impact on public attention to domestic policy, though the unweighted presidential mention variable is statistically significant. Moreover, the R^2 of the weighted equation falls short of that for the unweighted equation. When both variables are entered together into the equation, the R^2 improves about seven points (from .81 for the unweighted equation to .88). The impact of the unweighted presidential attention variable surges in impact, from .20 to .84, but the popularity-weighted presidential attention variable shows a perverse, negative sign, which is also statistically significant. Still, the coefficient for the weighted variable is quite small. This sign reversal is probably due to multicollinearity and interaction effects (Friedrich 1982).

To summarize, in two cases, foreign policy and civil rights, the evidence points to the conditioning effect of popularity on the ability of the president to lead public opinion. A third case, economic policy, shows no impact, while a fourth (domestic policy), shows quite confusing results. These impacts for foreign policy and civil rights are, however, quite modest, and the very high intercorrelation between variables weighted by presidential popularity with their counterparts that are not weighted makes disentangling their separate effects quite difficult.

Time Decay Effects

Presidents unequivocally lead public attention to policy concerns. Popular presidents seem only marginally better able to lead than less popular presidents. In this section, I raise the question, How long do these presidential effects persist? Are they ephemeral and fleeting, or does presidential leadership restructure public opinion, thus leading to longer-term, persistent effects?

Some scholars contend that the president's most formidable power is his ability to alter the political agenda (Peterson 1990). Anecdotal evidence suggests the ability of incoming presidents, such as Johnson and Reagan, to steer public opinion and the policy agenda down new paths. By focusing on some policy areas more than others, presidents may be able to redirect the policy agenda. They probably can push some items off the agenda or keep brewing problems from reaching the agenda by merely attending to other, competing policy areas. Thus, presidents play an important agenda gatekeeping role. This gatekeeping may have prolonged effects, filtering some issues into or out of public consciousness and concern. In this sense, the president can restructure the agenda.

In contrast, some view presidents as captives of uncontrollable events (Rose 1991; Light 1982). In this view, uncontrollable events and crises impinge on the president, forcing him to attend to issues and concerns that he would either prefer to avoid or is unprepared to deal with. Though presidents may try to structure debate and the agenda, they cannot sustain their efforts because of the diversionary power of uncontrollable events and crises.

Thus, we are presented with two competing models of presidential leadership of public opinion. The first suggests that the leadership effects witnessed earlier should persist over a long period, even in the face of interceding events and crises. The other suggests that presidential leadership effects do not last for long, as uncontrollable events and crises push onto the agenda, crowding out presidential concerns. Moreover, the weak agenda position of discretionary policy areas should lead them to be pushed off the agenda faster than the required policy areas.

I test these competing notions by looking at the impact of the president's Address on the last public opinion reading prior to the next Address, which comes about a year after the president's Address. Does presidential leadership of the public's agenda persist for a year or not? I also enter controls for war, inflation, and unemployment into the equation. The results are presented in table 2.5.

Presidential leadership effects decay for economic and civil rights policy by year's end, but they persist for foreign policy and weakly persist for domestic policy. The economic policy equation, like previous ones, shows the strong impact of objective economic conditions on public opinion. Unemployment again has a greater impact than inflation, but both are potent sources of public concern with the economy. Also repeating earlier findings, war has no impact on economic concern, but neither does the past year's presidential Address. The b coefficient declines from .40 (see table 2.3) to $-.01$. The coming and going of economic conditions seems to have more effect on what

TABLE 2.5. Long-Term Impact of Presidential Policy Emphases on the Public's Most Important Problem, 1953–89

Policy Area	b	SE	t
Economic policy			
Constant	−25.65	9.16	−2.80
Inflation	2.40	.62	3.91
Unemployment	8.66	1.47	5.88
War	−3.52	4.90	−.72
President's economic mentions$_{(t-1)}$	−.01	.14	−.08
R^2/Adj. R^2/equation type	.82	.79	AR1
Rho	.16		
Lagrange multiplier	.64		
Foreign policy			
Constant	59.98	12.90	4.57
Inflation	−3.19	.63	−5.06
Unemployment	−4.03	1.65	−2.45
War	4.18	6.00	.70
President's foreign policy mentions$_{(t-1)}$	.23	.11	2.11
R^2/Adj. R^2/equation type	.73	.69	OLS
Lagrange multiplier	.56		
Civil rights policy			
Constant	21.11	8.06	2.62
Inflation	−.51	.55	−.93
Unemployment	−2.02	1.22	−1.65
War	1.28	5.00	.27
President's civil rights policy mentions$_{(t-1)}$	−.21	.37	−.57
R^2/Adj. R^2/equation type	.31	.22	AR1
Rho	.26		
Lagrange multiplier	.26		
Domestic policy			
Constant	6.44	7.99	.81
Inflation	−.56	1.27	−.44
Unemployment	1.98	.54	3.68
War	6.75	4.98	1.36
President's domestic policy mentions$_{(t-1)}$	.17	.11	1.60
R^2/Adj. R^2/equation type	.59	.53	6LS
Rho	.24		
Lagrange multiplier	.23		

people think about the economy than nearly year-old statements by the president about the economy. We see this with George Bush as the nation began to sink into recession during the middle of his term. Bush's economic optimism, based on the long expansion of the Reagan years, was not able to buoy the spirits of public opinion as the economy began its slide into recession.

Civil rights replays the basic thrust of the economic policy findings. Unemployment diverts attention from civil rights, repeating an old finding, while neither war nor inflation affects concern with unemployment. But neither does previous presidential attention. By year's end, the *b* coefficient for presidential civil rights policy attention drops from .50 to −.21, reversing in sign and no longer statistically significant. Like the economy, interceding events have strong impact on public concern with civil rights, but these events are more volatile and unpredictable than the more slowly evolving economic conditions.

For foreign policy, however, the past year's presidential Address significantly affects public opinion. Unemployment and inflation dilute attention to foreign affairs, but curiously war has no effect, although the sign is in the correct direction.[16] The presidential variable remains statistically significant (*t* = 1.97), and the *b* coefficient hardly decreases (from .23 to .21). The president seems more able to structure the public agenda in foreign policy than in either economic or civil rights policy.

The domestic policy results resemble the foreign policy ones but in weaker form. Of the objective conditions, only unemployment affects attention to domestic policy, but here increases in unemployment stimulate public attention to domestic policy. Unmeasured variables may be causing this result. Commonly, unemployment is associated with increases in crime and other social disruptions. Rather than being responsive to unemployment per se here, the public may be responding to the consequences of unemployment. Presidential attention has a modest ability to keep public attention focused on domestic issues across a year's time. The coefficient drops slightly from that found earlier, from .20 to .17. However, in this equation, the variable is marginally significant, with a *t* value of 1.60. Better measurement of the consequences of unemployment may dramatically alter this presidential leadership effect.

Overall, the president's ability to structure the agenda across a relatively long term through the State of the Union Address is modest at best. Clear effects are only found for foreign policy, no persistent effects are uncovered for economic policy or civil rights, and at best only weak effects are noted for domestic policy.

We can also see here why presidents generally prefer foreign policy, and perhaps why they are more successful in foreign policy than other policy areas. They are able to restructure opinion about foreign policy matters. This restructuring persists for a considerable time, unlike other policy areas where presidential leadership effects, though noteworthy, are fleeting and ephemeral.

Conclusions

The theory being tested in this study suggests that presidents will be responsive to the public when responsiveness does not cost them later control and discretion over the substance of policy-making, and the ability to lead the public has implications for presidential responsiveness. The problem identification process, the subject of this chapter, allows presidents to both respond and lead. Responsiveness is mostly symbolic and void of specific policy content during the process of problem identification. The results indicate that presidents are responsive to the public during problem identification. The results also indicate that presidents lead public opinion in the process of identifying policy problems. This may allow presidents greater leeway in the more substantive aspects of the policy-making process, as pressures to respond to public opinion pressures may be lessened.

An important mediating variable that conditions presidential responsiveness and leadership is policy type. We found that presidential responsiveness seemed restricted to required policies, such as war and the economy. Presidents did not seem to respond to the public on discretionary policies.[17]

I also investigated the "presidential context" of leadership. Popular presidents were only slightly more persuasive than unpopular presidents when it came to setting the public's problem agenda. Similarly, presidential leadership effects seem to decay quite rapidly. They are gone by year's end for economic and civil rights policy and are substantially weakened for domestic policy, though they persist for foreign policy.

These findings allow us to address other theoretical concerns not mentioned earlier. The first concern is the process of agenda building. Cobb, Ross, and Ross (1976) identify three processes of agenda building, the outside initiative model, the mobilization model, and the inside initiative model. The leadership and responsiveness dynamics investigated here resemble the mobilization and outside models of agenda building.

Cobb, Ross, and Ross argue that for the outside model to succeed in placing an item on the agenda, its proponents must "create sufficient pressure or interest to attract the attention of decision makers" (1976, 128). They go on to stress the importance of issue type, but they focus more on whether the issue threatens established groups and leaders (131). The results here point to another important dimension of issue type, whether the issue is discretionary or required. The inability of public concern over civil rights or domestic policy to induce a presidential response illustrates the vulnerability of discretionary policy areas. Often sufficient pressure cannot be placed on decision makers because they can divert public concern to other issues and because public attention on discretionary areas may be quite volatile and unstable.

Presidential leadership of public opinion is analogous to the process of expanding an issue from the formal or institutional agenda to the public agenda. We found presidents to be very persuasive, but results also indicated that presidents may have a hard time keeping the issue on the public agenda, unless they repeatedly rally the public and institutionalize the mobilization process. Cobb, Ross, and Ross suggest that lack of leadership resources, poor planning, and inappropriate organizational structure may doom mobilization efforts (134–35). The results here point to other factors that may doom mobilization efforts. These include uncontrollable events and crises and the short and easily diverted attention of the mass public. Sustained efforts at keeping the issue in the public's eye long enough to institutionalize the problem with a policy may be required for successful agenda building through mobilization.

A second theoretical concern relates to the impact of presidential drama and activities on public opinion. Most research finds those efforts to have ephemeral effects, if such efforts produce any effects at all (e. g., MacKuen 1983). Such a finding is repeated here. Presidential policy emphasis in the State of the Union Address clearly sets the public's problem agenda but not for long. This demonstrates both the potential and the limitations of presidential leadership of public attention. Presidents can grab public attention, but they may not be able to hold that attention for long. Thus, they may develop a false sense of power and influence from the ease with which they find listeners when speaking but fail to note how swiftly those listeners shift their attention. Underestimating the resources and efforts needed to sustain public attention to a problem may account for many of a president's policy failures.

Like Light (1982) and Pfiffner (1988), presidents may best be advised to "hit the ground running." This advice may hold not only early in the president's term (Light 1982) but also early in the life of a policy problem or soon after the president has sought public attention. Not long after, public concern may recede as other problems arise and crises erupt. These results present additional advice: "keep on hitting until the policy process is played out."

Thus, we may understand Carter's failure with Congress. Not only did he overload the agenda, but he continually undermined his agenda. Soon after the announcement of a major policy initiative, he would offer another policy initiative, steering attention in a new direction. In effect, Carter undercut himself. In contrast, Reagan kept to a more limited agenda, one that he hammered away at. We see this in Reagan's refusal to adjust his economic policy stance or outlook when the severe recession of the early 1980s hit the nation. Instead, he urged the nation to "stay the course." In part, Reagan's reputation as the "great communicator" may derive from his focusing on a limited agenda, repeating and reinforcing the message of that agenda, and resisting the impulse to move to other issues. As a result, the public seemed to follow him, and he developed a reputation as a great leader of the public. His successful leadership may have been more a function of this strategy of action than his personality, public persona, or choice of words and symbols.

Presidential persistence may be required to see non–foreign policy initiatives to their enactment. Presidential persistence may be required to keep public attention focused on the policy topics that the president wants to emphasize. Either presidential silence or presidential attention to other policy problems may dissipate public attention on the original policy concern. Controlling the agenda may thus be a vital presidential resource in the policy-making process.

CHAPTER 3

The Substantive Content of
Presidential Agendas

In chapter 2 we looked at the process of problem identification, an important aspect of agenda building. In that chapter we assessed the impact of public concern on presidential attention to policy problems. We found presidential responsiveness to public concern but only for the required policy areas of economic and foreign policy. Presidents seemed unresponsive to public opinion on discretionary policies, like civil rights and overall domestic policy.

The previous chapter also looked at the impact of presidential policy attention on public opinion. Here we found that public concern with a policy area followed presidential attention, that presidents are able to lead public opinion. That leadership impact, however, was short lived, extinguishing or diminishing across all of the policy areas save foreign policy by year's end.

The analysis in chapter 2 did not, however, distinguish among different types of presidential attention. All presidential mentions of a policy area were treated equally. Not all presidential mentions of a policy area or problem are alike, however. Some merely mention a problem. Others offer solutions or information about the policy direction that the president is likely to take. These latter are more substantive. In this chapter, I ask the following questions: When presidents talk about a policy problem substantively, will they still be responsive to public opinion? Moreover, does substantive rhetoric enhance presidential leadership of public opinion? Does the public pay more attention to the president when he is being more substantive, and presumably more serious about a policy problem, than when he is merely pointing out a problem? Can mere symbolism lead the public, or must the president invoke substantive reasons to move public opinion?

Let me reiterate a point made in the previous chapter about substance versus symbolism. I do not want or intend to convey the idea that symbolism is void of policy content. Some symbols impart policy information. Terms like *liberal* or *conservative* can be thought of as symbols in their own right and suggest important policy differences. We do not possess a good terminology for contentless symbols. Thus, for convenience's sake, I use the term *symbol* or merely *symbolic* to indicate that I am talking about nonsubstantive presidential rhetoric, reserving the term *substantive* to indicate that I am talking about substantive rhetoric. Substantive rhetoric may employ symbolic manipulation, as I detail in this and subsequent chapters.

This substantive-symbolic distinction has implications for presidential responsiveness to public opinion. That theory proposed in this book hypothe-sizes that once presidents begin to make substantive policy decisions and choices, they will become less responsive to the mass public than when their words are mostly symbolic. This dynamic transpires because the public holds the president responsible for the conduct and outcome of public policy, which creates an incentive for the president to try to retain control over the public policy-making process. He intends to ensure, as much as possible, that posi-tive and beneficial policy outcomes emerge from the policy-making process. Consequently, his reputation with the public will improve if he can point to and take credit for policies that are performing well. Also, his popularity levels may rise, along with his odds for reelection and his ability to move other policies through the thickets of the legislative process.

When presidents talk about policy problems substantively, and not merely symbolically, they begin to indicate positions that they will take. Doing so may commit the president to a course of action (or inaction), which may constrain later presidential policy choice. In fact, many come to look upon a substantive statement by a president as a presidential policy or at least as an indication of the policy that the president will pursue.

A president cannot, without good reason, alter his policy stance. And even if he has good reason to change his policy position on an issue, he may have to bear some costs from doing so. The public and other political elites may view him as waffling, indecisive, weak, uncommitted, and/or duplicitous. This seems very much to be one of the major charges against Bill Clinton's presidency. After abandoning his campaign promise of a middle-class tax cut because of budget deficit pressures, Clinton reoffered a tax cut in the wake of the devastating 1994 midterm elections, in which his party lost control of Congress. From being publicly cool toward the North American Free Trade pact during his presidential election campaign, he became an ardent promoter of that policy once in the Oval Office. From these, and many other occasions, Clinton has developed an image of a waffling politician, one who is forever changing his mind, perennially trying to stake out the most popular position with the public and not necessarily a president who is able to lead.

The upshot of the dynamic under investigation here is that we should not find substantive presidential rhetoric to be as systematically responsive to public opinion as we found for symbolic rhetoric.

The distinction between symbolism and substance in presidential speech may also have implications for presidential leadership of public opinion. If presidents cannot mobilize public opinion with symbolic rhetoric, they have to resort to substantive rhetoric. This may lock them into positions taken to mobilize the public, with the result that they may be less able to compromise with other policymakers later on. Using substantive rhetoric to mobilize the public may require presidential commitment to a course of action. There may be major costs to presidents who later attempt to alter their policy course. The public may feel sold out or it may view the president as weak and ineffective, as incapable of delivering on the policies that he offered and that it rallied to support. Moreover, if the president tries to move public opinion to his side and it does not budge, his overall position in the political system may be weakened. Congress may be able to point out that the president's policy positions are unpopular and thus charge that he is out of step with the nation, asserting that it is a better representative of the people than the president.

None of these problems arises if the president can move public opinion with symbolism that is relatively void of substance. Moreover, if the president can move public opinion with symbolic appeals, he can create the impression of being responsive to the mass public without undermining his ability to make substantive policy choices. He can thus more clearly separate policymaking responsibility from responsiveness, which is the heart of the dynamic being investigated here.

This chapter proceeds as follows. First I discuss the coding of substance in presidential rhetoric from the State of the Union Address data. Second, I ask whether such substantive presidential rhetoric is responsive to public opinion. Third, I readdress the question of presidential leadership of public opinion. Specifically, what has more impact over public opinion, symbolic or substantive rhetoric? Can presidents mobilize public opinion with mere symbolic rhetoric or will only substantive rhetoric mobilize public opinion?

Detecting Substantive Positions from Public Presidential Speech

The State of the Union messages allow us to assess the substantiveness of presidential rhetoric (for a different approach see Light 1982). Clearly, the State of the Union Address is not the only opportunity for presidents to speak substantively to the public. Throughout the year, presidents have occasion to give speeches to the public that are dedicated to specific policies. Presidents are often highly strategic in the use of these policy-specific speeches, using them to rally the public behind their policies and sometimes to direct that mobilized public opinion to pressure Congress to enact their policies, in what Kernell (1993) labels "going public." Such "going public" activities have been found to affect public opinion, often building support for the president.

The question that I am dealing with here is quite different. We found that presidential concern with a policy area in his State of the Union Address affected public concern. But what is it about the rhetoric in that speech that so affected the public? Did the president's emphasis of a policy area itself move the public, or are presidents more persuasive when they take stands and positions on policies and issues? Moreover, as I will demonstrate later, presidents vary in how symbolic or substantive their State of the Union Addresses are. What accounts for this variability? Is it a matter of presidential style, context, or public pressure?

The last chapter used data on presidential mentions of a policy area. In this chapter, I refine that coding, distinguishing sentences in which the president merely mentioned a policy area from those that also indicate a presidential *position* on the issue.

Presidents incur costs when they begin to talk about issues substantively. First, the president expends time, effort, and other resources deciding whether to take a position and what that position should be. Opportunity costs are also imposed, limiting presidential attention to other issues and other activities. Political costs may also arise, as voters and interest groups react to the president's position. Some may be repelled, while others may be mobilized in support of the position. Taking a position on a issue may lock in the president to that course of action, limiting his ability to compromise and maneuver across the rest of the policy-making process.

Mere symbolism may not involve as many costs. Symbolic, empathic activities may help the president forge a strong relationship with the mass public. Importantly, symbolic activities and speech may have few implications for presidential discretion over policy choice later in the policy-making process. Expressions of sympathy with the public about a problem or concern do not impel the president to take a position or develop a policy to alleviate the problem. Presidents may suggest that the states and localities are the best sites for policy action on such concerns. But the symbolic gesture that lacks in policy direction or stance may allay public fears and anxieties (Edelman 1964), reducing the need to develop a policy response, while simultaneously creating a presidential image of responsiveness, leadership, and concern.

To capture the substantive emphasis of presidential sentences, I coded each sentence with respect to whether the president took a position that could be classified as either liberal or conservative. For each policy area, I counted the number of these positional sentences and then divided this number by the total number of sentences that referred to the policy area.

Many scholars distinguish symbolism from substance (e.g., Edelman 1964). Here I suggest that position taking on issues that raise ideological debate is a form of substantiveness. Sentences in which the president merely mentions the policy area, as opposed to taking a position, lean in the symbolic direction. Substantiveness can also be thought of as offering details concerning a policy. Policy detail is conspicuously lacking in State of the Union Addresses, but presidential positions on issues that divide liberals from conservatives are present and apparent and provide a type of substantively relevant information about the policy direction that a president intends to take.[1] Because of the controversy that attends liberal-conservative divisions, presidents often must go to greater lengths to justify their positions and to undermine the opposition, and thus the quality of information provided to the public is often stronger and clearer than that for other types of statements. Thus, these types of positional statements provided the clearest indicators of presidential policy intentions, an important type of substance, in a speech where the tendency is not to offer policy or programmatic details (see Hinckley 1990). They also offer us the strongest test of the impact of substantive emphasis on public opinion, when detail and specificity is often lacking. (In the next chapter I go into more detail on coding whether a sentence is liberal or conservative.)

From the State of the Union data, I created five indicators of substantive presidential emphasis. The first divides the total number of sentences with positions by the total number of sentences that refer to any policy area. This gives us an overall sense of the symbolic or substantive emphasis of the president's Address. The other indicators focus on specific policy areas. For the economic, foreign, domestic, and civil rights policy areas, I divided the number of sentences in which the president took a position by the total number of sentences for each respective policy area. Thus, one can look at the substantive or symbolic emphasis of each policy area.

There is one important difference in the quality of the overall measure of presidential substantiveness with the policy-specific ones. This relates to the substantive-symbolic focus or mix of these indicators.

In the previous chapter, I argued that presidential mentions of a policy area are a relatively and substantively free action, that is, an almost purely symbolic action. At least, the symbolic aspects of mentioning a policy area far outweigh its substantive element. I also remarked in the previous chapter that many draw a too firm distinction between symbolism and substance. All activity has a symbolic flavor or character.

The point that I want to make here is that activity must be aligned against both its symbolic and substantive dimensions to reveal its true character. Even the most substantively focused activity, such as a detailed presentation of a complex policy proposal, has a symbolic attribute. In characterizing an activity such as those from presidential speeches, as I am doing in this study, it is important to understand the mix between substance and symbol. For some activities, symbol overrides substance, while for others the substantive aspect is the more important to the president. Some actions may be relatively void of substance, leaning toward being purely symbolic. This is how I characterized presidential attention to policy areas in the previous chapter. But in other activities there is a more even blending of these two attributes.

When looking at the substantiveness of presidential statements with regard to specific policy areas, like economic, foreign, domestic, and civil rights policy, I contend that the substantive element begins to outweigh the symbolic in importance to the president. At least, the substantive element becomes a prime presidential consideration. Still, such actions convey a symbolic message and have a symbolic meaning.

In contrast, the aggregate measure that looks at overall substantiveness, combining all policy areas, while containing an important substantive element, leans more toward the symbolic than the specific policy area indicators. Clearly, this overall substantive indicator is more substantive than the presidential attention variables of the previous chapter, which were nearly purely symbolic, if only because there was ambiguity about the substantive component. But the overall indicator is also more symbolic than the policy-specific indicators. That is, the symbolic message that the president is trying to set forth with the overall substantive indicator is greater than it is with the policy-specific indicators. Because presidents can adjust their overall substantiveness by varying the emphasis of specific policy areas, presidents manipulate the symbolic image of the aggregate indicator.

For example, a president may not want to convey the image of being interested in an expansive and specific legislative program, perhaps because he wants to scale down public expectations or because he faces a hostile Congress and does not want to face off with the legislature, a prospect that might entail defeat before Congress and erode his reputation. But he may also be interested in pursuing specific policies in one policy area. He can retain the image of being less substantively focused by beefing up mentions of policy areas for which he is being purely symbolic, for which he will offer no specific policy initiatives. Though being highly specific in one policy area, this substantive image may be diluted by more frequently mentioning other policy areas in which little of a substantive nature is being conveyed. Presidents can thus manipulate their overall substantive image.

This line of argument suggests two things. One, the crude categorization of the stages of the policy-making process with regard to substantiveness needs revision. We must be sensitive to the symbolic implications of each policy-making stage.

Two, as the overall measure of presidential substantiveness emphasizes symbolism somewhat more than the policy-specific indicators, we are more likely to witness presidential responsiveness with the aggregate than the policy-specific indicators. Moreover, as the aggregate substantive indicator balances substance and symbolism more than the presidential attention variables of the last chapter, presidential responsiveness should be somewhat less on the aggregate substantive measure than the presidential attention ones. In other words, in terms of degree of presidential responsiveness, we should see declining responsiveness from the presidential attention indicator to the overall substantive indicator to the policy-specific substantive indicators. The degree of presidential responsiveness to public opinion for the overall policy substance indicator should fall somewhere between the presidential attention and policy-specific substantive indicators.

These data will allow us to ask what factors lead the president to be more or less substantive in his speeches to the public. We will also be able to look at the interrelationships across issue areas. Do policy areas compete for substantive attention from the president or are policy areas substantively packaged in sets? Moreover, does substantive attention to one issue area pave the way or restrict such attainment by another issue area? Or, is substantive emphasis across policy areas independent of what happens to other policy areas?

Comparing the Substantive and Symbolic Content of Presidential Speech

Table 3.1 and figure 3.1 present descriptive data on the substantiveness of the president's State of the Union Address. About one-third of sentences in the State of the Union Address that refer to a policy area contain a specific presidential position. These figures are similar to ones that Hinckley (1990, 72–73) reports in citing a study by Ragsdale. Ragsdale's study, which uses the State of the Union Address and other major speeches, finds that 62 percent of sentences are policy discussions, 24 percent are calls for action, and 14 percent are nonpolicy statements. Calls for action are probably similar to my coding of policy positions. Excluding the 14 percent that are nonpolicy, calls for action constitute 28 percent of presidential statements, a figure that is quite

TABLE 3.1. Descriptive Statistics on Presidential Substantive Policy Emphases, 1953–89, Overall and by Policy Area

	Overall	Economic Policy	Foreign Policy	Domestic Policy	Civil Rights Policy
Mean percentage	31.04	45.79	27.14	21.35	56.90
Minimum	13.25	11.11	6.67	2.08	0.00
Maximum	57.80	83.33	66.08	41.41	100.00
SD	11.17	15.95	14.76	10.12	32.38

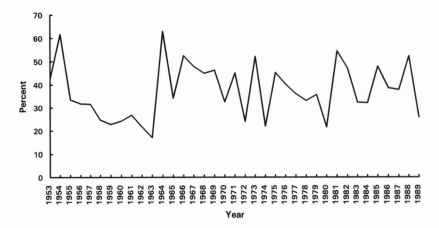

Fig. 3.1.   Substantive content of presidential sentences in the State of the Union Address, 1953–89. (Data compiled by the author from presidential State of the Union addresses.)

close to my 31 percent, though the universe of speeches and the coding rules and categories differ.

The State of the Union Addresses, however, vary considerably in their substantiveness. Table 3.1 indicates that the percentage of substantive sentences can fall to a low of 13 percent or rise to a high of nearly 58 percent. Moreover, there is variation across presidents and within administrations. Lyndon Johnson is the most substantive president, a finding that accords well with our historical understanding of Johnson (see table 3.2). Johnson possessed a specific and expansive legislative program, the Great Society. It appears that he used the occasion of the State of the Union Address to explain and sell that program. Ronald Reagan is another president with a well-specified policy program, and he ranks relatively high among presidents with 34 percent of his sentences offering a position. This places him third, closely behind Ford at 35 percent.

Kennedy is the least substantive president, tying with Bush at 19 percent. Historical accounts present such a portrait of Kennedy. With the exception of foreign policy, Kennedy was detached and uninterested in most policy areas (Giglio 1991, 36). In civil rights, he had not formed a policy position, and it seems that events moved him into his later support and activity in that policy area (Giglio 1991, 159–87; Stern 1989). He was even relatively uninformed about economic policy. It took the efforts of his economic advisers, especially those on the Council of Economic Advisers, to teach Kennedy about eco-

TABLE 3.2 **Presidential Rhetorical Policy Symbolism and Substance, 1953–89;
Average Percentage Substantive by President and Policy Area**

President	Overall	Economic Policy	Foreign Policy	Domestic Policy	Civil Rights
All	31	46	28	21	57
Eisenhower	30	40	22	25	72
Kennedy	19	32	13	16	83
Johnson	43	45	40	31	63
Nixon	28	50	30	16	36
Ford	35	57	32	18	20
Carter	26	51	26	14	90
Reagan	34	52	32	22	50
Bush	19	26	26	23	15

nomic matters and convert him to Keynesian fiscal policy (Giglio 1991, 135–36; Flash 1972).

Political conditions may have also constrained Kennedy from taking positions. He barely possessed a working majority in Congress, where the Conservative Coalition held the cards. He was in the difficult position of being elected by a generally liberal electorate, who expected liberal policies from him, but also needing support from conservative Southern Democrats in Congress. Position taking could easily alienate either element of his governing coalition (Seligman and Covington 1989). Thus, he refrained from offering the public much in the way of concrete policy direction. A strategy of ambiguity (Shepsle 1972; Page 1976, 1978) seemed to serve him better, allowing him to negotiate and bargain with both elements to secure legislative victories.

Viewing George Bush as nonsubstantive is quite conventional. He was roundly criticized for not having a "vision." He tended to be "unwilling to make initiatives in domestic policy . . . because of an obsessive desire to maintain public support" (Barrilleaux 1992, 17). Instead, his strategy was to lower public expectations (Kenski 1992, 94; Jones 1991). If speaking out on policies, taking the initiative, and staking out positions all heighten public expectations, which Bush wanted to cap, then Bush's lack of substantiveness is easily explained. Thus, these data seem to conform to our understandings of the substantive emphasis and policy agendas of these presidents.

Presidential substantiveness also varies within administrations. Figure 3.1 plots the relevant data. For instance, Eisenhower was considerably more substantive in his first two Addresses, a pattern that seems general across other administrations. Kennedy's abbreviated administration shows a slight decline in substantiveness over time. Johnson, Nixon, Carter, and Reagan all seem to demonstrate a similar pattern of relatively high initial levels of substantiveness, which then drops off, usually bottoming out near the end of their tenure. Although initial years are generally high and late years low, the middle years swing back and forth but usually do not surpass the early highs or late lows.

Substantiveness and Policy Area

The substantive orientation of presidents also varies by policy area. The overall substantive thrust of a president may derive from varying substantive emphases across policy areas. Some presidential agendas are more focused on one policy area than another, and this may be reflected in the substantive tone of their State of the Union Addresses. Also, as there are political costs and benefits to taking policy positions, presidents must calculate whether to take a position as well as decide which position to take. Differences across policy areas may affect these cost/benefit calculations.

For instance, the public is often characterized as less informed and more indifferent to foreign policy than other policy areas (Erikson, Luttbeg, and Tedin 1991, 65–70). Under such conditions, the president has few incentives to take a position. Few, if any, votes can be generated, and the possibility exists that he may activate opposing elites. In fact, too much attentiveness to foreign policy may alienate voters, who might come to believe that the president is neglecting domestic issues. Such was George Bush's plight.

In contrast, presidents have greater incentives toward position taking on economic policy, although strong disincentives also exist. First, economic policy is perhaps the most salient policy to the public. The salience of economic policy increases when times are bad. Salience and importance provide incentives for the president to take positions on economic policy, as he must show the public that he has ideas and policies that can solve the economic problems. But presidents also want to insulate themselves from blame during economic downturns. This may lead them to hide from the public or try to deflect public attention to other problems. Still, the importance of the economy to the public impels presidents to address it.

Distributive policies afford the greatest relative benefits from position taking. Distributive policies are characteristically low in conflict, and presidents may rally support by offering distributive benefits to important interests. These distributive-interest-based policies, however, require a degree of specificity because the targets of the appeals are often well-informed members of an interest, who recognize the implications of specific policy proposals. When presidents play the distributive politics game, they have incentives to take positions, as mere symbolism may lead to charges of "playing politics." To be credible, presidents must tell what they intend to do. There are limits, however, to the distributive politics game for presidents. The group to which the president is targeting must be large enough for him to reap some electoral benefit on the national stage. Many interests do not measure up to this standard.

The comparative characteristics of the policy areas lead to the prediction that presidents will be more substantive in civil rights and domestic policy than economic policy and least substantive in foreign policy. Civil rights and domestic policy share some distributive attributes, as I discussed earlier. Relevant data are presented in table 3.2. The data partially support this expectation. Presidents took positions on 57 percent of civil rights sentences, 46 percent of economic policy sentences, and only 27 percent of foreign policy sentences, but the policy area with the least substantive tone was domestic policy at 21 percent.

Several factors may account for this domestic policy result. First, the policy area here combines many different subpolicy areas, including agriculture, government administration, social welfare, energy, environment, science, and technology. It may be that many of these areas do not possess large enough interests for presidents to attend in the State of the Union Address. Pulling small interests into the president's orbit may not have enough political benefit. Moreover, by "catering" to all manner of interest, presidents may incur political costs. Rather than looking national or presidential in outlook, presidents may look like captives of special interest when they offer too many policies to too many interest groups. Further, many of the policy areas that make up the global domestic policy area, as coded here, might be more conflictual than the distributive game can handle. This should result in presidential withdrawal from taking positions on such issues. When interest group politics is highly conflictual, presidents have almost no incentive to become active.

Thus far, the discussion presents each policy area as if the conditions affecting presidential substantiveness are constant. This is surely not the case, and inasmuch as these conditions change, the incentives for presidential position taking should also vary. Moreover, presidential preferences and interests may vary across policy areas, which might also lead to differences in presidential position taking across policy areas.

For instance, wars may increase the incentives for presidents to take positions in the foreign policy area. Wars directly affect the populace and may lead to public interest in the war policy and attendant foreign policies. Presidents may also feel compelled to explain, rationalize, and justify their war policies. This may lead them to be more forthright in their rhetoric, forcing them to detail their foreign policies. Furthermore, the two major wars of the period, Korea and Vietnam, were pursued often without public support. To generate support for these relatively unpopular policies might require presidents to be more specific about their foreign policies.

There is a hint of this in the data in table 3.2 and figure 3.2. Johnson is

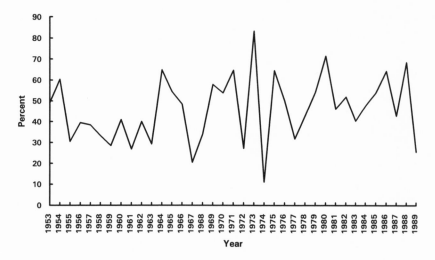

Fig. 3.2. Substantive content of presidential sentences that refer to international affairs, 1953–89. (Data compiled by the author from presidential State of the Union addresses.)

somewhat more specific on foreign policy than other presidents, though he has been described as being less interested in international and foreign affairs than domestic policy (Kearns 1976). Figure 3.2 also indicates that Eisenhower was more substantive while the Korean War was ongoing than after the war's conclusion.

The secular decline of the economy that began in the early 1970s may also motivate presidents to be more specific about their positions on the economy, although being blamed for the economic slide may provide disincentives to position taking. The data in table 3.2 and figure 3.3 provide some support for this notion. The presidents from Nixon on, who presided during the decline, were generally more specific on economic policy than the early presidents. The only exception to this is George Bush, but we have only one year of data on Bush and that is during a year of economic growth. Figure 3.3 displays an upward slope in economic policy position taking but also shows dramatic swings within administrations.

Civil rights policy has transformed and evolved (Carmines and Stimson 1989) across the period. It was an area of ferment, activism, and public concern from the mid-1950s through the late 1960s. By the 1970s, concern had died down, a backlash had set in, and civil rights was pushed off the top of the political agenda. After years of neglect and Republican rule, Jimmy Carter was elected, in part because of strong support from black Americans. He indicated early in his administration that he wanted to elevate civil rights as a

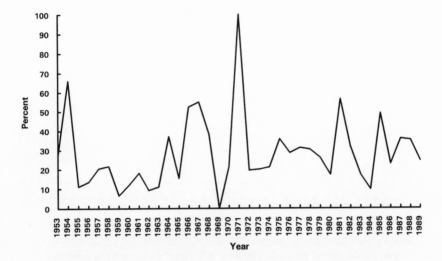

Fig. 3.3. Substantive content of presidential sentences that refer to economic policy, 1953–89. (Data compiled by the author from presidential State of the Union addresses.)

government priority. His successors, Reagan and Bush, had less interest and reason to pursue activist civil rights policies, and some even suggest that they played the game of moderate civil rights rhetoric but conservative civil rights actions (Shull 1993).

This historical rendering is evident in the data in table 3.2 and figure 3.4. The presidents of the "civil rights era," Eisenhower, Kennedy, and Johnson, were all relatively specific in their civil rights rhetoric. Public concern may have made them so. Nixon and Ford, in contrast, were much less specific on civil rights, while Carter, who felt he owed his election to black voters, was the most substantive president of all. Lastly, specificity strongly declined under Reagan and Bush. Figure 3.4, however, indicates that presidential substantiveness in civil rights varies within administration, often by considerable magnitudes.

Domestic policy shows no definite temporal pattern, though one could argue that presidents might become more attentive to interests during the era of the ascendancy of interest groups in American politics, the period from the late 1970s on. This does not seem the case. But Lyndon Johnson emerges as more substantively oriented on domestic policy than any other president (see table 3.2 and fig. 3.5). Again, this may be a function of Johnson's Great Society, which aimed to offer all types of government benefits to all Americans.

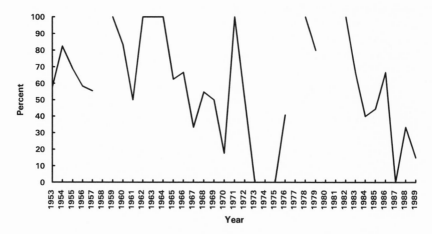

Fig. 3.4. Substantive content of presidential sentences that refer to civil rights policy, 1953–89. (Data compiled by the author from presidential State of the Union addresses.)

Johnson's high level of substantiveness in his State of the Union Address, not only in domestic policy but all policy areas here save economic policy, may indicate his attempt to build the "grand coalition," a national consensus around his program. And he aimed to build such a coalition through the style of coalition building that served him so well in the Senate. This style was not

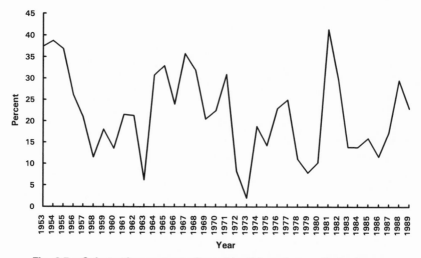

Fig. 3.5. Substantive content of presidential sentences that refer to domestic policy, 1953–89. (Data compiled by the author from presidential State of the Union addresses.)

built upon symbolic manipulations so much as on political trading, compromising, and the like, toward the end of enacting policy. The substantive orientation of Johnson is also consistent with his image of being result oriented and concrete in his treatment of public policy (Kearns 1976; Skowronek 1993).

In this section, I have described the presidential substantiveness in the State of the Union Address overall and by policy area. That description indicates much variation and hints at several factors that may account for this variation. These factors include the presidents themselves, real-world conditions, and public concern. But this discussion did not test these notions systematically, nor did it directly address the responsiveness of presidents to public opinion. The next section takes up those chores.

Presidential Substantive Responsiveness to Public Opinion

The theory being tested here suggests that presidential responsiveness to the public declines as presidents make substantive decisions about public policies. Presidential desire to maintain discretion and control over the public policy-making process is the major reason for this lack of responsiveness. When symbolism, as opposed to substantiveness, can be employed, presidential responsiveness to the public is more likely. Such symbolic responsiveness is possible in the problem identification process because acknowledging that something is a problem does not compel a president to take action or to develop a policy position.

Substantive decision making may lock a president into a course of action, thereby limiting later policy choice, or it may impose costs if the president finds it necessary to alter his policy. Presidents may change their policy stance because of resistance from Congress, new information about policy impacts, changes in the public mood, and/or other factors that might affect presidential decision making about policy choices. As a consequence, presidents desire to maintain as much discretion, maneuverability, and control as possible in the policy-making process.

Talking about an issue substantively and publicly may limit later presidential policy choice for several reasons. First, presidents may create expectations of action when they take an issue position. Failure to follow through may lead those whose hopes were raised to criticize the president for lack of action. Second, taking a position may mobilize proponents and opponents of the president's position in anticipation of presidential activity. Proponents may try to propel the issue's priority higher in the agenda than the president prefers. Opponents may try to undercut presidential popularity and reputation (Neustadt 1964) and otherwise attack the president and his proposal. Discussing issues substantively, especially as defined here, looks to many people like the president committing to a course of action.

Presidents, speechwriters, and other presidential advisers seem to feel that even offhand presidential remarks on a topic or issue may raise public expectations about presidential involvement and commitment to that issue. Thus, White House operatives and others with a policy agenda often lobby or otherwise maneuver to get their pet ideas incorporated into formal presidential speeches. Walcott and Hult report that Eunice Shriver, President Kennedy's sister and an advocate for mental health reform, would actively lobby to get the president to mention mental health just for this reason (1995, 220).

Thus, to avoid these constraints on behavior and choice, we are likely to witness lower levels of presidential responsiveness here than we noticed in problem identification.

Analysis Issues

To test for presidential responsiveness in issue prioritization, I will regress the indicators of presidential substantiveness on the public's most important problem. The analysis starts with the aggregate indicator of presidential substantiveness. Then I go on to the four policy-specific indicators. We expect, based on the earlier discussion, to find somewhat more responsiveness for the aggregate than the policy-specific indicators, but even the aggregate indicator of presidential substantiveness should demonstrate lower levels of responsiveness than the presidential attention variables, which were the topic of the previous chapter. Also, as I discussed in chapter 2 and earlier in this chapter, more than public opinion can be hypothesized to affect presidential substantiveness in the State of the Union Address. The fuller equations control for the contextual conditions of war, inflation, and unemployment. Moreover, I control for presidential attention to each policy area, hypothesizing that substantiveness might increase as presidential attention to a policy area increases. Lastly, each equation also controls for the time point and presidential dummies that were used in the analysis of the previous chapter. The inclusion of so many variables into an equation with a limited n (no more than 37) poses some important analytic challenges, and the inclusion of both the time point and presidential dummies raises some other estimation issues.

Having a large number of variables to cases makes estimation difficult and may result in variables explaining particular cases. The inclusion of all of the time point and presidential dummies, 11 variables in all, compounds this problem and may exacerbate multicollinearity. Furthermore, the simultaneous inclusion of the time point and presidential dummies complicates interpretation, as the criterion (omitted variable) becomes president-year, in this case, Bush-1989. Thus, each time point and presidential dummy, when all are included in the equation, is compared to this case. The cycle across the president's four-year term that the time point dummies pick up is effectively lost.

As in the previous chapter, to deal with these issues I experimented with an exhaustive number of estimation combinations, including all variables, only the time point dummies, only the presidential dummies, one time point or presidential dummy at a time, various combinations of time point and presidential dummies and the like. Throughout, the context, presidential attention, and public opinion variables are retained or dropped from the analysis as the logic of the process and findings dictated. Comparison of results across the estimations leads me to the results presented in table 3.3.

The results are reduced-form equations, which only present the variables that are statistically significant. In each case, the results were quite stable— addition of any variable or combination of variables to those found significant did not alter the results, except for minor changes in the size of the regression coefficients, standard errors, and *t* values. No change in status from significant to insignificant was observed, nor did any variable originally found to be insignificant become significant. The results in table 3.3 are quite stable. For presentation purposes, and because of the large number of estimations, I report the end result of that process rather than the myriad trials, just as I did in the previous chapter.

The presentation of the results begins with overall presidential substantiveness and then goes on to the substantiveness of the State of the Union Address for each of the four specific policy areas. I also discuss more substantively the various hypotheses under consideration.

Overall Presidential Substantiveness and Responsiveness

My earlier discussion in this chapter indicated that the overall substantive content of the State of the Union Address varied across and within administrations. How much of that variance is due to presidential responsiveness to public opinion? To provide for the strongest test possible with the data at hand, I control for other factors that the earlier discussion suggested might also affect presidential substantiveness. Real-world conditions and the electoral cycle may affect the substantiveness of the State of the Union Address.

First, real-world conditions, such as a falling economy or international strife, may stimulate presidents to be more substantive in their annual Addresses. When problems are great, presidents may have to build support for policies in order to deal with them. They are keenly aware that the fate of their administrations rests on their accomplishments in office. Successfully dealing with the great issues of the day are accomplishments to which they can point,

TABLE 3.3. Determinants of the Substantive Tone of Presidential State of the Union Addresses, 1953–89

Policy Area	b	SE	t
Overall address			
Constant	−52.35	5.71	9.17
War	10.21	3.35	3.05
Inflation	−1.32	.60	−2.22
Public opinion–foreign policy	−.42	.11	−3.83
Johnson dummy	9.80	4.19	2.34
R^2/Adj. R^2/equation type	.44	.36	AR1
Rho	−.39		
Lagrange multiplier	1.06		
Economic policy			
Constant	30.48	6.30	4.84
Presidential economic policy mentions	.37	.18	2.00
Presidential foreign policy positions	.20	.12	1.66
R^2/Adj. R^2/equation type	.23	.18	AR1
Rho	−.27		
Lagrange multiplier	.52		
Foreign policy			
Constant	.15	8.28	.02
Presidential economic policy positions	.25	.14	1.78
Presidential domestic policy positions	.73	.20	3.60
R^2/Adj. R^2/equation type	.30	.25	AR1
Rho	−.10		
Lagrange multiplier	−.26		
Civil rights policy			
Constant	−34.29	24.06	−1.43
War	28.03	8.85	3.17
Unemployment	12.85	2.74	4.69
Inflation	−4.84	1.71	−2.80
Public opinion–civil rights	1.60	.40	4.00
Eisenhower dummy	36.94	11.10	3.33
Kennedy dummy	42.69	12.60	3.39
Carter dummy	96.50	14.10	6.84
R^2/Adj. R^2/equation type	.73	.65	AR1
Rho	−.36		
Lagrange multiplier	3.85		
Domestic policy			
Constant	8.58	2.16	3.98
War	6.05	1.72	3.51
Public opinion–domestic policy	−.62	.07	−9.11
President's domestic policy mentions	.50	.07	7.60
President's foreign policy mentions	.32	.05	6.17
R^2/Adj. R^2/equation type	.82	.80	AR1
Rho	−.22		
Lagrange multiplier	.72		

hoping to use them to secure reelection, promote other policies, and/or en-hance their historical reputations. When problems are severe, presidents may begin this coalition-building process in the State of the Union Address, using the great publicity and attention given to this speech as a springboard for later efforts.

Second, the cycle or pulse of presidential elections may also stimulate presidents to be more substantive than symbolic at some points in the cycle than others. Election years motivate presidents to offer policies to prospective voters. Thus, during presidential election years, we may witness increased presidential substantiveness in their Addresses. Similarly, after being elected, president's must consolidate their victory and build a governing coalition (Seligman and Covington 1989). Inasmuch as presidents view their election support in coalition-of-interest terms, they may feel induced to talk of the policy directions they are going to pursue. Thus, substantiveness may also increase in the first year of each administration.

The results of the analysis are presented in table 3.3. The public opinion data come from the Gallup poll immediately preceding the president's Ad-dress. Other variables are operationalized as they were in the previous chapter. First order autocorrelation problems were corrected with an AR1 procedure. LaGrange multiplier tests find that this satisfactorily corrects the seriality problem.

Four variables significantly affect overall substantiveness in the presi-dent's State of the Union Address: war, inflation, public concern with foreign policy, and the Lyndon Johnson dummy variable. Overall, 44 percent of the variance is explained.

War affects the substantiveness of the president's agenda. As hypothe-sized, when the nation is at war, substantiveness increases by slightly over 10 percent. Inflation, however, has a contrary effect. Each one percentage point increase in inflation reduces substantiveness by 1.3 percent. Also, as I hinted at in my earlier discussion, Lyndon Johnson is more substantive in his State of the Union Addresses. The effect is quite large, nearly 10 percent, and suggests that Johnson may have tried to sell his expansive program by detailing it to the public. Johnson's Great Society was not offered merely as a symbolic gesture but was presented more concretely than other presidents' programs. Again, this underscores Johnson's orientation toward accomplishment.

The variables of most interest are the public opinion ones. Here we find one public opinion variable, concern with foreign affairs, statistically signifi-cant, but its sign indicates that as public concern grows, presidents become less substantive. Public concern about world situations may lead presidents to rally the public through symbols, to try to gloss over the divisions within society and present a common and united front to international adversaries. An Edelman (1964) type of reaction may account for this behavior.

International strife is threatening to the mass public, which responds with heightened concern. But as Edelman suggests, under such circumstances politicians do not always respond to the public with policies to address their problems but rather offer symbols aimed at reducing the level of public distress, which politicians hope will provide them with the greatest freedom or latitude to act. We may be seeing this dynamic in these data.

Presidents, however, may be responding to public concern in this issue area by offering symbols in another issue area. They may do so because the policy area of public concern is controversial or because the president and the public disagree about policy solutions. Thus, presidents may try to divert public attention to issues areas that are less controversial or ones in which policy agreement exists. In this way, presidents may defuse public concern in policy areas that are likely to impose heavy costs on them.

These data are much too highly aggregated to discern clearly the president's reaction to public concern with foreign affairs. Do presidents offer symbolic responses when public concern over foreign affairs increases across all types of policies, or is the response specific to one policy area, say, international affairs? We have to dissaggregate by policy area to answer this question.

Presidential Substantive Responsiveness across Issue Areas

The data series on presidential substantiveness across the four policy areas allows us to test more directly the connection between public concern with specific policy areas and the presidential response. This should help us sort out the several possibilities for the finding of counterresponsiveness to public concern with foreign affairs. Again, I employ real-world conditions, time point dummies, and presidential dummies as controls. Also, I add into each equation the percentage of presidential mentions (not positions) on the policy area under discussion. This lets us address the possibility that the substantiveness of presidential comments within a policy area is a function of his own concern with that area. When presidents speak more often about a policy area, is it because they are trying to sell a specific policy to the nation or does the quantity of rhetoric merely indicate increases in symbolism? Lastly, I add variables for presidential issue positions on the other policy areas to test for competition or linkage across policy areas. Does presidential position taking on one issue area inhibit position taking on other issue areas? Are policies competitive, bundled together in sets, or independent of one another?

Economic Policy.   What drives presidents to stake out positions on the economy, to treat that policy area substantively instead of symbolically? Does a faltering economy lead presidents to offer specific solutions to economic problems or do presidents try to insulate themselves from a bad economy by using political symbols or by diverting public attention to other policy areas, such as foreign policy?

Presidents have incentives to distance themselves from a poor economy. Popularity decays with a declining economy. Government revenues also recede, limiting the president's ability to offer new or expanded programs to voters. But presidents also have incentives to attend to economic problems. More than any other policy area save foreign affairs the public holds the president responsible for the state of the economy. Thus, he has strong incentives to attend to economic issues. And in the face of a poor economy presidents have others to whom they may try to point the finger of blame. For instance, presidents may be able to blame the economy's woes on the previous administration. Or, if the opposition party holds Congress, they can blame Congress for not cooperating in building an effective policy. Ronald Reagan mastered the art of blaming economic problems that cropped up during his term of office on his predecessor, and throughout his tenure George Bush tried the tactic of shifting blame onto Congress.

Table 3.3 presents the results, corrected for autocorrelation. Unlike the overall substantive equation, the fit here is less impressive, with barely one-fourth of the variance accounted for. Two variables are statistically significant, presidential economic policy attention (listed in the table as "Mentions") and presidential foreign policy substantiveness. The latter variable is only marginally significant. In the area of economic policy, presidents demonstrate no responsiveness to public concern with the economy.

As presidents mention the economy more often in their speeches, the substantive content of those mentions increases in frequency. Each 1 percent increase in the percentage of the speech devoted to the economy leads to a corresponding .37 percent increase in the substantiveness of economic comments. The economy provides the president with mixed incentives toward position taking. On the one hand, presidents would like to hide from a weak economy, blaming others for that problem. But on the other hand, the public holds the president responsible for the state of the economy, which may require a presidential response. Furthermore, that response must be specific, not just symbolic. Thus, we discern this modest presidential response. When presidents speak on the economy, they tend do so substantively.

Lastly, there is little evidence of substantive competition between economic policy and the other policy areas. Rather, foreign and economic policy seem to be packaged together. As presidents get more substantive in the foreign policy area, they get more substantive in economic policy. Each 1 percent increase in foreign policy substantiveness is associated with a .2

percent increase in economic policy substantiveness. Instead of pursuing a "guns or butter" approach, presidents seem to offer the public "guns *and* butter."[2]

Foreign Policy. Foreign policy presents issues that often rally the public to support the president. This is most likely when the international situation heats up to the point that the populace feels threatened. Then, politics stops at the water's edge, bipartisanship takes over, and manipulation of patriotic symbols rather than reasoned debate fills the public airwaves. Foreign policy has also been a policy arena of marked political conflict for much of the post–World War II period. In particular, two of the most important foreign policy events, the Korean and Vietnam Wars, were prosecuted by administrations that often lacked public support for those policies, sometimes even facing strident opposition.

The rally phenomenon may allow presidents to wrap their policy in patriotic trappings. If the public blindly rallies to support the president in the face of international danger, the president need not specify his policy. Patriotic, symbolic mobilization tactics are all that is required. But if the rally phenomenon does not universally hold, especially in the case of the Korean and Vietnam Wars, then presidents may have to resort to substantive explanation of their positions to build support.

Table 3.3 presents results for foreign policy. Very minor seriality was detected; AR1 corrections were employed. Like the economic policy case, the fit of this equation is far from overwhelming, with only 30 percent of the variance accounted for and only two variables with statistical significance: presidential positions on economic and domestic policy. As in the case of economic policy, presidents do not seem responsive to public concern on foreign policy, which continues to build the case for limited presidential responsiveness in the more substantive phases of the policy-making process.

The results suggest that as presidents become more substantive with regard to economic and domestic policy, they become more substantive on foreign policy. Again, we find a linkage between the economic and foreign policy realms. When presidents become more substantive with one, substantiveness with the other goes up. In this case, each 1 percent increase in economic policy substantiveness boosts foreign policy substantiveness by .25 percent, an amount somewhat proportionate to the impact of foreign policy substantiveness on economic substantiveness.

More impressive is the impact of domestic policy substantive rhetoric on foreign policy substantiveness. Each 1 percent change here increases foreign policy substantiveness a whopping .73 percent. What we may be seeing here is another indication of presidents pursuing both "guns" and "butter" at the same time. Perhaps to rally support for war or foreign policies, presidents must offer the public domestic policies that serve as compensations for the sacrifice of war and international policies.

Civil Rights Policy. Civil rights policy differs from foreign and economic policy. It rarely commands as much attention or concern from the president and the public as the other two issue areas (see details in chap. 2 and earlier in this chapter). Lower levels of public attention reduce the incentives for the president to respond to public opinion or to offer substantive proposals. Moreover, as economic and foreign policy issues increase in importance, the amount of substantive attention that the president can give to civil rights should decline. For instance, although Jimmy Carter promised to reelevate civil rights concerns to the top of his agenda after years of indifference under Nixon and Ford, the energy crisis and stagflation appeared, pushing civil rights concerns to the sidelines. Even a president strongly committed to civil rights and who owed his election in part to black voters allowed pressing economic worries to divert his attention away from civil rights.

The only incentive that the president has with regard to civil rights is rooted in interest group appeals during election campaigns. Presidents may try to build voter support by offering civil rights, and distributive policies to other types of interest groups, during their reelection years. This perspective views civil rights as one type of interest group policy. Consequently, real-world conditions associated with the economy and the international setting, plus presidential concern with those policy areas, should suppress presidential substantiveness on civil rights, as it would on any distributive or interest group policy area.

The results are displayed in table 3.3. Diagnostics revealed a seriality problem; an AR1 estimation was used as a correction.[3] The results indicate several major differences between civil rights substantiveness and the results for economic and foreign policy. First, the fit is very good, with nearly three-quarters of the variance accounted for.[4] Second, and theoretically more important, presidents seem responsive to public concern with civil rights.

First, consider the impact of the other variables also found to affect presidential substantiveness with civil rights. War impressively boosts the substantiveness of presidential civil rights rhetoric. When the nation is at war, civil rights rhetoric becomes more substantive by an amazing 28 percent.

Similarly, economic conditions affect presidential rhetoric here. Each 1 percent increase in unemployment increases the substantive tone of the president's message nearly 13 percent. Increases in unemployment disproportionately distress minority populations; these results may reflect this connection. But inflation has the opposite effect. Each 1 percent increase in inflation depresses the substantive tone of presidential civil rights rhetoric by nearly 5 percent. Although unemployment may raise concerns about fairness and distribution, inflation raises other kinds of economic concerns. These concerns seem to undercut distributional arguments, as combating inflation takes on paramount importance. Thus, the relationship between real-world conditions and presidential substantiveness on civil rights is more complex than originally hypothesized.

Three presidents also displayed greater substantiveness with civil rights than the others. Eisenhower and Kennedy, presidents who served during a period of heightening concern with civil rights, were more substantive by impressive margins, 37 and 43 percent, respectively. Importantly, they came from different parties, but both served during the early stages of civil rights legislative and political battles. Oddly, Johnson is no more substantive on civil rights than other presidents, despite his impressive civil rights legislative legacy. This may also indicate that Johnson's Great Society program extended quite far beyond civil rights.

The other president who is highly substantive on civil rights is Jimmy Carter. After a decade of assumed presidential neglect to the issue, Carter promised more, at least rhetorically. Moreover, by the time of his administration, the notion of civil rights had expanded beyond the concerns of blacks to include other minorities and women. Carter is the most substantive president on civil rights, a finding shown in table 3.2 also. When Carter talks about civil rights, he does so substantively. This may indicate that, at least for Democrats in this later period, civil rights may have transformed from a symbolic policy or moral movement to one suffused with interest group and electoral implications for Democrats. When we speak of the Democrats being captured by special interests in the post-Vietnam era, we often refer to the hold of minorities on the party. The substantiveness of Carter's rhetoric here may reflect that process. But it is important to note that Carter did not speak about civil rights voluminously, as I reported in the previous chapter. The modest frequency of his civil rights rhetoric was highly substantive nevertheless.

Lastly, and most importantly, presidents are responsive to concern for civil rights, the first such indication of presidential responsiveness found in this chapter. Each 1 percent increase in public concern with civil rights leads to a 1.6 percent increase in the substantiveness of presidential civil rights rhetoric. Why presidents would be responsive to the public on civil rights when they are not on economic and foreign policy is anomalous. One possibility is that the combination of the moral tone of civil rights policy, when coupled with public concern, may be too much for a president to resist, and thus he has to offer something concrete. But we also must bear in mind that presidents do not speak much about civil rights. When they do, it is often highly concrete and substantive, more so than any other policy area, as table 3.1 also shows.[5]

Domestic Policy. Domestic policy, like civil rights, raises interest group concerns, but it is rarely cast in moral terms, except perhaps when the environment is discussed. The interest group nature of this policy area may make it susceptible to election-year dynamics, as presidents offer policies to interest groups as they try to build electoral coalitions. The state of the economy and foreign policy may, however, push domestic policy off the president's agenda. Still, I remarked earlier on the "packaging" of domestic and foreign policy. As presidents' rhetoric on domestic policy became more substantive, so too did their rhetoric with regard to foreign policy. Thus, we might expect foreign policy substantiveness to affect the substantive tone of domestic policy rhetoric. We expect little presidential responsiveness to public opinion, our major theoretical concern.

The results are presented in table 3.3. Like the civil rights equation, this equation showed a good fit, with over 80 percent of the variance explained. Four variables affect presidential domestic policy substantiveness: war, presidential attention to domestic policy, presidential positions on foreign policy, and public concern with domestic policy. As I will shortly explain, the last finding indicates counterresponsiveness.

First, during wars, presidential domestic policy substantiveness increases by 6 percent, another hint of the "guns and butter" orientation that presidents may be operating under. There seems to be a reciprocating effect between domestic and foreign policy substantiveness; both covary positively. Each 1 percent increase in foreign policy substantiveness increases the substantive tone of domestic rhetoric about .3 percent, a result about half as potent as the impact of domestic policy rhetoric on foreign policy substantiveness.

Moreover, when presidents speak more about domestic policy issues, their rhetoric gets more substantive. Each one percentage point increase in the quantity of domestic rhetoric increases its substantive tone by .5 percent, a strong effect. Interest group issues, when talked about more frequently, are done so concretely. It may be more difficult to talk about such narrow issues in symbolic tones, as a president can when speaking of the economy or foreign affairs. Thus, perhaps the nature of domestic policies, conceptualized here as aggregates of interest group policies, may require more concrete rhetoric.

But oddly, the more the public is concerned about domestic policy issues, the less substantive the president's domestic policy rhetoric. Each 1 percent increase in public concern depresses the substantiveness of presidential rhetoric a hefty .6 percent. Thus, presidents are resisting, even contradicting, but not responding to the public here.

Why would presidents resist public concern so strongly in this case? One possibility is methodological. The match between the specific aspects of domestic policy over which the public is concerned may not resemble those domestic policies that the president is talking about. Without being able to disaggregate this policy area more finely, we cannot test this possibility.

Alternatively, when interest group pressures increase, presidents may find it in their interest to resist such calls. When faced with mounting interest group demands, presidents may find it prudent to resist those pressures, even to fight against them. In this way, presidents may appear presidential, speaking for the whole nation against narrow interests. Thus, this indication of counterresponsiveness may represent presidential resistance to interest group demands and not so much resistance to public opinion.

Summary.   The major hypothesis of this research is that we should see less presidential responsiveness to public opinion when the president's rhetoric is substantive than when it is symbolic. This is basically what we have found. Across the five indicators of presidential rhetorical substantiveness, only one, civil rights, exhibits any presidential responsiveness to public concern. Moreover, in two cases, overall and domestic policy substantiveness, we found indications of possible counterresponsiveness.[6] In contrast, in the previous chapter, where we looked at symbolic rhetoric, we found presidential responsiveness to public opinion on two of four policy areas, economic and foreign policy.

Earlier I hypothesized that presidents might be more responsive to public opinion on the overall measure of substantiveness than on the policy-specific measures. The ability to manipulate the overall policy measure by varying mixes of the specific policy area components was offered as one reason for this possible outcome. No direct responsiveness was found for the overall measure of presidential substantiveness, but the negative association between public concern with foreign policy and overall presidential substantiveness may indicate such symbolic manipulation. The main point—generally weaker presidential responsiveness when presidents are being more substantive—is substantiated.

The other important substantive finding was that rather than noticing policy competition, we found linkages across policies. In particular, presidential substantiveness in foreign policy was linked to substantiveness in economic and domestic policy. A "guns and butter" explanation was offered as one reason for this linkage. Interestingly, civil rights was the one policy area not linked this way to any other policy areas. Civil rights appeared to be the most independent of policy areas, and this was the one that appeared to occasion some presidential responsiveness. Perhaps this independence has something to do with presidential responsiveness. Presidents may deflect the public on the other policy area perhaps because they can call up other, linked policy areas. Thus, the manipulation of policy areas may enable presidents to immunize themselves from public pressures. Presidents may be able to divert public attention from one policy area to another, say, foreign to domestic, but they are less able to do this with civil rights. The moral implications of civil rights may have something to do with this policy area's independence from others—its specialness—and perhaps gives us a reason for presidential responsiveness to public opinion in civil rights but not the other policy areas.

To appreciate fully this presidential behavior, we must look further into the dynamics of presidential leadership of public opinion. Presidents may be able to "get away" with this sidestepping and substantive nonresponsiveness if the public is content to follow symbolic leads. If, however, presidents more effectively lead public opinion through substance, rather than symbol, this presidential behavior pattern may have dear costs. It may eventually lead to public discontent and disillusionment with the president. In the next section I address the question of presidential leadership of public opinion. Which is better able to move public opinion, substance or symbol?

Presidential Symbolic versus Substantive Leadership of Public Opinion

In this and the previous chapter, I characterized presidential policy rhetoric as either symbolic or substantive. Analysis in chapter 2 showed that presidential attention to a policy area in the State of the Union Address affects public opinion. In this section, I raise the question, What is it about presidential rhetoric that influences public opinion? Does the public respond to any presidential utterance, whether symbolic or substantive, or is substantive rhetoric more effective than symbolic appeals in mobilizing public opinion?

There are good reasons to believe that a president must take a policy position before he can focus public attention in that direction. Position taking signals to the public that the policy area is important, that it is a policy priority. When presidents take a position they usually explain the reasons for taking that position, which reinforces the message that the policy is an important one.

My analysis in the previous chapter indicated that factors other than presidential rhetoric affect public opinion. Real-world conditions, such as the state of the world and the national economy, also have an effect, depending on the policy area. Thus, the president must compete with these factors in influencing public opinion. It is likely that only clear policy messages with substantive content can compete with these other factors for the public's ear. Mere symbolism may get lost in the cacophony of messages.

Moreover, there is an inertial quality to public opinion, making it resistant to change. The most important inertial force is preexisting opinion. Preexisting opinion presents a barrier that limits the receptivity of the public to new information. Another barrier is lack of attention. The public is well noted for its limited attention to matters political. To convert those with preexisting opinions and awaken the inattentive, the president may have to resort to strong, clear, and substantive argument about public policies. Symbolic appeals may be too weak to overcome these barriers.

Conversely, one can make the case that presidential rhetorical symbolism is itself persuasive, that presidents do not have to resort to substantive argumentation to sway public opinion. First, the president stands alone in the political arena. No one can match the prestige that the president has with the public, the degree of attention that the public has for the president, or the responsibility for policy and governance that the public places on him. Miroff's (1982) phrase, the "monopolization of the public space," nicely summarizes the place of the president in the public's political consciousness. From a "priming" perspective (Iyengar and Kinder 1987), one can argue that the public is predisposed to pay attention to the president when he decides to speak out on an issue. Lastly, the political psychology arguments of Greenstein (1974) and Edelman (1964, 1974) suggest that the public often waits in anticipation for the president's words (and deeds) about policy issues. Thus, symbolic appeals may influence public opinion. Although symbolic appeals may not direct public opinion on the choice of policy options, they may help structure the public's problem agenda.

A third possibility is that the power of symbolic appeals will vary across issue areas. Symbolism may influence public opinion on some issue areas, while substance is required on others. Throughout this book, I have treated foreign and economic policy as required policy areas, differentiating them from the more discretionary civil rights and domestic policy areas. The public is already predisposed to attend to required policy areas; consequently it does not take much to direct its attention to problems in these areas. Thus, symbolic appeals may effectively mobilize public concern in the foreign and economic policy areas. In contrast, the public is less aware, attentive, and interested in the discretionary policy areas. To overcome these barriers, presidents may have to resort to substantive argumentation, pointing out the importance of the discretionary area to the public.

I test these hypotheses by adding the presidential issue position variable in the public's Most Important Problem equations that I estimated in the previous chapter. Presidential mentions of the problem are kept in the equation to compare its impact with that of the presidential position variable. Also kept in the equation are the economic and war variables and public concern for each respective policy area (taken from the Gallup poll just prior to the president's State of the Union Address). When diagnostics reveal first order serial correlation, an AR1 estimation was used to correct this problem. LaGrange multiplier tests indicate that each equation was satisfactorily free of autocorrelation. The results are presented in table 3.4.

The results are quite clear. None of the presidential issue position variables has any effect on the public's most important problem. Nor does inclusion of the position-taking variable affect the performance of the other

TABLE 3.4. Impact of Substantive Positions on the Public's Most Important Problem, 1953–89

Policy Area	b	SE	t
Economic policy			
Constant	−24.57	8.78	−2.80
Inflation	.53	.67	.78
Unemployment	6.43	1.82	3.53
War	2.90	4.19	.69
President's economic mentions	43.46	11.74	3.70
President's economic positions	−6.63	9.27	.71
Public opinion$_{(t-1)}$	.24	.16	1.47
R^2/Adj. R^2/equation type	.88	.85	AR1
Rho	.29		
Lagrange multiplier	2.10		
Foreign policy			
Constant	16.59	14.30	1.16
Inflation	.01	.72	.02
Unemployment	−1.81	1.46	−1.24
War	5.55	5.03	1.10
Presidential foreign policy mentions	.26	.10	2.01
Presidential foreign policy positions	−.06	.13	−.46
Public opinion$_{(t-1)}$	.51	.17	3.01
R^2/Adj. R^2/equation type	.81	.76	OLS
Lagrange multiplier	1.69		
Civil rights policy			
Constant	3.90	4.87	.80
Inflation	−.11	.32	−.35
Unemployment	−.88	.64	−1.38
War	1.06	2.03	.52
Presidential civil rights policy mentions	.59	.24	2.48
Presidential civil rights policy positions	.02	.03	.53
Public opinion$_{(t-1)}$	.51	.10	5.03
R^2/Adj. R^2/equation type	.78	.72	OLS
Lagrange multiplier	2.76		
Domestic policy			
Constant	−5.77	7.25	−.80
Inflation	.41	.53	.76
Unemployment	.57	1.00	.57
War	−2.55	4.57	−.56
President's domestic policy mentions	.22	.15	1.57
President's domestic policy positions	−.04	.21	−.18
Public opinion$_{(t-1)}$	.90	.21	4.24
R^2/Adj. R^2/equation type	.81	.76	OLS
Lagrange multiplier	.94		

variables in the equation (compare table 3.4 with table 2.3). Adding the position-taking variable into the equation does not increase its explanatory power. Substance does not influence public opinion any more than symbolism. Thus, the public responds directly to anything the president says. It does not distinguish between presidential mentions of a policy area and taking a position on the policy area. Both symbolic and substantive presidential statements equally influence public thinking about what issues to think about. In this regard, we can call the president the "Great Mentioner."

Conclusions

This chapter has focused on the dynamics and determinants of presidential position taking in the State of the Union Address. The theory proposed in this book offered some theoretical expectations about those processes. Primarily, presidential responsiveness to the public should decline as the president's decision or action affects his ability to control and direct the public policy-making process.

Problem identification, the topic of chapter 2, has few implications for the substance and/or timing of policy-making. Problem identification does not require a president to take a position nor even to commit to any unspecified action. Position taking, the topic of this chapter, has just such implications. Position taking sets policy priorities and may create expectations for future presidential action. Position taking commits the president to a particular course of action, a course that can only be altered with effort and cost. Thus, subsequent discretion is limited.

My analysis in chapter 2 found initial support for this hypothesis. Presidents were found to be responsive to the public in the problem identification process but only on the required economic and foreign policy areas. No responsiveness was detected in the discretionary civil rights or domestic policy areas. Analysis in this chapter offered further support for the responsiveness hypothesis. We did not expect to find high levels of presidential responsiveness to public opinion when the president's rhetoric is substantively focused, as is position taking. Analysis detected only mild responsiveness in one case, civil rights, and potential counterresponsiveness in two cases, overall substantiveness and domestic policy.

Moreover, we found another reason for this nonresponsiveness in the substantive aspects of policy-making. Presidents do not have to resort to substantive arguments to lead public opinion. In terms of building public concern for a policy area, symbolism seems as effective as substance. Hence, the president can lead public opinion by merely identifying problems. He does not have to offer solutions. Thus, he can restrict public mobilization to the problem identification stages of the agenda-building process. He does not have to integrate the public into the process of "coupling" problems and solutions (Kingdon 1984) in order to lead it. This leaves him freer to act as he chooses when discussing policies substantively, when he publicly exposes how he has coupled solutions and problems.

CHAPTER 4

Presidential Responsiveness and Policy Formulation

In the policy formulation process, decision makers construct and select solutions to the policy problems and issues that they identified as priorities. Time, energy, and other resources are committed in developing a policy response. In choosing policy solutions, presidents begin looking away from public opinion and toward those elites who can affect the progress and shape of the policy under question. Thus, the mix of incentives facing the president shifts in this process, and presidential responsiveness to the public, consequently, should decline.

Several processes dilute direct presidential responsiveness to public opinion in policy formulation. First, the public may not be a good guide in deciding which policy alternative to adopt. It is notoriously ill informed (Erikson, Luttbeg, and Tedin 1991), and even if it is informed it may not understand the technicalities involved in shaping a policy response. For instance, which is a better solution to a problem, coercive regulation or inducements? Which level and agency of government should administer the program? How big should the program be? The public lacks the information and resources to answer these questions. Rather, the public asks that a problem be dealt with effectively, timely, and responsibly once it has become a public concern. Determining how that should be done is usually left up to political leaders, especially the president.

Even when the public has some idea of the direction that the policy solution should take, that notion may still be too general to provide guidance on more technical and detailed matters of policy formulation. The public may prefer more or less government involvement, a bigger or smaller program, a fairer or more efficient policy, but it may not know how to shape a program to fulfill that vision.

For example, in the debates over health care during the early months of the Clinton administration, it was clear that the public was worried about health care as a public issue. The public was especially concerned with the spiraling cost of health care and the large number of people lacking coverage. It desired widespread, affordable coverage that provided reliable, effective access and treatment. But it is not clear that the public knew what kind of policy would best realize those goals.

The role of the public in the policy-making process is more that of spectator than policy developer (on this public role see Kingdon 1984; Light 1982). Public opinion does not devise policy solutions. Political elites and policy specialists do. These policy competitors then try to win public support for their proposal, which they do through reasoned debate and/or symbolic manipulation. Thus, the public is a poor guide for presidents in detailing the substance of policy options.

In the policy formulation process, presidential concern turns to two questions: (1) Can the president build support with other authoritative decision makers, like members of Congress, to get his policy alternative implemented? and (2) Once implemented, will it succeed or fail? There are major costs to failure on either count. The president may not be elected to a second term, or if already in that term his party may lose the presidency in the next election. Negative fallout may affect other policies. The president's position may be so weakened that he will be unable to build winning coalitions behind those initiatives. His reputation may be tarnished, and he may become the scapegoat for the nation's political and policy woes. In such an atmosphere, policy and political competitors may raise their voices, further undercutting the president's position.

Thus, presidents are vitally concerned with implementing effective policies. Anything that interferes with successful implementation will be shunned or resisted, including public opinion. Presidents cannot afford to follow public opinion if doing so results in congressional defeat or disastrous policy.[1] Rather than follow public opinion in the policy formulation process, presidents aim more to mobilize public support behind the policy paths already chosen.[2]

In this chapter, I test whether or not presidents respond to public opinion in the policy formulation stage. I develop a data series on presidential policy stands, using the State of Union Address, as in the previous chapters. This series identifies the president's ideological positions on issues. I call this series *presidential ideology*. Then I relate this liberal-conservative presidential stance to a data series tapping liberalism and conservatism in the mass public that James Stimson (1991) has developed.[3] I ask, Does the president move in a liberal (conservative) direction when the public moves in that direction?

Measuring Presidential Ideology in Public Statements

In this section I present data on presidential ideology. Here ideology refers to the positions that presidents take on a liberal-conservative continuum. It is not meant to convey a sense of the constraint or degree of sophistication of presidential thinking about public policies (Converse 1964). Further, I define

liberalism and conservatism in terms of policy positions not as attitudes toward change (Reichley 1981, 6–7) or personality (McClosky 1958).

I view liberals and conservatives as groups of competing politicians and
policy advocates with differing policy positions on many issues of the day.
The debate between liberals and conservatives helps structure most of the
political debate of the nation. One can think of a liberal-conservative dimension dividing the political world, and most policies can be arrayed along that
dimension. Further, one can identify the liberal or conservative position on the
policy in question. Some policies may present stark and extreme differences
between liberals and conservatives; other policies may present differences that
are less pronounced. People whose preferences fall somewhere in between are
moderates.

For the purposes of this study, I identify the direction of the policy
positions that were analyzed in the previous chapter, using the position of the
liberal interest group, the Americans for Democratic Action (ADA), to identify the liberal position on an issue. Yearly reports by the ADA and two
histories of the organization (Brock 1962; Gillon 1987) provide detail about
the ADA position on specific policies and public issues.[4]

The coding scheme is quite simple. Using sentences in the president's
State of the Union Address, as I have done in earlier chapters, I categorize
each sentence as either liberal or conservative, or neither, according to this
ADA standard. The number of liberal sentences divided by the number of
liberal plus conservative sentences produces a percent-liberal score. This percentage of liberalism will be the focus of attention in the analysis that follows.
The appendix to this chapter presents a detailed and technical discussion of
the reliability and validity of this measure.

Relying on an ADA standard has several virtues. First, the ADA is
considered the upholder and definer of modern American liberalism. Whatever intellectual and abstract connections may exist between the ADA position and liberalism, if the ADA calls a position liberal that is how it is
perceived.

Second, congressional roll call studies find that ADA indexes are highly
correlated with indexes of other interests groups that also try to assess ideological support, like the Americans for Constitutional Action (ACA) (Smith,
Herrera, and Herrera 1990). Shelley (1983, 18) finds that the ADA scores
correlate in the −.82 to −.96 range with Conservative Coalition support
scores of members of both congressional chambers.[5]

Third, the ADA standard can be used to assess liberalism (conservatism)
across a wide array of behaviors, from the rhetorical positions used in this
chapter to roll call positions, which I use in chapter 6. Such a standard will
enable me to assess the validity of the measures employed as well as provide a
view of how rhetorical position taking affects roll call position taking. Thus,

TABLE 4.1. Presidential Rhetorical Liberalism, Overall and by Policy Area, 1953–89 (in percentages)

President	All	Economic Policy	Foreign Policy	Domestic Policy	Civil Rights
Eisenhower	66	30	94	49	94
Kennedy	84	52	94	100	96
Johnson	70	71	57	98	100
Nixon	35	32	26	39	100
Ford	26	22	37	28	18
Carter	57	34	89	59	100
Reagan	10	5	5	19	34
Bush	37	0	0	62	83
Average	47	32	53	52	81

different decision processes can be linked together, something that most studies of the policy process fail to do (Sabatier 1991).

Lastly, the ADA positions correspond quite well to the liberal and conservative alternatives on the public opinion polls that Stimson used to construct the public opinion series (1991, 35). This comparability is important if we are to assess the impact of public opinion on the president. We do not require that either the president or the public understand the term *liberal* or *conservative* or know about the ADA and its adversaries. All that is required is that I code the same position on an issue the same way for the president and the mass public.

Table 4.1 presents the ideology data for each president, across the whole Address and broken down by the four policy areas. Figures 4.1 through 4.5 present the time paths of the series.

Kennedy anchors the left and Reagan the right. Johnson leans strongly left (perhaps somewhat less so than one might expect). Carter, the most moderate Democrat, is only slightly left of center. On the right, Ford is slightly less conservative than Reagan, and Nixon is somewhat less extreme than Ford. Bush, while still conservative, is hard to compare because only one year of data is used for him. The only apparent anomaly is Eisenhower, who is moderately left of center.

Using historical and biographical materials, I will later discuss the ideological positions of the presidents. This will provide a sense of the common understandings of the presidents, and how well my data fit with those understandings. In several cases, such as the Eisenhower anomaly mentioned earlier, the interaction of the two types of information will help resolve some

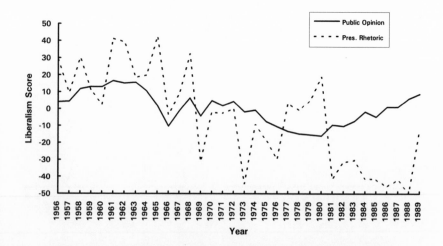

Fig. 4.1. Presidential rhetorical liberalism and public opinion liberalism, 1956–89. (Data for the presidential series was compiled by the author from presidential State of the Union addresses. Data for the public opinion series is from Stimson 1991.)

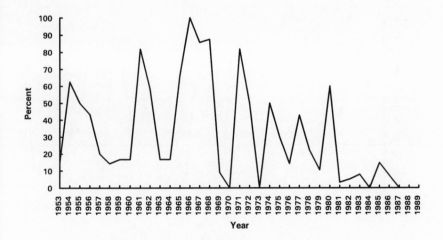

Fig. 4.2. Presidential rhetorical liberalism, 1953–89: economic policy. (Data compiled by the author from presidential State of the Union addresses.)

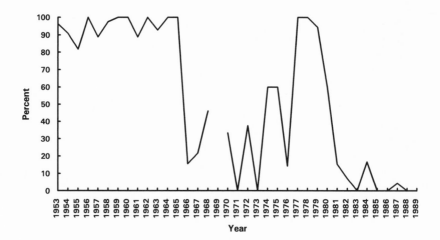

Fig. 4.3. Presidential rhetorical liberalism, 1953–89: foreign policy. (Data compiled by the author from presidential State of the Union addresses.)

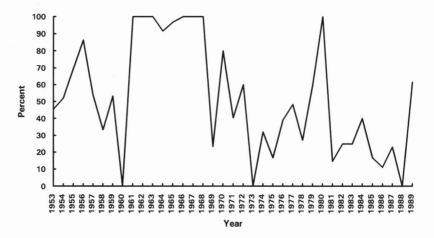

Fig. 4.4. Presidential rhetorical liberalism, 1953–89: domestic policy. (Data compiled by the author from presidential State of the Union addresses.)

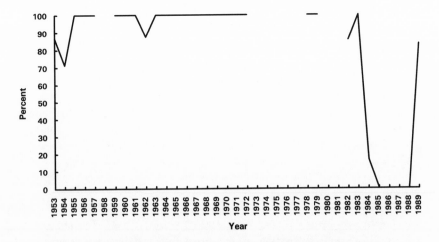

Fig. 4.5. Presidential rhetorical liberalism, 1953–89: civil rights policy. (Data compiled by the author from presidential State of the Union addresses.)

interpretive disputes. Moreover, the qualitative data will help flesh out the numerical renderings of the presidents, putting the numbers into historical context, thus providing a better sense of what the numbers mean as well as their limitations. This helps sensitize us to the complexity of presidential ideology, the impact of context, and the possibilities and probable causes of change in presidential positions. Using such descriptive and contextual knowledge will strengthen the quantitative analysis that follows, offering possible hypotheses about presidential behavior as well as guiding interpretation of findings.

The Ideological Leanings of American Presidents: A Qualitative Discussion

Eisenhower

The thinking about the Eisenhower presidency has changed considerably in recent years. Revisionists view him as a more skilled president and leader than did early appraisers (cf. Greenstein 1982; Ambrose 1990). There has also been a reevaluation in the thinking about Eisenhower's political beliefs and policies in recent years. This new thinking portrays a less conservative and more moderate president than was earlier thought. Close inspection of Eisenhower's beliefs and policies reveals a president who is at one time liberal and another time conservative. It is not so much that Eisenhower's positions on policies evolved over time but that he held different views depending on the policy area.

Looking at Eisenhower in one policy area, one may get a view of Eisenhower as a liberal. Turning to another policy area, one may see Eisenhower as more conservative. Summed across policy areas, Eisenhower looks moderate, but this hides his distinct liberal and conservative leanings on some very important policy areas. Eisenhower leans in the liberal direction on foreign affairs, but in a conservative direction on economic policy. Data in table 4.1 give Eisenhower a 94 percent liberal score on foreign policy and a 30 percent score on economic policy.

There is more controversy about his civil rights policies, with some viewing him as liberal, others as moderate to conservative. Tension existed between his beliefs (conservative) and his willingness to listen to his major civil rights adviser (Herbert Brownell, a liberal). This tension accounts for this mixed portrait of Eisenhower on civil rights, though the quantitative data indicate strong liberalism at 94 percent. Eisenhower's apparent liberalism in civil rights, discussed in more detail later, seems to fit well into the portrait of the Republican Party of the 1950s, as described by Carmines and Stimson (1989). They argue that the party was liberal on this issue during the 1950s and did not turn to its present conservative position until 1964.

Eisenhower's foreign policy beliefs were quite liberal for the time. In-spection of figure 4.3 shows that his foreign policy liberalism equaled that of Kennedy and the early Johnson years. Moreover, Eisenhower's foreign policy liberalism was quite stable. He stood for internationalism and foreign aid when conservative elements in his party wanted to retreat into another postwar isolationism and decried giving foreign aid (Hoxie 1983, 603). Ambrose (1990), the leading Eisenhower biographer, reports that "Eisenhower was so much closer to the Democrats than the Taft-dominated Republicans on foreign policy" that some Democrats held out hopes of Eisenhower as their party's choice in 1952 (p. 259). Eisenhower's first inaugural "sounded far more like Truman announcing the containment policy than . . . like Taft or indeed any other Republican" (Ambrose 1990, 297–98). The speech was roundly ap-plauded by Democrats. Even on Yalta, an issue on which the Republicans had bashed Democrats repeatedly, Eisenhower "maintained that Roosevelt had entered into the best possible agreement" (Ambrose 1990, 305). On foreign aid, Eisenhower ran into strong opposition from Senator Taft, who objected to proposed aid levels that were "only slightly less than those of Truman" (Am-brose 1990, 320), and throughout his administrations he worked hard to get his foreign aid packages through Congress (Ambrose 1990, 437–38).

In economic policy, Eisenhower held classically conservative beliefs, though they were tempered by his refusal to dismantle the New Deal. Eisenhower's economic policy beliefs were grounded in the idea that the budget must be in balance. This, more than any other factor, accounts for his economic and budgetary policies. He also feared that the economy would expand too fast, leading to inflation (Weatherford and McDonnell 1985).

Consequently, he resisted government intervention into the economy as much as possible. He refused to stimulate the economy in 1958 and later in 1960, which Nixon partially blamed for his defeat in the 1960 presidential election. But Eisenhower also wanted the party to shed its label as the party of Depression. Thus, in 1954, when the nation hit a mild recession, he made plans to stimulate the economy if unemployment rose above 5 percent (Ambrose 1990, 348). It didn't and Eisenhower didn't act.[6]

Yet he did not attempt to dismantle the New Deal (Prothro 1956, 736; Weatherford and McDonnell 1985, 111) and used some public spending programs to smooth out the fluctuations of the business cycle, as long as those policies had other benefits. For instance, he supported the massive highway construction project because he believed it was needed and that only the federal government could do it but also because it would put people to work on a government project without it being labeled "make-work" and could help modulate fluctuations in the unemployment rate (Ambrose 1990, 387). In all, he leaned in a conservative direction on economic policy, but he was a far cry from the self-help conservatism of Herbert Hoover or the radical deregulation of Ronald Reagan.

On domestic policies, Ambrose (1990, 346) characterizes Eisenhower as a moderate who "angered the conservatives as well as the liberals" but sometimes sponsored liberal expansions, such as his legislative victory that added Social Security protection to "ten million people not previously covered" (Ambrose 1990, 346). Eisenhower even wrote in his diary that his secretary of the interior, Douglas Weeks, "seems so completely conservative in his views that he at times seems to be illogical" (Ambrose 1990, 290). The ADA data support Ambrose's contention, scoring Eisenhower a decidedly middle-of-the-road 49.

In civil rights, Eisenhower's personal inclinations resided with white southerners, but several forces, including his beliefs about the presidency and the influence of his attorney general, Herbert Brownell, pushed him in a more liberal direction. Hoxie (1983, 601–2) is one who views Eisenhower as a moderate activist in civil rights, pointing to his efforts to eliminate job bias in the federal government.

Kahn (1992) also views Eisenhower as relatively liberal on civil rights, making the case that Eisenhower knew of the liberal civil rights positions of his appointees to the Supreme Court (Warren, Harlan, Brennan) before their nominations. Moreover, Eisenhower knew what he was doing when making those nominations. Ambrose (1990, 338) lifts this quote from Eisenhower's diary on the Warren nomination: "[If the] Republicans as a body should try to repudiate him, I shall leave the Republican Party."

Perhaps the most important liberalizing force acting on Eisenhower on civil rights was his attorney general, Brownell. Eisenhower did not want his attorney general to express his opinion on the unconstitutionality of segregated schools before the Supreme Court, then deliberating on *Brown v. Board of Education*. But he accepted Brownell's advice that it had to be done (Ambrose 1990, 340). Brownell was eager to sponsor a civil rights bill in 1956, and though Eisenhower had "gone to great lengths to divorce himself from the problem of race relations" (Ambrose 1990, 405), he "told Brownell to get to work on it" (Ambrose 1990, 406). Eisenhower later accepted Brownell's proposal, against the objections by some in the cabinet (Ambrose 1990, 408–9), confessing that "I'm at sea on this. . . . I want to put something forward that I can show as an advance" (Ambrose 1990, 414)

Stern (1989a) echoes the view of Eisenhower as basically supportive of civil rights. The case against Eisenhower's liberalism on civil rights is founded on Eisenhower's own privately stated sympathy with white southerners, in part a result of his upbringing in Texas; his sluggish response to the Little Rock crisis; the weakness of the civil rights legislation that he supported; and his reluctance to speak out on the *Brown v. Board d*ecision. Ambrose (1990, 335) reports that Eisenhower shared most of the prejudices of white southerners toward "Negroes." But he also felt that as president, he was "President of all the people. That included Negro Americans" (Ambrose 1990, 336). Eisenhower needed to be prodded to action on civil rights, either by the pressure of events or the insistence of his trusted attorney general, but in most cases when action finally came it promoted civil rights expansion. Thus, it is not unfair to call him a reluctant liberal or, as Ambrose sums him up, moderate (1990, 409). And whatever his private opinions, publicly he almost always took up the mantle of civil rights. My data show this liberalism as well.

Eisenhower's somewhat liberal aggregate score is now easily explained. He ties with Kennedy as the most liberal president on foreign policy (94). Moreover, foreign policy comprises a large proportion of Eisenhower's sentences, further pushing his aggregate score to the left. Foreign policy loomed so large for Eisenhower because of the intraparty debate over the policy area and Eisenhower's background and natural interest in that area compared to the other areas.

Kennedy

In two senses Kennedy differs from Eisenhower. Generally, Kennedy's positions were more tightly bounded, with a liberal cast, and unlike Eisenhower, whose policies seemed somewhat stable over time, Kennedy's evolved. This is especially true on economic and civil rights policy.

Kennedy's evolution is especially apparent in the economic policy area. As a member of Congress, he was influenced strongly by his father's economic conservatism. Thus, he believed in and supported measures to keep the budget in balance and voted for cuts in appropriations to the Tennessee Valley Authority and the Agriculture and Interior Departments. But pressures from his working-class congressional district led him to support "bread and butter" liberal issues, such as more low-income housing, increases in the minimum wage, and extension of Social Security benefits (Giglio 1991, 7–8). Perhaps the best characterization of Kennedy upon his assumption of the presidency was that in economic policy he held no firm beliefs.

It was in the tax cut proposal of 1962 that Kennedy's economic views began to take root. Initially, liberals did not support the proposal, arguing that it did not benefit the poor (Giglio 1991, 119). But the tax cut laid the groundwork for the acceptance of Keynesian-styled fiscal policies, which would provide the basis for liberal economic policies over the next two decades. The tax cut proposal, which would unbalance the budget, undercut JFK's earlier fiscal responsibility stance and his belief that "unsound fiscal policy" had harmed previous Democratic administrations (Giglio 1991, 124–25). He also feared that Republicans might label him another "reckless spender," as they had "every Democratic candidate since Roosevelt" (Giglio 1991, 125). The tax cut proposal marks an important turnaround on Kennedy's part.

Once he had adopted the tax cut proposal, Kennedy became a stable supporter of Keynesian macroeconomic policies. His adoption of the policy came as his economic advisers, especially Walter Heller, educated Kennedy on economic policy. Kennedy not only took their advice, he learned their lessons and their economic theory (Flash 1972; Stein 1972). He was converted to their point of view. But his emphasis on investment and productivity as economic goals does not mark him as a classic liberal, where redistribution concerns override all else.[7]

He showed some populist leanings in his clash with the steel industry over price hikes in 1962. He was ready to use the full force of the government to move steel to rescind the price hikes, but his willingness to intervene in the economy was not so much antibusiness as motivated by a desire to stabilize and rationalize the economy (Giglio 1991, 132). Still, Kennedy was no enemy of business. In the aftermath of the steel crisis, he offered the business community some assistance in the form of tax breaks (Vogel 1989, 16–23), and throughout his term he displayed a willingness to work with big business to expand the economy, employing conservative economic rhetoric and appointments in his attempts to woo them (Giglio 1991, 128). This balance between liberal and conservative economic views is evident in the quantitative data; Kennedy scores a 52.

Kennedy's evolution in civil rights policy is no less dramatic than his evolution in economic policy. Initially Kennedy was silent on civil rights, though he offered one early concession by appointing a civil rights adviser to his staff (Giglio 1991, 161–62). He made other minor moves in a liberal direction when he urged the Coast Guard, then all white, to recruit blacks and when his executive order created the President's Committee on Equal Employment Opportunity (Giglio 1991, 162–63). It was, however, the University of Mississippi crisis of 1962 and southern violence that pushed Kennedy strongly to the left on civil rights. He began to view civil rights in moral terms, something that the pragmatic Kennedy did rarely on public policies. But he was not above exploiting the political benefits of associating with the movement. He supported the march on Washington, providing government assistance. This, he hoped, would ensure a safe, peaceful march, one that would help his efforts to secure civil rights legislation, fearing as he did that violence or disruption would only undercut his efforts with Congress as well as his growing political reputation (Giglio 1991, 185). Kennedy's liberal leanings and pragmatism became a liberal commitment to civil rights by the end of his life (Gilbert 1982). (On Kennedy's civil rights pragmatism see Stern 1989b, 1992.)

In other domestic policy areas, he showed a cautious willingness to support liberal causes. He promoted women's equality by directing the chair of the Civil Service Commission to ensure that federal employment was based solely on merit. Moreover, he submitted legislation, which Congress accepted, to assist the states in establishing daycare facilities and ended the quota on female military officers (Giglio 1991, 142–43)

In foreign affairs, in which he was more interested, Kennedy showed greater stability in his beliefs and policies. He was staunchly anticolonial (Giglio 1991, 14), supported the liberation movements in the Third World (Giglio 1991, 222), and the United Nations (Giglio 1991, 86), all of which give him a liberal tenor. But he was equally anticommunist, at times militantly so, part out of belief, part opportunism, and part to weaken charges that Democrats were soft on communism. Thus, he chastised Eisenhower for allowing a "missile gap" with the Soviets and challenged the Soviets in Berlin and Cuba. He fired State Department official Chester Bowles, a liberal darling, and though the ouster was not ideologically motivated, it hurt his relations with liberals (Giglio 1991, 93). In all, his foreign policy leanings were quite liberal, a point that the quantitative data reinforce with Kennedy's 94 percent showing.

Johnson

Although Lyndon Johnson was aligned with the conservative elements of the Democratic Party as a member of Congress, his ambitions and entry into the national scene moved him in a decidedly liberal direction, especially on the issue of greatest division within the Democratic Party, civil rights. Throughout his service as president, Johnson shows relative stability in his policy positions, which are almost uniformly liberal. On foreign affairs, however, the strains of the Vietnam War tugged him in a conservative direction. Thus, like Eisenhower, but unlike Kennedy, Johnson is relatively stable in his policy beliefs and positions, but unlike Eisenhower and more like Kennedy, his policy positions are almost uniformly liberal. In fact, were it not for Vietnam, Johnson would be the most liberal president of all those studied here (see table 4.1).

Johnson shows little interest, understanding, and concern for economic theory or policy. His general inclinations were liberal, owing to his upbringing and maturation during the New Deal era. Even as New Deal support among Southern Democrats was fading in the second half of the 1930s, Johnson showed an unflagging support for FDR and his policies. As president, his economic policies retained that liberal heritage but added both Kennedy's newfound Keynesian and lack of animosity toward the business sector. Johnson displayed his Keynesian inclinations when he sought the income surtax, a policy he felt was necessary to fight the inflation that his war policy was fueling. His support for the business sector is evident in his refusal to raise economic class divisions and his view that the economy was a positive sum game. Overall, Johnson is the most liberal president in the economic realm at 71.

The relative moderation of this score, coupled with Kennedy's 52, indicates how much liberals in the United States have to answer to the free market mentality and support for capitalism that is so ingrained in the culture and the polity. The rightist tilt in U.S. economic policy-making that so many analysts detect (cf. Lehne 1993) is repeated in these data on presidential rhetoric.

On civil rights policies Johnson demonstrates his strongest adherence to liberal values. He has been credited with revolutionizing race relations in the United States through his words and deeds. Even after support for civil rights began to wane, he continued to push expansive policies. In the aftermath of the race riots of the mid-1960s, he called for a restoration of civility and respect for the law but also for an increase in the Great Society programs aimed at ameliorating the conditions that he felt partially led to the civil disturbances (Calder 1982). And public opposition to civil rights did not deter him from pushing legislation in his last year in office (Altschuler 1990, 27; Stern 1992). In all, Johnson was personally committed to civil rights (Altschuler 1990, 21). His social welfare positions also strongly attest to his liberal proclivities. He pushed for Medicare, attacked poverty through his Great Society programs, and supported the expansion of government regulation (Vogel 1989).

His Vietnam War policies, however, undercut the view of Johnson as an across-the-board liberal. On other foreign policy issues, he showed a loyalty to the liberal creed, believing in foreign aid and arms control talks with the Soviets. But when liberals began to back away from the militant anticommunist containment that they had believed in since the early Cold War period, moving to a more accommodating and less confrontational stance, Johnson seemed cemented to the earlier way of thinking. Thus, his war policies made him appear to be moving right, or at least not staying in step with liberalism as its foreign policy views evolved. In 1965, before Vietnam began to dominate his foreign policy statements to the public, his Addresses registered a 93.8 percent liberal score on foreign matters. The next year, his foreign policy score shifted to 46.7, due mostly to the need to justify the war, which was losing public support. Figure 4.3 dramatically details the slide in Johnson's liberalism on foreign policy. By the end of his term of office, Johnson's foreign policy stance becomes a curious mixture, keeping the internationalism of liberalism but not adopting its newer approach to the Cold War.

Nixon

Nixon's policy positions are very complex, showing considerable drift over time, partly as a result of his lack of firm belief outside the foreign policy area. Usually a conservative, he was willing, perhaps for political reasons, to adopt liberal policies and positions. Once those positions paid off or lost their political advantage, Nixon swiftly abandoned them. This lack of commitment makes Nixon appear to be a moderate who usually leans toward the right.

In economic policy, Nixon shows a pattern of movement from right to left and back to the right. His early policies were traditional Republican, viewing inflation as the chief economic problem (Genovese 1990, 63). Nixon was, however, not wedded to that course. He moved to the left, stimulating the economy to boost his reelection chances. Moreover, he allowed a host of new regulations, according to Herbert Stein (1984, 190), the most of any president since FDR, although Nixon had been a long-standing critic of government regulation, feeling they were too intrusive and complex to implement (Genovese 1990, 66). Nixon also took the most radical economic policy actions of any president during the period under consideration here with his wage and price controls. Prior to that action, he publicly claimed that "I am now a Keynesian" (Genovese 1990, 67). After the reelection bid, he slipped back to his more natural moorings, following conservative economic policies (Genovese 1990, 71).

The quantitative data pick up the volatility in Nixon's economic policy. His traditional conservatism at the onset of his administration is revealed in scores of 9 percent and 0 percent during his first two years in office. In his third year, the era of the wage and price controls, Nixon's rhetoric moves markedly leftward, to 82. That is much higher than any Republican president, fully twenty points more liberal than Eisenhower in 1954 (at 62). After the controls are lifted, Nixon moves right, with a 50 (1972), 0 (1973) and back to 50 (1974). What appears moderate overall is a series of extreme swings from right to left and back to the right.

Nixon's complexity is also apparent in his handling of civil rights. Never a conservative on the issue, and usually associated with moderates, Nixon concluded that his election owed more to southerners and racial conservatives than blacks and their civil rights supporters. Thus, he engaged a "Southern Strategy," which aimed at wresting the once solid south from the Democrats. He nominated conservatives on racial matters to the Supreme Court, but two early nominees, Carswell and Haynesworth, failed to be confirmed, forcing Nixon to seek more acceptable moderates. Although Nixon could point to some expansionist civil rights policies, such as developing minority participation in the construction industry, attempts to eliminate discrimination against women and minorities in college hiring, and creating voluntary councils to promote desegregation in the South (Genovese 1990, 82–83), the overall thrust of his policies by late 1970 was anti–civil rights. For instance, he favored limiting enforcement powers in the extension of the 1965 Voting Rights Act and proposed a moratorium on school busing in 1972 (Genovese 1990, 85–87).

This is not at all evident in the quantitative data. His first four years demonstrate perfect liberal credentials on civil rights, with uniform 100 percent scores. But he offered few statements. Nixon was silent on civil rights the last two years in office. This silence might indicate his retreat from liberalism on civil rights.

On social policies he showed the same inclination to first follow liberal directions, which probably ran against his grain, only to later abandon or weaken them. This is evident in his welfare reform proposal and his support for the environment. On crime, he took a more solidly conservative tack, brandishing the slogan "law and order" and offering several "get tough on crime" proposals (Genovese 1990, 89; Calder 1982).

After a moderately conservative start, Nixon moves to the left with a score of 80 in 1970. He heads right in 1973 (40), but his 1972 offering, perhaps to win reelection, moves him left to 60. Once reelected, the conservative Nixon comes to the fore with a 0 in 1973 and 32 in 1974. As Genovese (1990, 95) concludes about Nixon's domestic and economic policies, Nixon "was a conservative in a liberal era . . . His policy about-faces . . . reflect not so much a staunch conservative as someone who surveys the political landscape and acts accordingly. . . . Nixon was not a classic or extreme conservative . . . his policies did lean to the political right." Both the quantitative data and the historical account capture these swings and about-faces.

In international affairs, an area of greater concern and interest to Nixon,

Nixon again displays little ideological commitment and again strikes one as mixing liberal and conservative themes. He was always an internationalist, supporting such policies as the Marshall Plan (Genovese 1990, 100). This aligned him with the Eisenhower wing of the GOP. But he was also a conservative, and used red-baiting tactics to win some early electoral contests.

His conservative roots were underscored in his view that East-West tensions dominated world affairs and that Third World nations mattered little (Genovese 1990, 110), his willingness to support national movements aimed at resisting or overthrowing Communists (Genovese 1990, 106), his support of conservatives who overthrew the socialist Allende regime in Chile (Genovese 1990, 149), and the escalation of the Vietnam conflict into Cambodia. But his normalizing of relations with the Communist Chinese, his participation in arms limitations talks with the Soviets, his Eisenhower-like belief in military sufficiency and parity with the Soviets rather than superiority over them, and his reluctance to commit American troops into foreign conflicts, all demonstrate a retreat from strict foreign policy conservatism. He falls somewhere between conservative and liberal in foreign affairs in that the left criticized him for being too concerned about power and not enough about morality, while the right complained that he did not view the East-West rivalry in ideological terms and that he relinquished too much to the Soviets in his pursuit of détente (Genovese 1990, 164).

The quantitative data show Nixon striking a more conservative pose, but again the habit of policy shifts is evident in these data. In part because of the Vietnam War, Nixon stakes out a conservative posture during his first administration with a 33 in 1970, 0 in 1971, and 37 in 1972. With Vietnam out of the way and détente in full swing by 1974, Nixon's score hits 60.

Ford

Ford's brief tenure limited his opportunity to develop and change his policies. For the most part, Ford was a mainstream, conservative Republican of the post-Eisenhower era, and his policy leanings and initiatives showed many continuities with the late Nixon period (Reichley 1981). One sees this continuity through Ford's retention of some key Nixon policy advisers, such as Henry Kissinger at the State Department. Thus, while somewhat more conservative than Nixon, he is more moderate than Reagan (see table 4.1). Like most of the presidents reviewed here, Ford's ideological leanings vary across issue areas, but he is almost always positioned right of center. He is most conservative on economic policy, while his positions on foreign and civil rights policy are more centrist, though his rhetoric on civil rights leans conservative. He displays conservative tendencies on domestic policy too.

Ford's starkest application of conservative principles comes in the economic policy area. Presiding over the first oil shock, inflation became the administration's top economic priority, but unemployment, which also rose as a consequence of the oil shock, was less important to Ford. He instituted the Council on Wage and Price Stability (COWPS) to review and comment on "Inflation Impact Statements" that federal agencies were required to write when considering new regulations. He also offered his "Whip Inflation Now" campaign, which amounted to little more than exhorting the public to hold down inflationary pressures and to demonstrate support for the "program" by wearing a lapel button with the "WIN" acronym affixed to it. Like a conservative on economic matters, Ford's ventures into economic control and direction were modest and often symbolic, like the WIN button, though he tried to stem the tide of increasing public expenditures through his profligate use of the veto and his active support of proposals to deregulate many industries, including the airlines (Bierce 1974; Derthick and Quirk 1985). The quantitative data demonstrate his conservatism, with an overall 22 that is relatively stable across both of his Addresses (30, 14).

On foreign policy he continued the internationalist policies that Nixon pursued, such as the Strategic Arms Limitations Talks (SALT) with the Soviets. He was not, however, loathe to challenge the Soviets in other spheres, such as in Angola (Hodges 1976), and in Southeast Asia he willingly used troops in the Mayaguez incident. Thus, during the period of détente his foreign policy rhetoric is liberal at 60 in 1975, but it shifts in a conservative direction in 1976 as the election campaign nears and he seeks his party's nomination.

In the civil rights area, Ford steered a moderate course, rarely acting to restrict civil rights but also rarely working to expand them (Shull 1989, 48). Thus, he opposed busing but supported federal aid to school districts that were trying to desegregate as well as the extension of the Voting Rights Act. His rhetoric is decidedly more conservative here at 18 (with no positions taken in 1975), perhaps to appeal to the backlashers who comprised a large voting block within the Republican Party. His domestic utterances are also quite conservative, with a 17 in 1975 and 39 in 1976.

Carter

Jimmy Carter is a president who often found himself at odds with his own party. This is especially the case on economic policy. Like the other presidents discussed previously, Carter's leanings vary across issue area. Unlike most of them, though, he shows considerable differences in his policy views, from conservative economic leanings to very liberal positions on civil rights and foreign affairs (see table 4.1). When asked if he was a liberal or a conservative, Carter answered, "I was a fiscal conservative but quite liberal on such issues as civil rights, environmental quality, and helping people overcome handicaps to lead fruitful lives" (Carter 1982, 73–74). And what often looked like policy shifts in the economic realm may be better understood as his attempt at balancing his own conservative views with liberal pressures from his own party (Hargrove 1988, 107).

In economic policy, Carter was more conservative than typical Democrats and often looked as if he were a conservative Republican. He fought to hold back funding levels, being a strong supporter of fiscal conservatism and budgetary restraint (Hargrove 1988, 69). Thus, he openly supported conservative economics on "fiscal/monetary/budget affairs" and "deregulation" (Hargrove 1988, 22), positions that often led to strife with his congressional copartisans (Kaufman 1990, 110). His fiscal conservatism is also evident in some of his social policies. His early effort at welfare reform was submitted to Congress to demonstrate how his conservative fiscal posture could be used to further liberal policy goals (Hargrove 1988, 54), and his urban policy budget has been described as "frugal" (Kaufman 1993, 76) and drew criticism from black leaders (Kaufman 1993, 149).

Still, at times he had to respond to liberal elements in his party on spending matters. At the end of each budget cycle, Carter would meet with advisers, like Stuart Eizenstadt, to find several billion dollars that would be divided among liberal programs (Hargrove 1988, 80). But this represented a small part of a multi-hundred-billion-dollar budget. Further, it was politically motivated, as Carter sought to help and repay administration supporters. Carter also resisted growing protectionist sentiment and rejected efforts to impose tariffs. Tariff advocates wanted them to offset the weakening dollar and the declining competitiveness of American goods in world and domestic markets (Kaufman 1993, 152).

The quantitative data reveal Carter's relative conservatism in economic policy. He scores a 34 (compared to Kennedy's 52 and Johnson's 71). On economic policy, his score is hardly distinguishable from Eisenhower (30) or Nixon (32). The data also show Carter trying to respond to his party. His three initial scores are 42, 22, 10. Then, in 1980 he shifts left, to 60 percent, perhaps in an attempt to appeal to those whose support he would need to secure the nomination and fend off Edward Kennedy's challenge.[8]

His attempt to steer a course between his conservative views and his party's liberalism was strained in perhaps the most perplexing domestic issue of his time, energy. Carter supported decontrol of natural gas, as well as liberal efforts at conservation and a centralized government approach to dealing with the energy problem. Thus, his energy program was "too liberal for conservatives in its willingness to continue price regulation and too conservative for liberals in its plan for price increases" (Hargrove 1988, 52).

On the civil rights front, Carter was more attuned with the liberal moorings of the Democratic Party (Shull 1989, 48), and he furthered women's rights and environmental causes during his tenure, though the pressing economic and energy problems pushed those social problems down in priority.

When he spoke of civil rights, he did so liberally (with an overall score of 100), but twice (1977, 1980) he failed to take any positions on civil rights. His domestic policy record shows the same drift to the left found in his economic policy pronouncements. His first year shows moderate domestic policy proposals with a 48 score. This is followed by a strong rightward drift in his second year (27) and may be a major source of the building tension between Carter and his party. Here the data seem to capture Carter mixing liberal programs with conservative financing and reform. By 1979, his domestic proposals have become decidedly more liberal at 60, and by the reelection year they reach the 100 percent mark. Again, nomination and election pressures may have pushed him in that direction.

In foreign policy, Carter held some strongly liberal views, but he also rejected the post-Vietnam, antidefense attitudes of many of his co-partisans. Carter's view of the world was more multipolar than conservatives of his era, who viewed all foreign policy in terms of the Cold War rivalry. Thus, he aimed to deemphasize the rivalry with the Soviet Union while increasing U. S. attention to the Third World (Hargrove 1988, 113). He championed black nationalism, reimposed sanctions against the white-supremist government in Rhodesia (Kaufman 1993, 90), pushed on the Panama Canal Treaty, and worked for a Middle East settlement, where he won his greatest foreign policy victory with the Camp David Treaty between the Israelis and Egyptians.

His overall worldview has been portrayed as "Wilsonian" because of its idealism and support for human rights (Hargrove 1988, 111), a stance that "realpolitik" advocates often criticized as naive. Yet Carter also demonstrated a harder-nosed, seemingly conservative bent, as he began the defense buildup that Reagan would later accelerate and took strong, if unpopular actions, in response to the Soviet invasion of Afghanistan. His Achilles' heel in foreign affairs was the Iranian hostage crisis; his handling of it was roundly criticized from all quarters, but the incident conveys little information about his ideological leanings.

One sees Carter's liberalism on foreign affairs in an overall score of 89, a close third to Eisenhower and Kennedy's 94. Unlike economic and domestic policy, the shifting that Carter evidences on international policy matters is to the right, not the left. He begins with strong liberal showings of 100, 100, 94 in his first three years. By 1980, with the Iranian hostage crisis, confrontation with the Soviets over Afghanistan and Cuba, and the defense buildup, his score settles at 60.

Reagan

Ronald Reagan is the most consistent president in terms of ideological leanings. His economic and foreign policies both register 5s across his eight years, and while less extreme, his civil rights rhetoric is still conservative at 34. And his domestic policy rhetoric mostly hovers in the most conservative quartile of 0 to 25. There is also little drift or change of direction across his long tenure. His is a consistent conservatism.

Economic and defense policy were the cornerstones of his administration. His economic policy was a radical departure from recent practice and was considerably more conservative than any Republican administration's since Hoover (McNiven 1988). That policy contained four main themes: tax cuts, federal budget cuts, anti-inflation actions, and deregulation. Alone and together, the aim was to reduce federal involvement in the economy (Niskanen 1988; Tobin 1988; Weatherford and McDonnell 1990). The tax and budget cuts also had important redistributive ends—toward the benefit of the upper, rather than, the lower classes (Hibbs 1987, chap. 9; McClure 1990) and toward military spending and away from domestic spending. The combined effect of reduced taxes and increases in military spending (and the inability to control other budget increases) led to huge deficits. Reagan's solution for the deficit problem was a balanced budget amendment, that notion harkening back to budget theory in the pre–New Deal, pre–Keynesian era (Peterson and Rom; 1988). Quantitatively, he demonstrates little drift, each year scoring tightly in the 0 to 15 range.

Reagan also took a strong conservative tack on social and civil rights issues. Many social programs saw massive budget cuts (Champagne and Harpham 1984; Gottschalk 1988; Weaver 1988). On civil rights, he spoke out against busing and affirmative action in sometimes strident language (Shull 1989, 1993). He opposed pro-choice abortion policies, and his judicial nominations reflected that policy stance.

Civil rights often forces presidents to take rhetorically liberal positions. This happens to Reagan in his second and third years in office with scores of 85 and 100, but these figures are based on very few statements. More typical is his second term, where for each year in which he refers to civil rights positions, they are perfectly conservative at 0 (he makes no such mentions at all in 1987). Again, small ns constrain this analysis.

His conservatism is more clearly shown by looking at his domestic policy rhetoric, where we have large ns of sentences every year. Generally conservative, most of his State of the Union Addresses fall in the 0-to-25 range. Only once does he move further left, in 1984 at 40. Perhaps reelection pressures induced his leftward drift that year.

His foreign and defense policies were also decidedly conservative. He viewed foreign policy in bipolar, Cold War rivalry terms (Ignatius 1988; Destler 1988). He jettisoned the efforts of three previous administrations at arms limitations talks, replaced the talks with increased defense spending and a high-technology weapons development program nicknamed "Star Wars" (Stevens 1988). Later new talks were opened with the Soviets, which ironically resulted in massive arms cutbacks by the end of the Reagan term. Reagan saw the uprisings and unrest in Latin America as a part of East-West competition; thus he supported the Contra movement in Nicaragua against the leftist-styled Sandinista regime (Pastor 1990). In all, Reagan shows a remarkable coherence in worldview across policies, time, and space.

The quantitative data underscore this portrait. Overall, that score is a 5; it never surpasses 17, and only twice does it surpass 10 (1981 at 15, 1984 at 17). Even the prospect of a successful arms limitation treaty with the Soviets does not moderate his rhetoric. From 1985 to 1988, his foreign policy scores are 0, 0, 4, and 0.

Bush

Bush is quite a complex figure. His early political career associated him with the moderate elements of the Republican Party. As a representative from Texas, he supported passage of civil rights legislation in the 1960s, and in the 1970s supported the pro-choice abortion alternative. His ascendancy to the presidency on Reagan's coattails and sponsorship left an enduring, conservative mark on him. By 1988 a staunch conservative, he did not view government service as negatively as Reagan, though he continued Reagan's conservative policies almost unerringly.

His conservative inclinations are apparent in his economic policies. He ran for office in 1988 on an antitax pledge, echoing themes from Reagan's successful presidency. He caved in, breaking that pledge in 1990 because of a budget fight with the Democratically held Congress. The recession of 1991–92 also revealed his traditional conservative economic stripes. He resisted and rebuffed attempts to stimulate the economy, citing inflation and the deficit as more important problems. He appeared Hooverian in his belief that government would further harm the economy and that the economy could right itself if left alone. In the regulatory front he also revealed his conservative inclinations with his veto of the Cable Reregulation Bill.

In domestic policy, he pursued the Reagan agenda in bold outline, though his rhetoric was less strident and his proposals more moderate. Funding for some programs was increased (environment), plans to eliminate others dropped (education), and moderates were appointed to office where Reagan often appointed conservatives (Barilleaux 1992, 19). These actions raised doubts among conservatives about Bush's fealty to their side (Malecha and Reagan 1992, 59; Moen and Palmer 1992, 133).

Civil rights illustrate Bush's domestic policy stance well. His rhetoric was moderate, often sounding liberal. His actions tell a different story (Shull 1993). He battled with Congress over the extension of the Voting Rights Act and nominated a conservative black, Clarence Thomas, to the Supreme Court to replace Thurgood Marshall, the liberal anchor on the Court. On environmental policy, he sounded liberal at times, but in international meetings the United States often resisted environmental policies that liberals deemed necessary. According to two scholars, Bush's domestic policies "have built much more on the Reagan policy initiatives than they have differed from them" (Thompson and Scavo 1992, 150).

Bush's true interest was in foreign affairs, but the leveling of the Berlin Wall, the cessation of the Cold War, and the emergence of democracies from the old Soviet bloc in Europe left Bush with the task of charting a "new world order" (Berman and Jentleson 1991). Here Bush's record was again uneven but leaned in a conservative direction. He failed to rap the Chinese too hard after the Tiananmen massacre, though liberals loudly called for strong action (Duffy and Goodgame 1992, 183). He committed troops to liberate Kuwait from the Iraqis, again against liberal opposition. And he opposed trade barriers that liberals from the industrial heartland wanted; instead, he worked to secure free trade agreements with Canada and Mexico.

The quantitative data cannot do much justice to Bush. I have only one year of such data for him. Still, they are useful and reiterate some of the themes just addressed. In economics and foreign policy, Bush scores 0s; more than a strong hint of his desire to continue the Reagan programs there. But his civil rights rhetoric is softer, with an 83, and his overall domestic policy score is a 62. Thus, Bush's kinder-and-gentler theme is restricted to these domestic concerns, and some would say to his rhetoric, not his policies (Shull 1993).

Summary

As my discussion throughout has indicated, there is generally a close correspondence between the descriptive and quantitative data. Table 4.2 presents a summary of that discussion. In most instances both render the same assessment of the president in question. They both also tend to agree at the policy level. And very often the quantitative data pick up trends and changes in presidential positions on the issues. This exercise also builds some confidence in these quantitative data.

Does Public Opinion Move the President?

The previous pages outlined a method for measuring presidential ideology from public statements. These statements can be taken as indicators of presidential policy choices in the policy formulation process, though at a highly aggregated level. These statements are not yet policy commitments, nor do they indicate that actions necessarily have or will be taken. But they are indicative of what direction the president might move if he sought to convert these statements into public policies.

TABLE 4.2 Summary of Presidential Ideological Leanings as Based on Descriptive Accounts

President	Overall	Economic Policy	Foreign Policy	Civil Rights Policy
Eisenhower	M	C	L	L-M
Kennedy	L	M-L	L	L
Johnson	L	M-L	L-M	L
Nixon	M-C	V	M	M
Ford	C-M	C	M	M
Carter	M	C	L-M	L
Reagan	C	C	C	C
Bush	C	C	C	C-M

Note: C = Conservative; M = Moderate; L = Liberal; V = Variable.

Aggregating these statements, giving each president an ideology score for each Address, has an important analytic use. The ideology score can be thought of as representing the overall thrust of the administration along the liberal-conservative dimension. Thus, we can relate the president's liberalism to the liberalism of the mass public and in this way test for the responsiveness of the president to public opinion during the process of policy formulation. As there is little policy specificity included in these statements, the proposed test is not whether specific policy proposals or details are responsive to a general public mood but whether the president's policy mood, as captured by the ideology indicator, is responsive to the public's mood. In other words, does the president get more liberal (or conservative) as the public gets more liberal (or conservative)?

To measure public opinion liberalism, I use a series that James Stimson developed (1991). Stimson's series is computed from aggregating public opinion responses across nearly eighty different policies and about nine hundred measurements. The series spans the 1958–90 period and has been used in research, both as something to be explained (Durr 1993) and as an independent variable (for instance, as an influence over judicial decisions [Mishler and Sheehan 1993] and over election outcomes [Stimson 1991]).

Figure 4.1 plots both the presidential and public opinion series. Each series was shifted so that both would have a common midpoint. I did this to make visual comparison easier for the reader. Thus, the natural midpoint for each series was identified and subtracted from every value. Specifically, as 50 marks the midpoint for the presidential series, I subtracted 50 from each presidential ideology score. Positive values indicate presidential liberalism, negative scores conservatism, and the size of the resulting figure the degree of liberalism (conservatism). The Stimson series uses 100 as the midpoint. Thus, I subtracted 100 from that series. Again, positive and negative values have the same interpretation as for the presidential series. However, as the Stimson metric is different from the percentage metric used in the presidential series, the two are not ideally comparable. As the plot shows, the presidential series fluctuates around a broader range, while the public opinion series is more constrained. And while it is fair to say that President X is Y percent liberal (but see the caution in interpreting this series that I offered earlier), one cannot offer a similar statement for the opinion series. What one can do, however, is compare the general shape and direction of the two series. Do they tend to move in the same ideological direction in tandem or not?

The answer seems to be sometimes yes, sometimes no. In the early part of the series, with some exceptions, it appears that the public and the president were both getting more liberal (until about 1964). Afterward, liberalism moderates. Beginning in 1970, a notable divergence between the president and the public appears, as presidents in the 1970s seem to get more conservative before the public does. Then when Carter is elected, the public continues along a conservative path, while the presidential series heads in a liberal direction. Matters reverse in the 1980s, as the presidential series moves strongly toward the conservative pole, but the public begins heading in a liberal direction by the early 1980s.

Eyeballing is an especially crude method of analysis, but it does offer us the opportunity to inspect the data closely. Statistical techniques are more precise in determining the relationship between the two series. Very simply, I regress the presidential series on the public opinion series, lagged one year, to test for the responsiveness of presidential rhetoric to public opinion. The lag is employed for two reasons. First, we cannot determine the causality between the two series when both are measured simultaneously. The lag specifies temporal order, which allows us to make certain statements about causal direction. Second, the Address comes early in the year, while the opinion data come from aggregations of polls taken throughout the year. Thus, much of the opinion data of a calendar year come after the president's speech. Finding a relationship between the two unlagged series would not indicate presidential responsiveness to public opinion but probably the reverse. Finally, autocorrelation of the residuals was detected. To correct for this problem, I use a first order Generalized Least Squares (GLS) procedure. Equation 4.1 presents the results (standard errors in parentheses):

$$\text{Presidential Ideology} = 64.48 \text{ (Constant)} - .20 \text{ (Public Opinion}_{t-1}) \quad (4.1)$$
$$(22.66) \qquad\qquad\qquad (.22)$$

$R^2 = .24$ Adjusted $R^2 = .22$ Rho = .60

The results detect no association between public opinion lagged one year and presidential ideology. The regression coefficient for the public opinion variable falls very short of statistical significance ($t = -.90$); moreover, the sign is in the wrong direction.[9] This simple test may, however, be unable to pick up any relationship between presidential ideology and public opinion. In chapter 5 I deal with alternative specifications and hypotheses about the relationship between opinion liberalism in the mass public and presidential ideology.

A Note on Presidential Leadership of Public Opinion

The core task of this book is to test for the varying degree of presidential responsiveness to the public across the policy process. Less critical, but still of interest, is determining the impact of presidential leadership of public opinion at different points in the policy-making process. Nowhere does the theory being proposed here suggest that presidential leadership will vary. Instead, it suggests that presidents may be potent leaders of public opinion throughout the policy-making process. In contrast, presidential responsiveness to public opinion varies across the policy-making process as the mix of presidential incentives changes. Thus, in the process of problem identification, I demonstrated presidential responsiveness to public opinion on a symbolic level but found that presidents can also lead public opinion in that process. In contrast, when presidential rhetoric turned substantive, presidents display less of a tendency to respond to public opinion.

Since the publication of Stimson's work on public opinion, one study has tried to model influences over public opinion (Durr 1993). Durr's study emphasized how public expectations about the economy affect the public mood. When the public is more confident about the economy, it usually is more liberally bent. Moreover, the whole question of what moves and influences public opinion has a much longer heritage (cf. Page and Shapiro 1992; Page, Shapiro, Dempsey 1987). In this section, I will show that while presidents were not responsive to public opinion, presidential rhetoric may help direct the course of public opinion. The analysis here is not meant to be definitive but merely suggest that presidential rhetoric should be incorporated into an understanding of why the public thinks the way that it does about public policies. That the president commands such a looming presence over the mass public (Miroff 1982) argues for such incorporation.

I test for the impact of presidential ideology on public opinion using the two aggregated series, Stimson's public opinion series and the presidential ideology series. I regress public opinion on presidential ideology without using lags, contrary to the procedure employed earlier in this chapter. As I stated earlier, the State of the Union Address comes early in the year, and most of the polls used to create the opinion series followed the Address. Thus, one can use both observations of the same year to initially test for the causal impact of the president on the public. The using of a lagged approach, however, distances the public opinion reading for a significant period of time after the Address, allowing other events, including another presidential State of the Union Address, to intervene between the president's Address and the opinion reading. This may weaken and/or obscure any relationship between the two. Equation 4.2 (with a GLS solution to correct for first order autocorrelation) presents the results (standard errors are in parentheses):

$$\text{Public Opinion} = -2.49 \text{ Constant} + 8.51 \text{ Presidential Ideology} \qquad (4.2)$$
$$\qquad\qquad\quad (5.36) \qquad\qquad\quad (4.57)$$

$$R^2 = .60 \qquad \text{Adjusted } R^2 = .59 \qquad \text{Rho} = .80$$

As hypothesized, presidential ideology directly and significantly affects public opinion liberalism.[10] Each 8.5 percent shift in presidential liberalism produces a corresponding 1 percent public opinion shift in the same direction. The relationship is statistically significant at the .05 level ($t = 1.86$), but it is not overwhelming in magnitude. Still, it suggests that the public may be responding directly to major presidential speeches. Presidential leadership of public opinion through the State of the Union Address may have an impact beyond agenda setting. This result suggests that presidents can marginally, but noticeably, move public opinion toward their side. I must caution, however, that the effect is modest and that the inclusion of other variables may depress or even wipe out this effect. A fully specified model is required, but that is not the task of this study.

Still, one may peer into this relationship more closely by asking if the public is more responsive to some types of rhetoric than to others. Specifically, do some policy areas capture public attention more strongly than others? Using three policy areas (economic, foreign, and domestic), I expect presidential leadership effects to be greater on economic policy than the other two policy areas. First, public awareness and concern with foreign policy is usually less than it is for policy areas that more directly touch the daily lives of average citizens. Second, the domestic policy areas may be more appealing to interest groups than the mass of voters. Two factors should enhance the president's ability to move public opinion with his economic rhetoric. The first is the importance of economics to the voter. As seen earlier, economic policy often pushes other policies off the agenda. Second, the public places great responsibility for the health of the economy on the president. Lastly, the public opinion measure is based exclusively on domestic, not foreign, policies, while the aggregate presidential measure mixes foreign, economic, and domestic concerns. Inclusion of the foreign policy component may statistically dampen the impact of the president on public opinion, especially if there is no connection in public opinion between economic (and domestic) policy liberalism and foreign policy liberalism.

I test these ideas by regressing public opinion (not lagged) on the three presidential rhetoric series. Equation 4.3 indicates that no policy area directly affects public opinion. I also regressed the public opinion series on each rhetorical series one at a time in three separate equations. Again, no effect was discerned for any policy area.

$$\text{Public Opinion} = \text{Constant} + \text{Economic} + \text{Foreign} + \text{Domestic} + e \quad (4.3)$$

$$\begin{array}{cccc} 8.04 & -2.85 & +5.19 & +.12 \\ (6.62) & (3.74) & (4.13) & (4.39) \end{array}$$

$$R^2 = .60 \qquad \text{Adjusted } R^2 = .57 \qquad \text{Rho} = .84 \qquad \text{Type} = \text{AR1}$$

These results starkly contrast with the finding that the overall ideology series affects public opinion. It appears that the public creates an overall image of the president from the State of the Union Address and reacts to that overall image rather than responding differentially to only some part of the president's message. It is also possible that no relationship was detected because the public opinion measure is aggregated across numerous policy areas. Using more discrete policy areas that match those I constructed for the president might reveal a more policy-specific response, that is, presidents may be able to change public opinion on specific policies when they talk about those policy areas. These data are not up to that task, and that chore lies outside the central interest of this study.

Conclusions

This chapter has focused on the relationship between presidential ideology and the public mood in the policy formulation process. The bulk of the chapter described a measure of presidential ideology that utilized the State of the Union Address as the database. The major objective of this chapter was to provide an initial test of the impact of public opinion on presidential ideology. Initial analysis did not find presidents being responsive to public opinion; that analysis was quite simple and bivariate. A fuller model specification is required to say with more certainty that presidents do not respond to the public in the process of formulating policies. Moreover, it may be the case that responsiveness is conditional. This, and other hypotheses, are presented and tested in the next chapter.

Appendix: The Validity and Reliability of the Rhetorical Liberal Measure Coding Procedures

The sentence is the coding unit.[11] The coding procedure requires that the sentence explicitly indicate a presidential preference for the liberal or conservative position according the ADA standard. Rarely do presidents use the words *liberal* or *conservative*. But in their Addresses they do take general positions on policy questions or otherwise indicate what their policy direction would look like on particular and general policy questions. It is from these types of statements that I code liberal versus conservative tendencies.

In the economic policy area, mentions of increasing the federal role, expanding federal programs, or employing Keynesian-styled macroeconomic policies are coded liberal. Explicit mentions of contracting federal economic regulation, scaling back programs, ceding programs and services to the states, mandating a balanced budget, or supporting policies that would let markets rather than government solve problems are taken as conservative. Attacks on federal bureaucrats are also coded as conservative.

The following are examples of sentences that could be coded either liberal or conservative. The president who made the comment, the year it was offered, and the coding (liberal or conservative) are also noted. As one can see from these selections, presidents can be very specific and directional in their State of the Union Address rhetoric without being highly detailed.

> *The first order of business is the elimination of the annual deficit.* (Eisenhower, 1953, conservative)

> *I will propose to Congress within the next 14 days measures to improve unemployment compensation through temporary increases in the duration on a self-supporting basis.* (Kennedy, 1961, liberal)

> *Last January, and again last September, I recommended fiscal and moderate tax measures to try to restrain the unbalanced pace of economic expansion.* (Johnson, 1967, liberal)

> *We must balance our Federal budget so that American families will have a better chance to balance their family budgets.* (Nixon, 1970, conservative)

> *We unbalanced our economic system by the huge and unprecedented growth of Federal expenditures and borrowing.* (Ford, 1976, conservative)

> *The fact is, our deficits come from the uncontrolled growth of the budget for domestic spending.* (Reagan, 1983, conservative)

In the foreign-defense policy area liberal sentences are those that call for greater participation and support of international agencies, foreign aid (especially nonmilitary), accommodation and détente with the Soviets and other Communist nations, and nuclear parity. Conservatives take the opposite position on these issues.

On foreign and defense policy, however, the division between liberals and conservative has changed over time. Through the early 1950s, liberals were more supportive of a large military and confrontation with the Communist nations than afterward, whereas conservatives were more suspicious of a large military establishment in the 1950s than later. From the mid-1950s until the Vietnam War commenced, liberals and conservatives both held a promilitary posture, with little disagreement between them over this issue. This was a consensual period concerning matters of military might. But they still differed over other foreign policy issues, such as foreign aid. As a result of the Vietnam War, liberal support for military solutions for dealing with Communism waned, while conservative support for a large military establishment showed no signs of abating.

The following sentences are examples of foreign and defense policy statements that could be coded as either liberal or conservative.

We must continue to support and strengthen the United Nations. (Eisenhower, 1955, liberal)

It makes little sense for us to assail, in speeches and resolutions, the horror of communism, to spend $50 billion a year to prevent its military advance—and then to begrudge spending, largely on American products, less than one-tenth of that amount to help other nations strengthen their independence and cure the social chaos in which communism has always thrived. (Kennedy, 1963, liberal)

We achieved, in 1967, a consular treaty with the Soviets, the first commercial air agreement between the two countries, and a treaty banning weapons in outer space. (Johnson, 1967, liberal)

In the coming year, however, increased expenditures will be needed. (Nixon, 1974, conservative, on defense increases)

The Defense budget I will submit to the Congress for fiscal 1977 will show an essential increase over last year. (Ford, 1976, conservative)

I believe that my duty as President requires that I recommend increases in defense spending over the coming years. (Reagan, 1981, conservative)

Other policy areas also have divided liberals from conservatives. In the broad area of civil rights and liberties, liberals have supported school integration and busing; abortion rights; and, in the 1950s, statehood for Alaska and Hawaii—all positions that conservatives opposed.[12] Although both liberals and conservatives converge on many crime-related issues, conservatives tend to emphasize victims' rights more, while liberals argue that crime prevention is most successful if the causes of crime, poverty for instance, are ameliorated.

The following selections provide examples of codable domestic policy sentences.

There will be presented to the Congress a recommended program of Federal assistance for school construction. (Eisenhower, 1956, liberal)

Second, I renew my request that the principle of self-government be extended and the right of suffrage granted to the citizens of the District of Columbia. (Eisenhower, 1955, liberal)

The right to vote, for example, should no longer be denied through such arbitrary devices on a local level, sometimes abused, as literacy tests and poll taxes. (Kennedy, 1962, liberal)

We must enact Youth Employment legislation to put jobless, aimless, hopeless youngsters to work on useful projects. (Johnson, 1964, liberal)

But let us also establish an effective work incentive and an effective work requirement. (Nixon, 1971, conservative, on welfare reform)

We cannot realistically afford Federally dictated national health insurance providing full coverage for all 215 million Americans. (Ford, 1976, conservative)

I will continue to work with all my strength for equal opportunity for all Americans—and for affirmative action for those who carry the extra burden of past denial of equal opportunity. (Carter, 1979, liberal)

The 100th Congress of the United States should be remembered as the one that ended the expulsion of God from America's classroom. (Reagan, 1987, conservative, on prayer in schools)

Thus, the substantive understanding of liberal versus conservative used here is quite conventional (see Stimson 1991; for a similar substantive definition and a similar procedure and understanding of liberal and conservative in presidential speeches, see Goggin 1984). Liberal and conservative are not meant to relate to the philosophic underpinnings of the two "ideological" viewpoints. Nor are they meant to address how internally coherent the two are. Rather, present needs require a definition that relates to common understandings, to the ways that liberal and conservative help to structure political debate.

Each sentence is also weighted equally. This coding decision requires some justification. Here I assume that each liberal or conservative policy indication has a probability of occurring in direct proportion to the president's true ideological tendency or to that image he wants to present. Thus, aggregating across sentences gives us a fair representation of the president's ideological leanings or the image he wants to project. Still, presidents might assign different weights to different sentences. How appropriate this choice is, however, is a matter of validity. In the sections that follow, I provide an extended discussion of the validity of this indicator.

Reliability

Content analytic data recovery can vary from the literal to the intentional. Most content analyses of presidential rhetoric use the first approach (see the studies cited in note 6), in part because matters of coding interpretation are less severe (Weber 1985; Krippendorf 1980). Simple and literal word counts, however, may miss valuable information. Word counting cannot ascertain the ideological direction of presidential statements as our needs here require, nor can concordances between words. We need to unearth the meaning of the sentence not merely the words used.[13]

There is a tradeoff between literal and intentional content analytic designs. What the intentional design gains in information, it may lose in increased measurement error. I tried to anticipate this problem by making the coding rules as explicit as possible and by refusing to read meaning into a sentence. Explicit references to positions that one can associate with liberals or conservatives are required in order to code a sentence directionally. Coding rules were developed to determine whether a sentence was liberal, conservative, or neither based on the policy-related discussion in the previous section. When coders were unsure, they were instructed to code the sentence as ambiguous.

The coding scheme seemed quite able to discriminate among liberal, conservative, and neutral statements, and intercoder reliability was quite high. Two codings of a random selection of four presidential State of the Union Addresses elicited agreement on 95.3 percent of sentences. Disagreements at the sentence level occurred, not because a liberal sentence was thought to be conservative, but rather because a liberal (or conservative) sentence was thought to be neutral. The primary coder also recoded a sample of Addresses some time after the major data collection period to check for reliability through time, that is, the ability of the same coder to employ the coding scheme at different points in time (Prothro 1956, 729). Agreement at the sentence level topped 98 percent, signifying strong reliability. Thus, while some coding error may exist, the variable seems quite reliable.

Validity

Validity raises the question, Are we coding what we say we are? I employ several different tests to determine the validity of these data. These include tests of face and construct validity.

Face Validity

Face validity is generally a weak test. It asks one to compare the data collected with conventional understandings of what one expects the data to look like. Thus, a face validity test here would ask, Are the presidents as conservative or liberal as one would expect based upon common understandings of the presidents and liberal-conservative comparisons? Moreover, Is the ordering of presidents from liberal to conservative sensible? The weaknesses of face validity are many. It relies upon common understandings, and these understandings may be wrong. If the data do not correspond to these common understandings, do we go with the data or the common understandings? Moreover, what happens when there is no common understanding, but several competing understandings?

Nevertheless, face validity has its uses. It helps us assess the value of common understandings, and here it forces the data that I have collected to confront these common understandings. It thus sensitizes us to the limits of these data. The description of the presidents' ideological leanings as gleaned from the historical and biographical accounts presented in this chapter provides one type of face validity test. In general, the ideology data correspond well to those common understandings and in several cases helped to resolve some disputes in the literature about the president's true position. Still, face validity is a weak test; other tests of validity are provided next.

Construct Validity

Construct validity is a stronger path to assessing validity than face validity. Whereas face validity only assesses whether the indicator appears valid by conventional and common understandings of the concept, construct validity tests how closely the indicator relates to other indicators that theory suggests it should be related to.

Shull (1983) has independently attempted to identify presidential positions on a cross section of policy areas using sentences as the unit of analysis. There are some important differences between Shull's approach and mine. First, whereas I relied exclusively on State of the Union Addresses, Shull used all public presidential papers. Insofar as these two samples differ, we may witness divergence between our assessments.

Second, Shull recorded presidential statements on only six policy areas (price supports, public works, crime, antitrust, civil rights, poverty), which contrasts with my use of the universe of policy areas mentioned in State of the Union Addresses. Although Shull's substantive policy set produces a reasonable cross section of domestic policies, foreign policy mentions arise frequently in the State of the Union Address, creating another source of sampling divergence between our studies. Moreover, his six policy areas may not be mentioned across all presidential public statements with the same frequency that they are given within the State of the Union Address. Lastly, our definitions of liberalism and conservatism differ. Shull based his on support for government action in each policy area, while I relied upon an ADA standard.

Still, noting these differences, remarkable similarity in the liberalism of Presidents Eisenhower through Carter (1978–79) emerges. Shull's average level of presidential liberalism (what he calls support) across the six policy areas are as follows: Eisenhower, 61.4; Kennedy, 96.3; Johnson, 91.3; Nixon, 60.6; Ford, 36.5; Carter, 64.4 (these figures are recalculated from several tables presented in Shull on pp. 46–51). The Pearson's r between the Shull scores and mine is .88, indicating strong construct validity.

Our rank orderings of these presidents is identical except for the switching of Eisenhower and Carter. Still, both of our measures found these presidents to be relatively close in ideological leanings. Only Nixon may be anomalous here—Shull finds him to be somewhat liberal leaning, whereas I find him slightly conservative, but in neither instance is Nixon very far from the center, and in both instances he is the second most conservative president after Ford. Even though our samples diverged quite sharply, and appreciating the possible impact of the different methods, one is heartened to see such relative correspondence between the two measures.

Another construct validity test compares the rhetorical data with behavioral data. One type of presidential behavior relates to appointments. Everything else being equal, liberal presidents should be more likely to nominate liberals to their cabinets and the courts than moderates or conservatives (Gates and Cohen 1988, 1989).[14] David McKay (1989, 192) presents data that ideologically profiles the court appointees of Presidents Johnson, Nixon, Carter,

TABLE 4.3.   The Ideological Leanings of Federal Judges (in percentages)

Leaning	Appointing President			
	Johnson	Nixon	Carter	Reagan
Liberal	65.4	16.1	54.5	00.00
Moderate	23.1	35.5	30.9	9.6
Conservative	11.5	48.4	14.6	90.4
n	(*n* = 26)	(*n* = 31)	(*n* = 55)	(*n* = 55)

Source: McKay 1989, 192.

and Reagan. Table 4.3 reproduces that data. We expect Johnson's nominees to be the most liberal, followed by Carter's. Nixon's nominees should be slightly conservative, and Reagan's should be uniformly conservative, and this is what McKay's data indicate.

The major problem with both the Shull and McKay data is that they use only a subset of the presidents used here. To rectify that sampling problem, I created another ideological indicator that spans across all eight presidents, is disaggregated by year, and uses the ADA definition of liberalism and conservatism. This indicator uses the president's position on roll calls before Congress that the ADA identified as tests of liberalism and conservatism. The roll call data will become the primary topic of chapter 6. For now they serve the useful purpose of construct validation. The Pearson's r between the two indicators of liberalism is .85, which is significant at the .001 level. This provides us with the strongest support for the validity of the rhetorical measure of presidential ideology. (The weakness of this test, however, is that I cannot disaggregate the roll call measure by policy area; there are too few roll calls, and in some years there are no roll calls for certain policy areas.)

CHAPTER 5

Presidential Ideology and Public Opinion:
A More Detailed Look

In the previous chapter I presented data on presidential ideology and the public mood. My analysis found that while the president's rhetoric did not respond to the public's mood, the public mood seemed responsive to changes in presidential rhetoric. As presidents got more or less liberal, so did the public. This echoed results of earlier chapters on presidential influence over the public's Most Important Problem. All told, not only does the president seem able to affect what problems people think are important, but he also seems to be able to affect what policy solutions they prefer in a general sense. The same cannot be said about public opinion's influence over the president. Although the president responds to public opinion by symbolically reaffirming its concerns, he seems to respond more weakly when offering priorities or issue stances, types of activities that are more substantive.

In this chapter I return to the finding reported in chapter 4, that changes in the public mood do not affect presidential ideology as expressed in their State of the Union Addresses. There are several possible reasons for this nonresult. First, presidential responsiveness to public opinion might be conditional and contextual. It may occur only at certain times and under certain conditions. Second, the exclusion of important variables may mask or suppress the effect of the public on presidential positions. Lastly, the presidential series may be too aggregated. In particular, it mixes all policy types, while the public opinion series is limited to domestic policy issues. Disaggregating the presidential series into different policy areas, as I did in chapters 2 and 3, may reveal presidential responsiveness in policy areas that more closely relate to the public opinion series.

Alternatively, we may find that once we control for other variables, the president is more responsive to the public on the overall measure of ideology than on the policy-specific measures. The ability to manipulate the image of the indicator of overall ideology, its symbolism, is inherently greater than when we disaggregate to specific policy areas. Our ability to disaggregate the ideology indicator into its constituent parts allows a test of this rival hypothesis.

In this chapter, I deal with each of these ideas. First, I test the context argument, that presidents will be responsive to the mass public only under certain conditions. Six conditions are tested—war, unemployment, inflation, popularity, popular vote totals, and year in the presidential cycle. Not one detects a significant presidential response to public opinion. Next, I control for other variables that might be masking the impact of public opinion on presidential ideology. This analysis focuses on the impact of presidential party and the person in office, two major ways of accounting for differences in presidential policy positions. With controls for these important variables in place, I am still unable to detect any presidential responsiveness to public opinion. Last, I disaggregate the presidential rhetoric series into discrete issue areas to test the final charge, that the rhetoric series contains many issue areas not represented in the public opinion measure, especially its inclusion of foreign policy. This analysis combines the disaggregation with the addition of variables that may be masking or suppressing responsiveness. The disaggregation again fails to expose a presidential response to public opinion. However, the attempt to build a fuller model of overall presidential ideology demonstrates strong presidential responsiveness to public opinion. That fuller model adds to the party and presidential effects, the effects of the international and economic context.

These results are placed in the context of the argument being made here, that responsiveness is more evident when presidential activities have a strong symbolic component. Even in the policy formulation stage, where substantive concerns are important, symbolism in presidential behavior is evident.

Presidential Responsiveness and Context

Context may have major implications for presidential responsiveness to public opinion in policy formulation. Some contexts or situations may compel presidents to follow public opinion; others may allow greater freedom of action. In this section I test for the contextual effects of war and the economy. The guiding hypothesis is that the better the times, the more responsive presidents will be to public opinion. I also look at the political context of election timing and presidential popularity. The argument here is that some presidents will need the public more than others. In particular, presidents with weaker political bases may adhere more closely to public opinion than those with wider political bases. Lastly, the rhythm of the presidential election cycle may affect responsiveness. As election day nears, presidents may become more attuned to public opinion.

The International and Economic Context

War and the economy represent the two most important objective conditions for the president to deal with. When the nation is at war and/or the economy is faltering, the public expects the president to produce policies to win (and/or shorten) the war and to improve the economy. Policy success is the public's overriding concern when these large threats appear. Consequently, the public may allow the president great leeway in developing policies to meet these challenges.[1] When times are not so perilous, when the nation is at peace and the economy is strong, the public may expect the president to follow its wishes. During tranquil times, the balance between responsiveness and policy performance may tip toward responsiveness.

I test these contextual effects by creating interaction terms between the war and economic variables on the one hand and, on the other, public opinion liberalism. The guiding hypothesis is that responsiveness is more likely when times are good than bad. For the war opinion interaction, I set the public opinion values to 0 when there is a war; otherwise the variable takes on the value of the public opinion measure. For the unemployment and inflation interactions, I set the public opinion variable to 0 when inflation and unemployment surpass the mean for the economic variables. Otherwise, the interaction variables again take on the value of the public opinion variable. In essence, when times are bad, I censored public opinion. When times are good, I allow public opinion to filter through to presidential rhetoric. Like the procedure when using the full public opinion variable, the interactions are lagged one year, and GLS is used to correct for first order autocorrelation.

Table 5.1 presents the results of the three regressions (labeled 1, 2, 3 on the table). In no case do the interaction variables significantly affect presidential ideology. I also added into each equation controls for presidential party, the four presidential dummy variables (Eisenhower, Kennedy, Carter, Rea-

TABLE 5.1.   Impact of Context on Presidential Responsiveness to Public Opinion, 1956–89

Equation Number and Variable	*b*	SE	*t*	Rho	R^2
1. Not at war * Public opinion	−.14	.22	−.65	.60	.23
2. Low unemployment * Public opinion	−.23	.21	−1.10	.60	.26
3. Low inflation * Public opinion	−.20	.22	−.93	.60	.24
4. Low popularity * Public opinion	−.007	.007	−1.02	.60	.24
5. Low popular vote * Public opinion	−.004	.005	−.88	.60	.24
6. Year 4 * Public opinion	−.09	.10	−.90	.59	.24

gan), and time point dummies.[2] Again, no equation finds any interaction variable affecting presidential rhetoric.[3]

The Political Context

Political conditions may affect presidential responsiveness to public opinion. Public opinion is a key presidential resource, and much presidential activity is aimed at cultivating and mobilizing it (cf. Edwards 1983; Kernell 1993). Presidents with weaker ties to and lower levels of support from the public have a harder time rallying the public behind their efforts. Those with strong ties and high levels of support may often take that support for granted. For instance, Ronald Reagan could always count on a core level of unflagging popular support. This served as a base from which to build winning coalitions. George Bush's support, though often higher than Reagan's (it reached 89 percent in March 1991), was less stable and evaporated quickly once the economy declined (see Edwards 1991, 132).

Presidents with high and strong levels of popular support may resist public pressures and may even go against the public because they feel they can expend some of this political capital (Light 1982) in pursuit of other objectives. Even if their popular support declines after such an action, such blessed presidents may feel that they had an excess of popular support and can afford to lose some; they would still retain enough support for future needs, and they could possibly regenerate the lost support through successful policies.

Presidents without this cushion may be more cautious about alienating the public. More of their effort may go into building public support. This may mean pursuing policies that the public prefers more for popularity than policy reasons. Thus, we may expect that presidents with weak public support will be more sensitive to public demands. Less popular presidents will be more responsive to public opinion than popular presidents in order to enhance their public support and/or to keep from further alienating the public.

Presidential responsiveness to public opinion may also vary with the election cycle. A large literature has investigated the impact of election proximity on the voting behavior of senators. That literature finds that senatorial voting behavior shifts as election nears. Kuklinski (1978) finds that California state senators become more representative of their constituents the nearer they get to the next election (also see Elling 1982; Thomas 1985; Wright and Berkman 1986, 1988). The same dynamic may hold for presidents. During the fourth year of their term, an election year, presidents may display greater responsiveness to public opinion in the hope they will secure reelection for themselves or their party's candidate (assuming the incumbent is not up for reelection or is a lame duck). We saw a hint of this in chapter 4. There I noted that Jimmy Carter seemed to "liberalize" his positions on the economy and domestic policy during 1980, presumably to attract voters and thwart Ted Kennedy's challenge from the left.

To test these ideas, I created interaction terms between presidential election results, popularity levels, and election timing with the public opinion series. I measure presidential public support in two ways. The first uses the percentage of the vote that the president received in the previous election. This taps electoral support. I also use the Gallup approval total for the president during the period just prior to the State of the Union Address. To create the interaction terms, I inverted each public support measure by subtracting it from 100 percent. I then multiplied the result by public opinion liberalism. These variables are inverted to allow low levels of popularity to take on high values in the interaction and make substantive interpretation easier. The election cycle variable is created in a manner similar to that used for the war and economy variables. In all years but the fourth, I censored the public opinion liberalism variable to 0, allowing it to take on its original value only during the fourth year of an administration.

Table 5.1 presents the results of regressing presidential ideology on these political context-public opinion interaction variables (see the equations labeled 4, 5, 6). The interaction variables are lagged one year, as I have done before, and GLS is used to correct for first order autocorrelation problems. The results repeat those found for the war and economy contexts: none of the political context interactions affects presidential ideology. I also entered into the equation the party and presidential and time point dummy variables as controls, and again the political context interactions failed to reach statistical significance.[4]

Lastly, I ran an equation that included all six context interaction variables (war, inflation, unemployment, election results, popularity, fourth year of term). These results repeat; not one of the interactions attained statistical significance.[5] The international, the economic, and the political context does not seem to affect presidential responsiveness to public opinion. The basic finding of this chapter remains intact: during the policy formulation stage, presidents are not systematically responsive to public opinion.

Party, President, and Public Opinion Effects on Presidential Ideology

My analysis in chapter 4 suggested that presidential ideology is not responsive to the public mood. That analysis was quite simple and bivariate. The theory of presidential behavior proposed in this study asserts that in the policy formulation process, presidents are keen to control the substance, direction, and timing of public policy decisions. Presidents want to ensure that their proposals gain congressional approval and that, once implemented, the result-ing programs will be successful. Responsiveness to the public may steer presidents away from these goals. The goals of congressional acceptance and program success are more important to the president than responsiveness to the public because, in the end, the public will judge the president more on the performance of his policies than how responsive he might have been. In fact, a successful program can regenerate whatever public support the president lost because of his limited responsiveness to the public in the policy-making process. In contrast, if a president is responsive to the public, and that results in poorly performing policies, the president may lose the public's support with no way to regain it.

In this section, I provide a stronger test of that assertion of presidential control by showing that factors wholly within the control of presidents go a long way toward helping us understand their ideological position as evidenced in the rhetoric series. In particular, I show that the ideological positions of presidents are strongly conditioned by the party and the person in office. Moreover, once party and the person in office are taken into account, public opinion still possesses little hold on the president.

Sources of Presidential Ideology: President and Party

What may account for the policy positions that presidents take in their State of the Union Addresses? From the literature on the presidency, one can identify several possibilities. First, much writing on the presidency focuses on the person in office. Here I follow that line of argument and suggest that the personal choices of presidents may determine their policy preferences. A second line of research suggests that much policy debate in the United States reflects divisions between the parties. This may be the case especially in economic policy and, during some periods of time, foreign policy (Clausen 1973; Hibbs 1987). In this section I test whether person and/or party affects the ideological leanings of presidents.

Party and Presidential Ideology. Although the differences between the American parties pales in comparison to Western European parties, numerous studies document party differences across a host of policies in the United States (cf. Clausen 1973; Hibbs 1987). Furthermore, recent research suggests that parties play a key role in organizing important political institutions, like the U.S. Congress (Cox and McCubbins 1993; Rohde 1991).

There are several processes through which party differences may be linked to presidential ideological leanings. First, presidents may be playing the role of party leader or spokesperson. Thus, when presidents give their State of the Union Addresses, they may be speaking to or for the whole nation when responding to the public's Most Important Problem (see chap. 2). But when taking positions on issues, they may be identifying more closely with their party. It is possible for one public speaking event to include several different audiences. These varying audiences may present the president with different incentives to which he may try to respond. Whereas public responsiveness dictates presidential symbolic agenda activity, coalition building dictates policy formulation behavior, elevating the importance of the party audience over the mass public audience in this stage of the policy-making process.

Other processes may also link party to presidential ideology. Presidents stand at the top of a recruitment structure. Critical to advancement in that structure is passing through gateways that party elites and primary voters control. These gatekeepers may winnow party candidates using criteria such as the ideological positions of the candidates. Thus, the ideological leanings of presidents may reflect the partisan biases built into the recruitment process.

Third, the interaction between the president and his advisers, who usually are fellow partisans, may instruct or indoctrinate the president into party orthodoxy on many issues. This is most likely the case for issues that receive considerable presidential attention and for which the parties have institutionalized their positions, such as economic policy and, in recent years, foreign policy and some social issues. Thus, biased presidential contact and learning may be reflected in these presidential rhetorical data.

An Alternative View of Presidents and Their Parties. All of these reasons for party influence on presidential ideology, however, fly against the more common notion that the parties in the United States are weak and that their weaknesses have mounted over the past several decades. Some of the earliest research on legislative voting behavior, now nearly a century old, documented the weak ties of parties on members of Congress when compared to the British Parliament (Lowell 1902), and this was supposedly during the high point of party strength in the United States. Since Lowell's pathbreaking study, study upon study has documented the comparative weakness of the U.S. parties in structuring policy in the United States, especially at the national and presidential levels.

The localism of the parties and, at the presidential level, their generally moribund state—except during periods of candidate nomination and election—partially account for this view. The candidate-centeredness of the political careers of members of Congress, and in recent years the president, further pull members away from their parties and toward their individual self-interested pursuits (these characteristics of U.S. parties are reviewed extensively in Sorauf and Beck 1988).

In recent years, scholars and observers of the U.S. political scene have suggested that the historically weak parties have fallen upon even harder times and are now feeble shells of their former selves. The party system has dealigned, and party has reduced its ability to structure the political world.

This is most evident in the mass public, where levels of party identification have dropped and ticket splitting has become a common occurrence. One consequence of this trend is the rise of divided government at the national level.

Dealignment away from the parties is also noticeable at the presidential level. The most common explanations for the decline of party pull on the president has to do with the new style of presidential nomination. Once controlled by party elites, the new system, which firmly rooted itself in the 1970s, is now one of contending candidates for primary voters. Party elites are less consequential in the process; thus, nominated candidates have less reason to look to them. Presidential campaigns are built anew with each candidacy.

One scholar, however, sees the roots of this personal and antiparty presidency in the development of the modern presidency and its managerial and administrative functions (Milkis 1993). Rather than build the presidency on a party base, presidents from Franklin Roosevelt on have looked at the administrative apparatus of the national government as the foundation upon which to build the executive office. As a result, presidents get a national view of problems and policies, while the localism of parties and their leaders undermines the direction the president desires to move in. In this modern era, presidents have helped erode the parties, which they view as antagonists or barriers to their nationalizing ends.

Whatever the source, nomination politics or administrative rationale, presidents, by this perspective, have little need for parties and should be relatively unfettered by party constraints. To find that party influences presidential ideology, then, would constitute a major finding.

Impact of Party on Presidential Ideology.   The data at hand cannot test these alternative linkage mechanisms between party and presidential ideology. But the data can test the strength of the party connection. Quite simply, I regress presidential ideology on party, again using a GLS estimation to correct for first order autocorrelation problems. The results are displayed on the middle columns of table 5.2.

The results speak quite sharply to the impact of party on presidential ideology. The regression results suggest that Democrats are more liberal than Republicans by about forty-four percentage points. This effect is quite robust, with a t value of 4.03.[6] Moreover, the combination of the autocorrelation correction and party account for nearly one-half of the variance in presidential ideology. Contrary to the party weakness or party decline perspectives, party is a major part of the explanation of the ideological leanings of American presidents.

Still, while party goes a long way in explaining presidential ideological differences, over half of the difference is yet to be accounted for. Other

TABLE 5.2. Presidents, Parties, and Presidential Rhetorical Liberalism, 1953–89: Effects Coefficients Analysis

Variables	*b*	SE	*t*	*b*	SE	*t*	*b*	SE	*t*
Constant	47.5	2.16	22.01	33.6	9.82	3.41	34.6	3.05	11.36
Party (1 = Dem.)	—	—	—	43.8	10.85	4.03	35.2	5.83	6.04
Eisenhower	18.9	3.71	5.12	—	—	—	31.5	4.41	7.14
Kennedy	35.1	5.53	6.35	—	—	—	11.9	6.66	1.78
Johnson	20.9	4.43	4.72	—	—	—	—	—	—
Nixon	−11.5	4.14	−2.78	—	—	—	—	—	—
Ford	−21.5	6.83	−3.15	—	—	—	—	—	—
Carter	8.3	4.89	1.70	—	—	—	−14.9	5.98	−2.50
Reagan	−37.7	3.80	−9.83	—	—	—	−24.8	4.48	−5.52
R^2/Adj. R^2		.85/.81			.45/.44			.83/.81	
Rho		−.27			.66			−.23	
Lagrange multiplier		.86			1.36			.50	

explanations present themselves, among the most prominent being president-centered or person-in-office theories.

Person in Office and Presidential Ideology. The party analysis suggests a strong party impact on presidential ideology, but party does not wholly account for differences in the liberalism of presidential rhetoric. Over half of the variance was not accounted for. There are good reasons to suggest that presidents themselves, and not merely their parties, may drive the positions that presidents take.

Anecdotally, presidents have been viewed at times as being out of step with their parties, either too moderate or too extreme (see the review of the presidents in chap. 4). Party regulars criticized John F. Kennedy for his tax cut proposal to stimulate the economy. The mainstream of the party wanted the president to increase spending, which would allow them to increase favored programs and at the same time stimulate the economy. It took the success of the tax cuts for most of the party to come around to Kennedy's view.

Lyndon Johnson seemed quite at odds with major elements of his party over the Vietnam War. Jimmy Carter was criticized by some Democrats for not being liberal enough, especially on economic policies (Hargrove 1988). Carter's relative conservatism has been cited as a reason that liberal Senator Edward Kennedy challenged him for the party's nomination in 1980. In each of these Democratic cases, liberals within the party attacked presidential policies that they felt were too conservative.

Republicans have been attacked for the opposite reason, for being too liberal. For instance, Eisenhower was thought too liberal on foreign policy by many party regulars, such as Senator Robert Taft of Ohio (Ambrose 1990). Eisenhower's popularity and influence is often credited with moving the Republican Party into a more prointernationalist posture on foreign policy matters.

And some presidents seem to have little connection to their party at all. Nixon, for instance, seemed to alter his policies, especially his economic policies, for pragmatic and electoral reasons and demonstrated little fealty to the standard Republican line on economic policy (Genovese 1990). Thus, there are many examples of presidents jousting with their party's mainstream over policy. The frequency, and sometimes ferocity, of these conflicts argue that party alone cannot explain presidential ideological leanings.

The person in office, more than party, may dictate presidential ideological leanings. Person in office may have several meanings. The most common approach to studying the impact of individual presidents looks at their personalities (Barber 1972). The personality approach, however, offers limited utility for understanding the policy positions of American presidents (but see Cohen 1980 and McClosky 1958). It may be more profitable to conceptualize the rhetorical leanings of American presidents as representations of their ideologies. This conceptualization identifies a direct link between the positions that presidents take on policy issues and the ideas that animated those positions. This is not an argument that ideology determines the policy positions that presidents take but only that ideology may influence those positions. Oddly, there has been little conceptual work on presidential ideologies (but see Langston 1992; McKay 1989; Weatherford 1987; Weatherford and McDonnell 1985, 1990).

If these rhetorical positions reflect presidential ideology, one should notice several patterns. First, presidential positions should be relatively invariant within administrations across time. This stability derives from the anchoring and structuring impact of ideology (belief systems) on issues (Converse 1964). Second, with party controlled, one should still observe presidential effects on their rhetorical positions. Third, not all presidents have to be ideological. Other factors, consistent with the notion that the person in office has some discretion in choosing which policy stance to take, may be more important for some presidents. Thus, one should find Reagan among the most ideological in the sense that his positions are relatively invariant over time, while Nixon should be much less ideological in that his positions shifted in accord with political times, circumstances, and opportunistic calculations. The nonideologues may be more responsive to public opinion than the ideologues for whom ideology creates a barrier to direct responsiveness.

I first test these notions by comparing the variability of presidential ideology within administrations. Table 5.3 presents the relevant descriptive

TABLE 5.3. **Presidential Rhetorical Liberalism, 1953–89, by Party and President**

	Mean	Range	SD
All Presidents	41.7	00.0–92.4	27.6
Democrats	68.8	46.7–92.4	16.7
Republicans	36.1	00.0–80.0	25.6
	65.7	52.0–80.0	11.0
Eisenhower			
Kennedy	83.1	68.6–91.3	12.6
Johnson	70.0	46.7–92.4	18.2
Nixon	35.1	5.9–50.0	18.3
Ford	25.9	20.5–31.3	7.6
Carter	56.6	49.3–68.8	8.5
Reagan	9.6	00.0–19.7	6.6
Bush	37.3	—	—

data. From these data, it is hard to establish a definitive standard for what constitutes stability. Still, two presidents stand out as being less stable than the others, Nixon and Johnson. In contrast, Reagan shows the most stability, as expected; the standard deviation for his positions is about one-third of those for Nixon and Johnson.

These data, however, raise some important issues in interpretation. It may be reasonable to suggest that stable positions over time reflect commitment to those positions and that commitment emanates from some ideological or anchoring principle. A static political environment might have the same effect on stability, but no president has served during such stasis.

More problematic is interpreting the meaning of instability. One interpretation is that the president lacked a commitment to a course of action and opportunistically shifted with the prevailing political winds. On the other hand, shifting could indicate conversion. Although conversion indicates a long-term change of commitment, it does not have to indicate lack of ideological underpinnings or short-term commitment. It is relatively easy to characterize Nixon as lacking policy commitment, especially in economic and domestic policy. Johnson is a different matter. His instability is due more to his resistance to change, his continued support of his Vietnam War policies. Although liberals shifted position on the war as it progressed, Johnson stood firm. One could argue that Johnson was not ideological enough to shift with other liberals as they redefined their view of the war. It is difficult to argue that Johnson was not committed to his policy; the nature of that commitment may not be ideology but perhaps sunk costs, inertia, or isolation. Perhaps the clearest case of conversion is Kennedy and the tax cut. From being a relatively conventional conservative on fiscal matters, Kennedy became a decided Keynesian. Deciding this issue—whether instability is a function of conversion or lack of commitment and opportunism—is not possible here, but it does muddy the analytic waters.

The second test for the impact of person in office regresses presidential ideology on "effects variables." Effects variables are similar to dummy variables, except that one category (Bush) is coded −1, while the rest of the variable is scaled as a traditional dummy variable (e. g., for Eisenhower, when Eisenhower, code 1; when not Eisenhower, code 0; when not Eisenhower but Bush, code −1). The advantage of effects variables over dummy variables is that the coefficients may be read as deviations from the average across all presidents, whereas dummy variables are read as deviations from the omitted category (on effects variables, see Dixon and Gaarder 1992, 162–64). This makes for easier substantive interpretation when a complex of variables is used.

Table 5.2 (the left-hand columns) presents the results of the effects variable analysis. The equation is quite potent, with 85 percent of the variance explained.[7] Six of the seven presidential effects coefficients are strongly significant, while the seventh (Carter) is marginally so. All signs point in the expected direction. In order of degree of liberalism, the results suggest that Kennedy is the most liberal, followed by Johnson and Eisenhower, with Carter as the most weakly leaning liberal. On the conservative side, from weakest to most conservative, are Nixon, Ford, and Reagan. Again these results suggest the relative liberalism of Eisenhower.

The effects coefficients analysis, however, does not allow us to suggest that ideology drives presidential positions. Rather, it lets us say that person in office may have a huge impact on the positions that a president takes. Importantly, person in office and party may insulate presidents from public pressure. Controlling for these effects may expose a relationship between presidential ideology and public opinion, an issue we now address.

Party, Person, Public Opinion, and Presidential Ideology.   The primary focus of this study is the relationship between the president and the mass public. My analysis in chapter 4 indicated that the positions that presidents take in their State of the Union Addresses, as a group, are not responsive to public opinion. There is no indication that as the public gets more (or less) liberal, the president will follow suit. One charge against the analysis in chapter 4 was its simplistic, bivariate nature. The relationship between public opinion and presidential positions may be masked because of the effect of confounding variables. Here I ask, If we control for party and/or person effects, which had a large impact on presidential ideology, will we find presidents being responsive to public opinion?

As suggested, party and person effects may insulate presidents from public opinion pressures. When these effects are weakened, presidents may find themselves more responsive to public opinion. We can conceptualize party, ideology, and public opinion as resources that presidents might like to acquire, perhaps for instrumental reasons, such as bargaining leverage with Congress. When presidents have party resources at their disposal, they need not refer to public opinion. In fact, the two may collide, with the president's party preferring one policy course but public opinion another.[8]

For example, during Ronald Reagan's time in office Republicans seemed to prefer much more conservative public policies than the public. By aligning himself with his party, Reagan may have been able to keep public pressures at bay, such as during the deep recession of 1981–82. With strong party support in Congress—a function of majority control in one chamber and strong party support of the president among legislators in both chambers—Reagan could "stay the course" on his economic program. Insulation from public pressure may derive from being able to call upon another source of presidential support, another type of resource.

Ideological thinking may insulate presidents from public opinion through another dynamic, the power of ideas. But ideological presidents, especially those who rise to the top in this new, open political nomination system, may still develop a core of support, an ideologically motivated support coalition, that acts much as party does. Beck and Jennings (1979) show how the ideological coloring of candidacies may mobilize activists into the nomination process. Because of his stance, McGovern attracted many first-time activists in support of his candidacy. Reagan had a similar, if more successful, ideological coterie behind him. Again, when challenged by public opinion pressures that try to push the president away from his ideological moorings, the ability to call to the ideological faithful may enable a president to resist public pressures while also readying his ideological supporters, which he utilizes as a political resource.

The main point is that party and ideology may effectively insulate presidents from public pressures, providing the president with an alternative reference point and political resource. Presidents without strong attachments to their parties, with only weak parties to work with, and without strong ideological tendencies or supporters may be more exposed to public opinion pressures, if for no other reason than that public opinion may be the only political resource open to them.

Analysis. One cannot simply enter the party variable and all seven presidential dummy variables into an equation together. They sum into the party variable, producing a singular matrix, which cannot be estimated. Thus, I had to find some way of reducing the number of presidential variables. I employed a two-step procedure. First, I ran seven equations, each containing the party dummy and one presidential dummy. Again, a GLS procedure was used to correct for mild first order autocorrelation. Presidential dummy variables that were not found to be statistically significant in the face of the party controls were dropped from further analysis. This tended to be the case for presidents near their party means.[9]

Next, I ran a reduced-form equation, which included the party variable and the remaining presidential dummy variables. After arriving at this reduced-form equation, I reentered each presidential dummy variable alone and in sets. None of the originally excluded variables showed any impact, and thus they were dropped from the presentation. Further, at each stage, I entered time point dummies into the analysis, as Brace and Hinckley (1992) prescribe. As with previous estimations in this chapter, no time point dummy emerged as a significant predictor.

That final equation is presented in table 5.2, in the far right columns. Though the R^2 of the reduced-form equation is slightly less than the R^2 for the full-effects variable equation (see table 5.1, the left-hand columns), an F test indicates that there is no significant difference in their explanatory power. The adjusted R^2 points to the same conclusion.

The results of the reduced-form equation are, in themselves, substantively interesting. First, Democrats are more liberal than Republicans, on average about 35 points. This coefficient is highly significant, with a strong t value of 6.04. Kennedy was found to be slightly more liberal than other Democrats, by about twelve percentage points, but the t value and the significance level are weak, barely passing the .05 threshold. In contrast, Carter is found to be more conservative than other Democrats. The difference is nearly fifteen percentage points. Also as expected, Eisenhower is more liberal than other Republicans by almost thirty-two percentage points, while Reagan is more conservative than other Republicans by nearly twenty-five points.

To test for the impact of public opinion, I add the public opinion liberalism variable, lagged one year, into the equation containing the party and four significant presidential dummy variables. I also experimented by adding the excluded presidential and time point dummy variables. None of these had any impact.

The results, presented in table 5.4, indicate that public opinion has no direct impact on presidential ideology when controlling for these factors. The t value is a paltry 1.05, and the coefficient's sign is in the wrong direction. None of the other variables is appreciably affected by adding the public opinion variable into the equation, and the R^2 hardly budges either.

It may be the case that ideology creates a barrier between public opinion and presidential positions. Nonideological presidents, who lack this barrier, may be more responsive to public opinion than more ideological presidents. I test this idea by creating an interaction variable where the public opinion variable is scored 0 if the president is ideological (Eisenhower, Kennedy,

TABLE 5.4.   Presidents, Parties, Public Opinion, and Presidential Rhetorical
Liberalism, 1956–89

Variables	b	SE	t	b	SE	t
Constant	34.47	3.14	10.98	34.26	2.98	11.50
Party (1 = Dem.)	35.60	6.00	5.94	34.38	5.73	6.00
Eisenhower	30.23	5.36	5.64	29.84	5.07	5.88
Kennedy	13.74	7.11	1.93	14.01	6.70	2.09
Carter	−16.75	6.38	−2.62	−15.21	5.91	−2.58
Reagan	−25.32	4.64	−5.46	−24.88	4.36	−5.70
Public opinion$_{(t-1)}$	−.12	.11	−1.05	−.09	.06	−1.31
Nonideol. pres. *						
public opinion$_{(t-1)}$	—	—	—	.47	.49	.97
R^2/Adj. R^2		.84/.81			.85/.82	
Rho		−.22			−.26	
Lagrange multiplier		.70			1.88	

Carter, Reagan, Ford), but takes on the public opinion liberalness values if the
president is not ideological (Johnson, Nixon). Here I used the variability in
presidential ideology to identify if a president is an ideologue or not. Johnson
and Nixon demonstrated considerably more variability than the other presidents (see table 5.3). Then I added the interaction term into the equation, along
with the party, four presidential dummy variables, and the public opinion
variable.[10] The results of the analysis (see table 5.4) indicate that nonideological presidents, as defined here, do not respond to public opinion in this stage
of the policy-making process.

The general point of lack of presidential responsiveness to public opinion
in the policy formulation stage holds under these various tests. Yet a simple
model incorporating two ideas, party and person, seems to account for an
overwhelming component of the variance in presidential ideology (with an
autocorrelation term included, it topped 80 percent).

The combination of party and person-in-office provides us with a powerful understanding of the ideological leanings of presidents, and may help us
understand the dynamics of party change and stability. On the one hand,
presidents are the products of their parties. Inasmuch as presidents respond to
these forces, parties are a stabilizing force on politics and presidents. This
allows for much historical continuity of parties and their issue positions and
policies over time, continuities that are reflected in the presidency, as well.

But presidents also leave their marks on their parties, thus enabling their
parties to change over time, but in the context of the party's heritage. For
instance, we have remarked throughout on the impact of certain presidents to

get their parties to adopt their policy views. At times, this had led to remarkable change in the party. For instance, Eisenhower realigned the Republican Party on foreign policy, moving it away from its traditional isolationism. Kennedy, similarly, seemed instrumental in his party's adoption of Keynesian approaches to economic policy-making, melding that approach with the Democrats traditional redistributive inclinations. Reagan, too, had great impact on his party, leaving it much more conservative than he found it on a whole host of policies, from relations with the Soviets, to economic policy.

The results of this analysis give us a sense of the process by which presidents affect their parties. First, as indicative of these presidents, not all presidents are perfect products of their parties. Some bring policy stances that may be at odds with the way the party has traditionally attacked an issue, while others may bring a whole new complex of issues to deal with. Furthermore, we suggested in the previous chapter that presidents may be able to lead public opinion, pushing it in a liberal or conservative direction, if only marginally.

The combination of these new issues and presidential leadership may reverberate strongly within the party, sometimes leaving a lasting effect. Presidents who are able to lead public opinion tend to be more successful presidents; at a minimum they are looked upon as popular leaders from the ranks of their co-partisans. Thus, some co-partisans may be especially sensitive to the views of these popular leaders, adopting the issues positions that these leading presidents have pushed. They view such presidents as revitalizing the party, and try to capitalize on this. Moreover, the appeal of these presidents may stimulate new participants into party activity. These new participants often find the president appealing because of the views that he took on issues. A new cadre is created in the party loyal to this new credo.

A president's party legacy, thus, can be infused into the party fabric through conversion of the old and mobilization of the new. But this all hinges on presidents taking positions that may be novel for the party and the president being able to demonstrate leadership of public opinion. Thus, into the mid-1990s, we still can see the influence of Ronald Reagan on the Republican Party, clearly someone who brought a new view of policy to the party, as well as having demonstrated strong leadership potential. In contrast, George Bush did not offer much new for the party, seeking to continue Reagan's successful approach instead. And while he demonstrated at times exceedingly high popular support, it is not clear that Bush was a strong or effective leader of the public. His reelection defeat underscores that point.

The data and results presented here do not directly test this notion, but only lead me to speculate along these lines. These points further tie into the lack of strong responsiveness pressures. Presidents see their opportunities tied more to leading public opinion. And by leading, some presidents may reshape their parties, revitalizing them, and thus making them a more potent presidential resource. Simple presidential responsiveness, passivity in the face of public pressure, may lose the president these leadership, party-building, and legacy-leaving opportunities. But not all presidents are equally able to lead, and thus, the quality and depth of their legacy and party-building efforts will vary, as the comparison of Reagan and Bush indicates.

Presidential Responsiveness and Policy Type

The analysis thus far has failed to detect a strong, direct relationship between public opinion and presidential ideology. The presidential data combine all positions across all policy areas, while the public opinion series is limited to domestic policies. This divergence in substantive content may be the reason that analysis has failed to discover a relationship.

First, presidential responsiveness to public opinion may be conditioned by type of policy area. Knowing that the public is liberal on domestic policies may not be relevant to the president when considering foreign policies. As the discussion in chapter 4 indicated, presidential positions across policy areas do not necessarily correlate very highly. The average correlation across the four policy areas is .48 and range from .28 to .69.[11] Moreover, it does not appear that the public is very constrained in the positions that it holds across policy areas. Converse's (1964) famous study found no appreciable correlation in the public's opinions across foreign, economic, and domestic policies. In a recent overview of public opinion, Erikson, Luttbeg, and Tedin (1991, 90–95) do not find much consistency in public attitudes across policies, either. Thus, it may be wise for us to disaggregate the presidential rhetoric series into components that more closely match the substantive content of the public opinion series.

Second, presidential incentives to respond to public opinion may vary across issue areas, as well. Of the economic, foreign, civil rights, and domestic policy areas, perhaps only economic policy presents strong incentives for responsiveness. The public is often characterized as disinterested in foreign affairs, or if not disinterested, at least uninformed about foreign affairs. Thus, few voters rely on their foreign policy beliefs as guides to their vote choice (but see Aldrich, Sullivan, and Borgida 1989).

Civil rights policy, while possessing somewhat stronger incentives toward responsiveness because of its domestic content, nonetheless only weakly motivates presidential responsiveness because it is more an interest group policy than a policy with broad, mass appeal. Yet in chapter 3 we detected some presidential responsiveness to public concern with civil rights; when public concern with civil rights increased, so did presidential attention. This might lay a foundation for policy responsiveness here also, with presidents getting more liberal on civil rights as the public mood turns more liberal.

The aggregate domestic policy indicator of presidential ideology is an amalgam of many interest group issues, some of which might be quite narrow in scope. It is possible for the president and the public to demonstrate similar levels of domestic policy liberalism while their policy leanings differ across the elements comprising the domestic policy indicator. For instance, the president may be liberal on agriculture and conservative on the environment, while the public holds reverse opinions. When averaged, both the president and the public may look similarly liberal (or conservative). This aggregation problem may show some presidential responsiveness, but may be masking the differences between presidents and the public when dealing with specific subareas that comprise the domestic policy indicator being used here.

For a policy area to provide incentives for responsiveness, it must be one that large numbers of voters are aware of and care about enough to cast their vote. Moreover, voters must view the president as responsible for that policy area. On this count, civil rights and domestic policies fall short; Congress is often held responsible for many of these types of issues (Davidson and Oleszek 1990, 251). Only economic policy fits the bill well. It is important to many voters, they hold the president responsible for the state of the economy, and it is primarily domestic in content. By disaggregating the presidential ideology series into the different policy types, economic, foreign, domestic, and civil rights policy, I can test this hypothesis.

An important alternative understanding of the difference between the indicator of overall ideology and policy-specific positioning suggests that disaggregating should not increase the likelihood of presidential responsiveness to public opinion. Specifically, the overall ideology indicator presents greater opportunities for presidential manipulation of symbols than the indicators that focus on specific policy areas.

Like the case for overall substantiveness, presidents can manipulate the overall ideology image by mixing the several policy areas in varying proportions. Presidents may want to do this because they are out of step with the public in one policy area that is important to them, but want to convey a sense of generally being in step with the public. Thus, a president who is pursuing, for instance, a policy course that is more conservative than the public on economic policy may amplify his discussion of other policy areas in which he is closer to the mass public to dilute the charge that he is being unresponsive. He may not offer many sentences for those policies that he cares about but is out of step with the public, while he may add sentences for other policies that demonstrate a closer congruence with public positions or the public mood. To compensate for deviations from public preferences in some policy areas and to create an image of being on average in accord with the public mood, the president may manipulate his statements across policy areas within his State of the Union Address. Thus, the symbolic element of the president's overall ideological position is highlighted.

In contrast, on specific policy areas presidents may feel more constrained to offer statements that truly reflect their positions and policy directions. Concerned elites and interest groups are more likely to pay attention to policy-specific statements than the general public, which is more apt to only register a general impression of the president's speech. Moreover, presidents may have these more attentive audiences in mind when remarking on specific policy areas and proposals, unlike the overall message, which is meant to reach out to the mass public, as well as these political elites.

Furthermore, presidents may have previously staked out specific policy positions, which they feel relatively bound to follow or reiterate in the State of the Union Address. Many of these positions may come from the election campaign, previous statements that the Executive made while in office, and from deals already cut with important leaders. Mentioning these deals in the Address may be a way of making public decisions that have previously been made in closed quarters.

Thus, as presidential statements get closer to actual policies, there is less room for the kind of symbolic manipulation that can be made when dealing with the overall image of the Address, which can be altered by varying the mix or space that difference policy areas receive. This process of aggregation may allow more presidential opportunities to manipulate with eyes on the symbolic dimension of the State of the Union Address, something that is more constrained when dealing with specific policy areas. Given this view, we should not witness strong policy-specific responsiveness if we take the non-responsiveness of overall ideology as an expectation baseline or upper limit.

I regress each policy area on public liberalism, again lagged one year. GLS procedures are used to correct for first order autocorrelation problems when present. The results, which are displayed in table 5.5, are quite plain—presidents demonstrate no responsiveness to public opinion across any of the policy areas.[12] This is much like the result for overall ideology.

The Determinants of Presidential Policy Rhetoric

In this section I combine the analytic perspectives of the context, variable omission, and disaggregation views used earlier in this chapter to test again for the impact of public opinion on presidential ideology. In this process, I also aim to build a more comprehensive understanding of why presidents take liberal or conservative positions in their State of the Union Addresses, placing the impact of public opinion within this overall context. To this end, I will develop a multivariate model to understand presidential ideology.

TABLE 5.5.   The Impact of Public Opinion on Presidential
Rhetorical Liberalism by Policy Area, 1956–89

Policy Area	b	SE	t
Economic policy			
Constant	29.29	7.61	3.85
Public opinion$_{(t-1)}$	.21	.72	.29
R^2/Adj. R^2	.19/.16		
Rho	.36		
Lagrange multiplier	.61		
Foreign policy			
Constant	49.16	15.06	3.26
Public opinion$_{(t-1)}$	1.13	1.06	1.05
R^2/Adj. R^2	.48/.46		
Rho	.66		
Lagrange multiplier	1.06		
Civil rights policy			
Constant	79.55	13.59	5.85
Public opinion$_{(t-1)}$	.63	1.03	.61
R^2/Adj. R^2	.30/.27		
Rho	.54		
Lagrange multiplier	3.19		
Domestic policy			
Constant	51.20	8.94	5.73
Public opinion$_{(t-1)}$	.40	.85	.47
R^2/Adj. R^2	.15/.12		
Rho	.35		
Lagrange multiplier	.33		

Several sets of factors identified earlier have or hypothetically may have
consequences for presidential rhetorical position taking. Party, person and the
international, economic, and political contexts were discussed previously.
Each of these, along with public opinion liberalism, are used to explain overall
presidential ideology as well as presidential liberalism in each of four policy
areas: economic, foreign, domestic, and civil rights policy. Although some of
these factors are expected to have consistent impacts across the policy areas,
others are not likely to affect each policy area or to have consistent impacts
across policy areas.

I expect party and president to have an impact across policy liberalism
overall and on three policy areas—economic policy, foreign policy, and domestic policy. Over time, we are less likely to see party effects on civil rights
because of the shifting positions of the parties on that issue. Carmines and
Stimson (1989) demonstrate that the Republican Party shifted from a supportive to a less supportive posture after the enactment of the 1964 Voting and

Civil Rights Acts. We have seen this in Eisenhower's civil rights liberalism, while subsequent Republican presidents have been less liberal, if not conservative, on the issue. Rather than party, president in office may be more important for understanding presidential positioning on civil rights.

The international and economic contexts are likely to have variable impact on presidential ideology. Overall, we would expect wars to move presidents to the right, as presidents try to justify their war policies by using militaristic and combative Cold War rhetoric. Similarly, inflation may move presidents to the right, but unemployment may move them leftward. Inflation and unemployment differentially fall on mass public and the economy. Creditors, banks and lending institutions, and the upper-income classes all abhor inflation. When inflation rises, presidents of either party will sound more conservative when they pursue policies to curb it. The costs of unemployment, in contrast, are felt more strongly in the working and poorer classes (Hibbs 1987). Policies to relieve unemployment and to stimulate economic demand are often cast in more liberal terms. Presidents who aim to pursue such policies will thus sound more liberal.

It is unclear whether the international and economic context will affect domestic or civil rights rhetoric. Pressing international and economic problems may push these policy areas off the agenda, as demonstrated in chapter 2, but these problems may not have much impact on those policy areas that make the agenda during international and economic strife. In the domestic arena, we may find presidents pursuing a "guns and butter" posture. To maintain support for their war policies, presidents may have to offer special interests the domestic programs or program increases they want. In other words, war opposition may be bought off with domestic policy offerings.

The political context may also affect presidential rhetoric. Here I focus on the electoral calendar and election-based incentives. The nearness of the next presidential election may have an impact on domestic policy rhetoric, moving it in a liberal direction. If presidents view their electoral bases as a coalition of interests, presidents may try to expand and solidify that base by offering policies to interests. Thus, we are likely to find presidents moving left on domestic policy. Similarly, in the first year after an election, presidential domestic policy rhetoric may move leftward as presidents reaffirm the promises made during the election campaign. The time point dummies are used to pick up this hypothesized cycle.

Lastly, presidents in their second terms may be insulated from these coalitions of interests pressures because of their lame-duck status, and thus their domestic policy rhetoric may move to the right. Rather than attempting to lure interest group support, presidents may feel freer to attack interests, alone or as a political sector. They may even feel the need to attack "special" interests, as outgoing presidents attempt to build a reputation for being statesmen and guardians of the public interest prior to their political retirement. Presidents may be motivated to shore up their place in history in their second terms.

Each equation thus contains the following variables: party, presidential dummy variables, war, inflation, unemployment, the time point dummies, term two, and public opinion. The public opinion variable is lagged one year, as I have done in earlier analyses. Such an equation presents two problems. First, I cannot enter simultaneously each presidential dummy variable and the party variable. The presidential dummy variables sum to the party variable. This creates singularity in the matrix, which cannot be inverted, and the equation cannot be computed. For each equation, I had to experiment with each and every combination of party and person to find the most parsimonious and best fit, as I did earlier in this chapter.

The second problem, which is related to the first, is the huge number of variables (17) compared to the available number of cases (34, minus 1 for the lagged term). Such a high variable-to-cases ratio may induce considerable instability in the equation as variables are added or dropped from the estimation, perhaps indicating multicollinearity. To check for this, I ran every possible combination of variables, comparing variable performance across equations. Luckily, the final, reduced-form equations (see table 5.6) proved highly stable.

The reduced-form equations are composed of only those variables that significantly added to the equation R^2. This was determined by inspection of the t values for each coefficient and a comparison of the R^2s of the equations with and without the variable in question. Lastly, after the reduced-form equation was found, I added, one at a time and in combination, each excluded variable to see if it had any impact on the equation. An F test is used to determine if the inclusion or exclusion of any variable significantly affects the equation's R^2. In no case did any excluded variable at this point have pronounced effects on the estimations.

The results of the five equations are presented in table 5.6. Each equation proved quite powerful, with adjusted R^2s ranging from .67 to .87. Also, each equation F was significant, owing to the exclusion of insignificant variables. All equations contain between two and seven variables; thus, rather simple, parsimonious, yet powerful statistical estimations resulted from this analysis.

No variable was significant across each equation, yet several were significant several times. Never did the time point dummies emerge as significant predictors, but the presidential dummies did in different combinations across the equations. Similarly, party, the international and economic context, and the lame-duck term were intermittently significant.

The Reagan variable was statistically significant for each equation save foreign policy. In each instance, the sign points in the expected direction.

TABLE 5.6. Impact of Party; Person; International, Economic, and Political Context; and Public Opinion on Presidential Rhetorical Liberalism, Overall and by Policy Area, 1956–89

Variable	Overall Liberalism			Economic Policy			Foreign Policy			Civil Rights Policy			Domestic Policy		
	b	SE	t	b	SE	t	b	SE	t	b	SE	t	b	SE	t
Constant	−29.27	14.47	−2.62	−86.49	32.99	−2.02	19.32	9.05	2.13	92.12	32.45	2.84	68.68	12.96	5.30
Eisenhower	40.48	6.34	6.38				70.26	18.97	3.70	55.81	16.03	3.48			
Kennedy				72.03	15.25	4.73							53.38	14.04	3.80
Johnson				51.22	10.51	4.88							46.76	9.28	5.04
Nixon										−96.90	16.91	−5.73			
Ford													−26.64	12.13	−2.20
Carter															
Reagan	−11.54	−6.17	−1.87	−36.95	8.67	−4.26				−58.61	15.85	−3.70	−24.77	7.05	−3.52
Party (1 = Dem.)	43.11	4.25	10.14				55.13	11.93	4.62						
War	23.44	5.63	4.16	47.52	10.90	4.36				14.70	8.69	1.69			
Unemploy.	6.67	1.58	4.21	9.53	3.48	2.74				8.70	3.69	2.36			
Inflation	1.96	.95	2.06												
Year 2															
Year 3															
Year 4															
Term 2				32.40	10.53	3.08				−45.33	14.45	−3.13	−17.01	8.43	−2.02
Pub. Op$_{(t-1)}$	1.41	.33	4.33	−1.47	.46	−3.20	.63	.66	.96	−.17	.35	−.48	−.44	.45	−.99
R^2/Adj. R^2	.90/.87			.74/.67			.73/.70			.91/.87			.81/.76		
DW d (Rho)	(−.36)			(−.24)			(.41)			2.14			(−.23)		
Lagrange multiplier	3.52			1.50			.70			.96			1.38		

Controlling for all other influences, Reagan's rhetoric is more conservative. This confirms our conventional portrait of Reagan. The coefficients indicate that, depending on the policy area, the rhetoric of presidential State of the Union Addresses is from 12 to 59 percent more conservative when Reagan is president, except for foreign policy.

Eisenhower also stands out. On three of five occasions his coefficient is statistically significant. Only on economic and domestic policy, where Eisenhower is a typical, mainstream Republican, does his coefficient fail to reach statistical significance. Unlike his co-partisan Reagan, Eisenhower demonstrates tendencies toward greater liberalism after holding all these other factors constant. These Eisenhower impacts are often quite strong, ranging from 40 percent overall to 70 percent on foreign policy.

Kennedy and Johnson were found to be significant for the same two equations, economic and domestic policy. In each case, holding all other variables constant, they are more liberal by 46 to 72 percent. Nixon was never found to be a significant impact, a result that corresponds to the opportunistic shifting of Nixon while in office. Gerald Ford was statistically significant on two occasions, domestic and civil rights policy. In each case, Ford's rhetoric was tilted in the conservative direction by considerable amounts (27 percent on domestic policy and 97 percent on civil rights policy).

Lastly, Carter, like Nixon, was never found to be a significant effect. Why this is so is unclear, but it might demonstrate that Carter was especially affected by the forces impinging upon him while in office, a view that seems to correspond well with some scholarly interpretations of his administration (Skowronek 1993).

Party was a significant influence only on overall liberalism and foreign policy. In both cases, Democrats are more liberal than Republicans by 40 to 55 percent. The striking aspect of this finding is the significance of party on international affairs but not economic policy. Past research has indicated that the partisan division is pronounced on economic policy (cf. Hibbs 1987), but bipartisanship often has ruled the day on foreign affairs. At the presidential level, at least, foreign policy sets important partisan divisions, divisions that may not always clearly resonate with the mass public. The public may usually be willing to rally behind the president on foreign policy matters, but at this highest political level competition among partisan elites is a fact of life.

Contextual influences vary in impact. War was an important factor for overall, economic, and civil rights policy, but rather than moving rhetoric to the right war moves presidents to the left. The effect can be pronounced, from 23 percent overall to 48 percent on economic policy and nearly 15 percent on civil rights. This may be another indication of a "guns and butter" approach in the Cold War era, where presidents tried to build support for their militaristic Cold War policies through appeals with economic policies that moderated class differences and stimulated demand in the less monied classes. A similar dynamic might hold with regard to civil rights policies and war, especially when wars in the modern era have been justified in terms of spreading or safeguarding democracy and civil rights and liberties of the affected nations. This may spill over into the domestic context, and some presidents, especially liberally oriented ones, may view war as an occasion to further a liberal civil rights agenda. Alternatively, the linkage between war and civil rights may increase civil rights pressures on presidents, and this move leftward during war may indicate presidential responsiveness to those pressures.

Unemployment was similarly important only for overall liberalism, economic policy, and civil rights. The results suggest that each one percentage point increase in unemployment leads to a presidential shift to the left of from nearly 7 to almost 10 percent. The unemployment effects of these policy areas also make sense. Unemployment pushes presidents to follow more liberal economic policies, and, very likely, the differential social impact of unemployment, which hits minorities harder than most other populations, may also lead presidents to suggest more liberal civil rights policies as a compensation or corrective. Inflation has one statistically significant effect; it pushes overall presidential ideology leftward, the opposite direction of what I originally expected, but the effect is modest—each 1 percent increase in inflation results in a 2 percent presidential shift.

Lastly, the lame-duck term has an impact on several occasions. Somewhat oddly, lame-duck presidents, holding all other effects constant, are more liberal on economic policy by about 32 percent. But on civil rights and domestic policy, lame-duck presidents harden their stance, moving to the right some 45 percent for civil rights and 17 percent for domestic policy. The domestic policy case may indicate presidential attacks or resistance to special interests, as hypothesized earlier. If presidents view civil rights in such terms, as many seem to have done during the past twenty years, then we also have a reason for the rightward shift here.

Before turning to the impact of public opinion, let us summarize the effects from another vantage point, that of the policy area, rather than from the perspective of the individual coefficients, as I did in the preceding paragraphs. Overall policy liberalism is a function of president (Eisenhower and Reagan), party, war, inflation, unemployment, and public opinion. Economic policy is a function of president (Kennedy, Johnson, and Reagan), war, term two, unemployment, and public opinion. The simplest model is found for foreign policy. It is a function of president (Eisenhower) and party. Civil rights rhetoric is a function of president (Eisenhower, Ford, and Reagan), war, unemployment, and the lame-duck term. Finally, domestic policy is a function of president (Kennedy, Johnson, Ford, and Reagan), and the lame-duck term.

Relatively simple yet powerful models of presidential ideology emerged from this analysis. Although the substantive results are interesting in their own right, the thrust of this study concerns the impact of public opinion on presidential policy choice. In two of the equations, I detected a public opinion impact.

First, public opinion influenced presidential rhetoric on economic policy, but rather than following public opinion presidential rhetoric moved in the opposite direction. Each one-point move of public opinion in the liberal direction motivated a presidential retreat to the right by about 1.5 percent.[13] Why presidents should be contrary to public pressures is unclear, but given the importance of economic policy to the success of an administration, this may indicate that presidents try to maintain some control over their economic policy. They may even be trying to moderate public demands by being somewhat out of step with the public—moving to the right when faced with liberal pressures on their economic policies and moving to the left when faced with conservative pressures. Thus, presidents may moderate expectations by telling liberals (or conservatives) that there are limits to how far he will move left (or right), perhaps because of economic policy dictates. This result may also be an attempt by the president to insulate his economic policies from demands of the right or left that emanated from other policy or issue areas.

The results indicate, also, that overall presidential ideology is responsive to the public mood, even though we needed a fully specified model to reveal this relationship. This finding is consistent with the notion that presidents have some symbolic leeway at this level of aggregation that is lacking when looking at specific policy areas. The lack of responsiveness detected when we disaggregate to the specific policy area reinforces this interpretation. It also demonstrates that even in this highly substantively charged stage of the policy process—policy formulation—symbolic politics is a critical ingredient, but that symbolism also does not override all activities.

The coefficient suggests that each one-point change in the public mood moves the president about 1.4 percent, about the same magnitude as the counterresponsiveness found on economic policy. Another way to assess the magnitude of this effect is to remove each of the statistically significant variables from the equation and compare the drop in the R^2.

Dropping the public opinion variable from the equation depresses the adjusted R^2 to .78, a nine-point drop. The R^2 declines associated with the other variables, in order of magnitude, are as follows: party, 36; Eisenhower, 16; war, 9; unemployment, 9; inflation, 2; and Reagan, 1. Public opinion stands tied for third place in impact, along with war and unemployment, and far ahead of the more modest predictors, Reagan and inflation. Thus, public opinion is not a dominant influence but is middling in power—significant, though not overpowering or determining.[14]

Conclusions

In chapter 4, I began the investigation of presidential responsiveness to public opinion in the process of policy formulation. Liberal or conservative stances on issues in the president's State of the Union Address were used to indicate the outcomes of the policy formulation process. The theory being tested here suggests that presidents should not be very systematically responsive to public opinion in this stage of the policy-making process because of the substantive implications of policy formulation, except for overall ideology, which affords presidents some ability to manipulate symbols without altering substance.

In this stage of the policy process, then, presidents turn away from public opinion for several reasons. First, the public's lack of knowledge and detail about issues and policy alternatives makes it a poor guide for choosing policy options. Second, the president must contend with other actors, like members of Congress, in the formal policy-making process. The strategic institutional placement of these competing actors enables them to block the progress of presidential policy proposals. Thus, the president must be sensitive to their policy demands and must often compromise with them to realize his policy goals. Third, the president, insofar as he is held responsible for the impact and success of policies implemented during his administration, must also balance public preferences with the impact and success of his policies. All these factors reduce the incentives for presidential responsiveness to public opinion in the policy formulation process.

My analysis in chapter 4 found support for the limited responsiveness hypothesis. That analysis, however, was too simplistic to prove definitive. This chapter opened with several critiques of the analysis of chapter 4. Those critiques charged that the relationship between public opinion and presidential positions might be masked because confounding variables were not controlled for, that presidential responsiveness might emerge under certain contexts, and that the presidential ideology series might be too aggregated to detect responsiveness. Each of these critiques was dealt with in turn.

Overall, tests of these critiques support the basic guiding hypothesis but with an important revision. Of all tests performed in this chapter, only one instance of presidential responsiveness to public opinion was unearthed— overall presidential ideology seems responsive to the public mood, but when the presidential speech is broken down by policy area that aggregate result vanishes. And in one case, that of economic policy, counterresponsiveness was found, with presidential rhetorical positions pointing in the opposite direction of public opinion. The vast bulk of the findings thus support the idea of limited presidential responsiveness to public opinion when substantive considerations predominate in an activity.

CHAPTER 6

Policy Legitimation and Presidential Responsiveness to Public Opinion

In the previous chapters I looked at the impact of public opinion on presidential problem identification, substantive rhetoric, and policy formulation. The findings thus far are generally consistent with the theoretical idea motivating this study: that presidents will be more responsive to the public when activities are more symbolic than substantive. Symbolic responsiveness does not force presidential choices about the substance of public policy. Presidents face strong incentives to control the substance of public policies. The most important incentive is that the public holds them responsible for the outcome of policy-making.

But presidents still face incentives to be responsive to the mass public. The president is seen as a representative of the people. To fulfill that expectation, presidents must demonstrate some level and type of responsiveness. They tend to do this symbolically rather than substantively, though as the discussion in previous chapters points out, it is a mistake to divide behavior and policy in symbolic versus substantive categories. All policy activities have both symbolic and substantive components, but the relative mix or emphasis may vary from one activity to another. Some may be almost purely symbolic, lacking any substantive content, while other activities may set the substantive element higher in importance than the symbolic. Symbolic responsiveness unencumbered by substantive commitment is most likely in the problem identification process. The findings reported in chapter 2 indicate some presidential symbolic responsiveness in problem identification. In later policy-making stages, when presidents offer substantive rhetoric and formulate policy positions, both of which have strong substantive implications, presidential responsiveness declines. This last point needs modification: when activities in these post–problem identification stages take on symbolic importance, presidents also tend toward responsiveness. This was most evident in the example of overall presidential ideological responsiveness to the public mood.

In this chapter, I look at presidential responsiveness to public opinion in the policy legitimation process. The ideas being presented here suggest that presidents will not be very responsive to public opinion in this process. First, presidents have fewer opportunities to symbolically manipulate their actions, in this case positions on roll call before Congress. Second, the presidential need to control the policy-making process increases as the process gets closer to congressional passage of legislation. Presidents must bargain with Congress, and they must also ensure that the congressional legislative output looks like the policies they want. Critically, presidents insist that policies so passed and implemented must work, must be effective. Ineffective and failed policies will redound onto the president in any event, harming his reputation, undermining his ability to generate popular support from implemented policies, and interfering with the accomplishment of a whole host of other presidential goals.

But an alternative perspective suggests that presidents might be highly responsive to public opinion in policy legitimation. Presidents will be responsive so they can use their public support to pressure Congress to support their policy proposals. The assumption here is that presidential responsiveness builds public support. In the pages to follow, I review this competing theory, which I call the "public opinion resource" theory.

Presidents, Congress, Public Opinion, and Policy Legitimation

Policy legitimation is the process by which public policies are chosen from competing policy alternatives. The final policy chosen in this process does not have to come from the set of alternatives originally offered. The dynamic interplay of policy advocates and antagonists may result in new, and perhaps novel, policy solutions. The legislature is a key player in the legitimation process. Without the passage of bills into law, no legitimation occurs, no policies can be put into effect.[1]

In the policy legitimation process, presidents who want to see their proposals become official policy must work with Congress and acquire the legislature's approval of their policy initiatives and proposals. Congress becomes a partner in building public policy in this process. In the other processes described earlier, presidents had some leeway in deciding how much they would allow congressional preferences to affect those decisions. In the legitimation process, the president cannot ignore Congress, even if he so desires. The president must be able to influence Congress if he is to get the legislature to enact the policies he wants. During policy legitimation, presidential attention and effort is directed toward influencing congressional decisions. This focus on Congress also constrains presidents' manipulation of the symbolic attributes of their behaviors.

Presidential Influence in Congress

The president's ability to influence Congress is among the most theoretically and empirically developed topics on the presidency. Richard Neustadt's

(1960, 1990) work serves as the theoretical foundation, though Neustadt offers a broader theory of presidential behavior. Neustadt argues that the gap between the president's institutional authority and resources and the governing expectations placed on him forces him to persuade others to follow his wishes. Professional reputation and public prestige constitute the resource base available to the president. Presidents with favorable reputations and high levels of public prestige will be more persuasive than presidents lacking those resources.

To Neustadt, public prestige entails more than just popularity, though popularity is one component of presidential prestige (Neustadt 1960, 87). And while much subsequent research has focused on the short-term ups and downs in popularity, Neustadt does not think that these temporary swings are particularly important. This is because Neustadt does not think that popularity directly affects the president's immediate power situation. Instead, for Neustadt public prestige "is a factor operating mostly in the background as a conditioner, not the determinant, of what Washingtonians will do about a President's request. Rarely is there any one-to-one relationship between the appraisals of his popularity in general and responses to his wishes in particular" (87). Thus, presidents concerned with their power relationships, with their ability to persuade others, will be concerned about their general prestige and standing with the public. They will not intentionally do things that undermine their prestige and/or popularity, while many activities will be geared toward building up their popularity and prestige.

Recent research suggests that presidential concern with popularity and prestige have become a presidential preoccupation and that this preoccupation has grown in recent decades. This growing preoccupation with popularity has come about because of changes in the bargaining structure in Washington. Kernell (1993) argues that the institutionalized pluralism that characterized the period of Neustadt's writing has evolved into individualized pluralism (Kernell 1993, 9–52; see also Edwards 1983 for a good review on the president and public opinion). Rather than build winning coalitions by bargaining with the handful of congressional party and committee leaders, who control blocs of congressional votes, presidents of the more recent individualized pluralist state must seek support from members of Congress one at a time. Mobilizing public support pressures a wide swath of legislators at once. It is an efficient, if blunt, method of building support.

Presidential Popularity and Congressional Influence

If, as Kernell claims, the Washington community has changed and the importance of popularity for presidents has increased, there might be an incentive for presidents to follow public opinion when bargaining with Congress. For presidents to use public opinion to influence Congress, they must first ensure that they and the public have the same policy preference or at least that the president and the public are closer in their preferences than Congress is to the public. Second, the president must be well regarded in the mass public; he must be reasonably popular. Only when both conditions hold will Congress feel that the president speaks for the public, and thus give in to his policy demands.

There are two paths to the congruence of presidents and the public over policies. First, the president can lead and mold public opinion. We have seen the potential for this in earlier chapters. Presidential rhetoric affects people's policy concerns and the positions the public favors with respect to those policies.

The second path is for the president to follow public opinion. Presidents follow public opinion but more symbolically than substantively. Nonresponsiveness was the norm for substantive rhetoric and policy formulation except when the symbolic importance of these activities was highly evident or when the political symbols associated with an activity were easily manipulated.

In the policy legitimation process, however, presidential responsiveness to public opinion may increase as presidents try to mobilize public opinion in their behalf. If presidential responsiveness to public opinion increases presidential popularity (or if nonresponsiveness erodes popularity), then presidents have an incentive to follow public opinion. Moreover, even if responsiveness does not directly boost popularity, but still gives the appearance that the president and the public are on the same policy wavelength, presidents may have an incentive toward responsiveness. The closer the tie between the president and the public, the better positioned the president is to mobilize public opinion when bargaining with Congress and to convince Congress that he speaks for the public.

This incentive to follow public opinion in the policy legitimation process stems from the importance of Congress in legitimating policy and the impact of public opinion on Congress. Without congressional assent, presidents will not see their policy proposals enacted into law. In this context of individualized pluralism, public opinion may improve the president's bargaining situation.

This argument contrasts strongly with the theory I have been offering in this study. That theory suggests that presidents also want to maximize their discretion over public policy and thus will not be highly policy responsive to public opinion during the legitimation process. Symbolic responsiveness itself is sufficient to forge the popular connection so important to presidents. Moreover, there are strong public pressures or expectations for presidential leadership, which lead the president to try to control the policy-making process. Presidents can afford to be symbolically responsive because such responsiveness does not entail a loss of presidential control over the policy-making process. The ability of presidents to manipulate symbols is one reason why presidents can be symbolically responsive without losing policy-making control. When symbols cannot be manipulated without ceding some control over policy-making, presidential responsiveness to the public will flag.

The Impact of Popularity

Popularity may not have the gross effects on legislative success necessary to motivate presidents to follow public opinion in the policy legitimation process. Considerable research has documented the quantity of presidential activity aimed at boosting popularity levels. Presidents travel to increase their popularity (Simon and Ostrom 1989; Brace and Hinckley 1993), speeches are strategically timed to affect popularity (Ragsdale 1984), and policies may be promoted with popularity payoffs in mind. In one important study, Ostrom and Simon (1985) find that presidential legislative success with Congress leads to increases in subsequent presidential popularity.

In contrast, findings about the impact of popularity on presidential success with Congress are mixed. One set of studies finds that short-term swings in popularity have no impact on congressional support once controlling for party seat ratios (Bond and Fleisher 1990; Edwards 1989). Peterson (1990, 193–94), in fact, finds that higher levels of presidential popularity lead to higher incidences of conflict with Congress in the legislative process.

Viewing popularity from a longer time perspective offers a different portrait of popularity's impact on presidential success. Rivers and Rose (1985) find that annual levels of popularity affect annual levels of success with Congress after controlling for party seat ratios. Each 1 percent increase in annual presidential popularity leads to a corresponding 1 percent increase in the likelihood that Congress will pass a presidential initiative. Similarly, Ostrom and Simon (1985, 349) find that each ten-point drop in approval results in a three-point decline in the rate of roll call victories.[2] Brace and Hinckley (1992) also find that popularity affects success with Congress.

We can attempt a reconciliation between the short-term no-effect findings of popularity on presidential success (Bond and Fleisher 1990; Edwards 1989) with the long-term studies that find a popularity impact on success (Rivers and Rose 1985; Ostrom and Simon 1985; Brace and Hinckley 1992, chap. 4). Recall that Neustadt argued that short-term popularity shifts are unimportant. Public opinion is often fickle, and the heat of the moment can cause large shifts in a short time that recede as quickly as they began. Rather, the background context of public standing is important. From this context, one can observe the stability or trend in presidential popularity. Hence, it is not too surprising that popularity, as for Bond and Fleisher or Edwards, has little impact on congressional support for the president. But taking a longer view, as

Rivers and Rose or Ostrom and Simon try to do, reveals a popularity impact on presidential success.

Thus, if popularity, at least in the longer run, is important to presidential success with Congress, presidents may have a strong incentive to stick close to the public's way of thinking about policies in this legitimation process. Policy responsiveness may boost levels of presidential popularity. If this is so, presidents may realize more of their policy goals in their dealings with Congress.

Policy responsiveness may also increase presidential success with Congress even if such responsiveness does not directly translate into increased popularity. By holding a policy position that is closer to the public's than the position held in Congress, the president can also claim to speak for the nation even if he is not overly popular. Congress can rarely resist a president who is thought to speak for the public on an issue of great concern to the public. Moreover, by appearing to take the public's side against a resistant Congress, the president may build a reputation for serving the public interest. The combination of increased success in Congress and the reputation of serving the public welfare may lead to future popularity gains.[3]

Summary

The theory of limited responsiveness suggests that presidents will not be very responsive to the public in the policy legitimation process. In contrast, the theory of popularity as a presidential resource suggests the opposite, that presidents will be responsive to public opinion in this process. In the remainder of this chapter, I test these competing theories. As I did in the last chapter, I here use the Stimson public opinion series to capture the public's ideological mood. I rely on a measure of presidential positions on roll calls before Congress to indicate presidential preferences in the policy legitimation process. Like the rhetorical measures used in the previous two chapters, this measure taps the degree of liberalism (conservatism) of presidential positions in the aggregate. I call this *presidential roll call liberalism,* and I describe its construction in the next section.

Measuring Presidential Liberalism
in the Policy Legitimation Stage

Most research on the presidency and the policy legitimation process looks at some form of presidential success with Congress, usually a type of roll call indicator. Presidential success with Congress is of only incidental interest here. My major concern is with the impact of opinion on presidential behavior and policy choice in the policy legitimation process. The idea being tested here suggests that public opinion should not affect presidential position taking very much in this stage of the policy-making process. In contrast, the public opinion resource theory suggests that public opinion may indeed affect presidential position taking. The positions that presidents take on roll calls before Congress and the way those positions relate to public preferences—not whether the president was on the winning side—are the relevant information here.

One can view presidential position taking on roll calls as a form of presidential lobbying of Congress. This type of "lobbying" is visible to Congress and the public. When presidents express roll call preferences, they are not only indicating their policy preferences but are also mobilizing public pressure on Congress.

Across roll calls or legislation before Congress, presidents will exert varying degrees of effort to mobilize public opinion. Sometimes presidents may travel around the nation giving speeches to stir public sentiment and activity. Woodrow Wilson's campaign to secure acceptance of the Treaty of Versailles ending the First World War is the most famous example of such intensive presidential lobbying. Recent major presidential campaigns to stir public opinion include Clinton's efforts on the North American Free Trade Agreement (NAFTA). Presidents may urge the public to take action directed at Congress, such as writing legislators to support the president's position. This was a repeated plea and ploy of Ronald Reagan on issues dear to him. But even when presidents merely announce a position and do nothing else to rally the public, the threat of presidential activity to stimulate public pressures if Congress fails to support the president lurks in the background. The presidential announcement of preferences on bills that Congress will vote on include most instances of presidential attempts to translate their popularity and public standing into legislative success.

Many sets of roll calls could be used in this analysis. Several factors affected the choice of roll calls. First, the roll calls should relate to the liberal-conservative continuum that underlies the public opinion series, much as the data on rhetoric used in chapters 4 and 5 did. Second, there should be a historically consistent, reliable, and valid way to identify the liberal or conservative side of the roll call.

I have selected those roll calls on which both the president and the ADA have staked out a position. Using the ADA standard builds some comparability between the roll call indicator and the rhetoric measure of presidential preferences used in the previous chapters. Having a measure of presidential liberalism on roll calls also allows us to compare presidential liberalism with public opinion liberalism, as I did in the previous two chapters. Thus, many of the virtues of using an ADA standard are repeated in this roll call analysis, along with the ease of identifying, without ambiguity, the liberal position on the roll call.[4]

Unlike most other interest group ratings of Congress, the ADA measure extends across the entire period I am studying. Only the Conservative Coalition support score extends as far back in time and also taps into the liberal-conservative division. As Shelley (1983, 18) shows, congressional ADA and Conservative Coalition support scores correlate at levels between −.82 and −.94 at the individual level between 1973 and 1980. In another analysis, Daniels (1989) shows that the ADA rating anchors the liberal end of a liberal-conservative dimension along which interest group ratings have been arrayed. Shaffer (1989) demonstrates the validity and reliability of the ADA rating for congressional roll call analysis, and Smith, Herrera, and Herrera (1990) find that ADA roll calls correlate at .90 with congressional self-reports of ideological position on a mailed questionnaire. ADA roll call scores have been used repeatedly in research on Congress, though less frequently on the presidency.[5]

One virtue of the ADA over the Conservative Coalition scores for my present purposes is the ease of collection for the president. With the ADA standard, all that is required is to match the expressed ADA position with such facts as whether or not the president took a public position on the roll call and which side he took. The Conservative Coalition scoring would require the statistical estimation of Conservative Coalition roll calls for the years in the 1950s, before the standard source, the *Congressional Quarterly,* began its analysis and identification of Conservative Coalition support. Moreover, part of the ADA data have already been collected and presented in usable form. (See King and Ragsdale 1988, 86–87, table 2-17, for a list of presidential ADA support scores from 1960–84. All I had to do was fill in the missing years 1953–59 and 1985–89).[6]

Yet there are some pitfalls to using the ADA standard. First, there are not enough roll calls per year to disaggregate by policy area, as I did in the analysis in chapter 5. Aggregation bias may distort the relationship between presidential roll call positions and public opinion. But the public opinion series is also an aggregate indicator across a host of different policies. The analysis that follows is limited to seeing whether the general tendency of the public to be liberal or conservative—the public mood—affects the general tendency of the president to take liberal or conservative positions on roll calls.

Another treatment would match public opinions on each issue at stake with the president's position. This raises not only daunting data collection problems but comparability problems. The wording of questions does not always closely match the way Congress deals with a particular issue by the time it gets to a roll call. Moreover, questions asked of the public close to the time of the roll call (or even after) may be contaminated by the attempts of policy activists to move public opinion one way or the other. This problem injects severe causality problems into the analysis. The aggregation procedure allows us to extract the "liberalism" of the public and the president without having to raise the issue of comparability. Furthermore, specifying a time lag in the analysis of the ADA scores and the public mood allows us to address the causality issue more satisfactorily.

There are several major critiques of the ADA index that must be addressed here. First, ADA scales, like all interest-group-selected scales, tend to force legislators into bipolar, opposed categories (Fowler 1982; Snyder 1992). The result is that members of Congress tend to look more extreme than they might in fact be. This problem may also hold true for the president. However, this should be a constant problem across time. It should not affect changes in presidential roll call liberalism over time. The criticism of forced extremism is more a problem for cross-sectional than for time series analysis.

Roll calls may imperfectly tap the preferences of presidents and legislators alike. Jackson and Kingdon (1992) argue that ADA scores as indicators of ideology will overstate the impact of ideology on voting and understate the impact of other factors, like constituency interests, because the roll call indexes are in part a function of these other nonideological factors. It is important to remember that in this study I am not equating the presidential ADA roll call score with presidential ideology. In fact, by asking what impact public liberalism has on presidential roll call positions, I am not even using the ADA roll call measure as an indicator of presidential ideology. Rather, following Jackson and Kingdon's suggestion (1992, 815), I have used a more direct indicator based upon presidential speeches—the ideology measures of the past two chapters—while still noting that the rhetoric measure of presidential ideology is an imperfect indicator of presidential beliefs in that it only taps into public statements. All that I claim for the roll call measure is that it taps into the general liberal or conservative positions of presidents on roll calls before Congress.

However, the ADA roll call measure, an aggregate indicator that combines positions across all types of policy areas, is not as amenable to presidential symbolic manipulation as the aggregate measure of overall presidential ideology I used earlier. The rhetoric measure used in chapters 4 and 5 enabled a president to moderate or modulate his stance by offering one sentence supporting the liberal option with the next supporting the conservative one. This is not possible on roll calls. Legislators and presidents are forced to chose between two opposed alternatives, yea or nay. (Overall moderation may be possible by refusing to stake out a position, but silence has its political costs. Members of Congress find themselves electorally vulnerable when they exhibit high levels of vote "absenteeism." Abstaining may alienate both sides of an issue; taking one side over the other may alienate only one group. Moreover, a president who "abstains" or "absents" himself from an important policy debate may generate hostility from a public that expects him to be active on all important policy debates.) Although roll calls are imperfect indicators of preferences, legislators cast ballots on roll calls, not preferences, and presidents must stake out positions on these roll call alternatives in their attempts to influence the policy legitimation process.

Moreover, Congress, not the president, determines what will be brought to the floor. Presidents often stake out positions early in the legislative history of a bill, sometimes even in the State of the Union Address or in previous years. Presidents can only imperfectly predict what will be brought to the floor, when it will be brought to the floor, and what the final bill will look like. Congress quite often amends the president's proposals. Thus, the president is less able to manipulate his symbolic image on roll calls than he was his overall ideological image in his State of the Union Address.[7] Hence, the aggregation properties that enhance the symbolic importance of an activity are less present with the roll call indicator, and consequently we should not witness as strong a presidential response to public opinion as occurred for the measure of overall ideology.

Presidential Liberalism on Roll Calls

Table 6.1 and figure 6.1 present descriptive information on presidential roll call liberalism. Superimposed on the presidential trend line on the figure is the public opinion liberalism series. Both series have been adjusted so that positive values indicate liberalism and negative values conservatism.[8] On the whole, the roll call liberalism series looks much like the rhetoric series presented in the two previous chapters. Those presidents classified as liberal by their rhetoric are similarly liberal in their roll call positions.

TABLE 6.1.   Presidential Roll Call Liberalism, 1953–89

President	Mean	Minimum	Maximum	SD
All	47.2	0.0	100.0	37.5
Democrats	88.2	66.7	100.0	12.6
Republicans	27.4	0.0	83.3	28.0
Eisenhower	61.0	33.3	83.3	18.4
Kennedy	96.3	88.9	100.0	6.4
Johnson	96.0	90.0	100.0	5.5
Nixon	22.5	8.3	50.0	16.2
Ford	14.3	0.0	28.6	20.2
Carter	72.5	66.7	77.8	4.5
Reagan	3.6	0.0	11.1	5.1
Bush	5.3	—	—	—

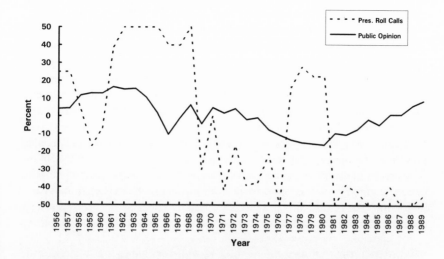

Fig. 6.1. Presidential roll call liberalism and public opinion liberalism, 1953–89. (Data for the roll call series was compiled by the author from various sources [see text for details]. Data for the public opinion series from Stimson 1991.)

Some minor differences exist, however. On roll calls, Johnson and Kennedy are nearly perfect liberals, though Johnson's rhetoric is a degree less liberal than Kennedy's. Carter also appears somewhat more liberal in his roll call positions than in his rhetoric. What we may be witnessing here is the way roll calls force politicians to the extremes, whereas rhetoric allowed presidents to moderate their positions and emphasize some policy areas more than others (which would be a better indication of presidential preferences than roll calls).

For Republicans, Eisenhower stands out as a liberal on both series. This serves as strong confirmation of the validity of the data collections. The other Republican presidents tend to behave similarly in their rhetoric and roll calls, except for a slight tendency to be more moderate in rhetoric than in roll calls, again possibly because of the aggregation bias of the ADA indicator. The greatest Republican gap between rhetoric and roll call is Bush's, a full 37 percent difference, but this is for only one year. Reagan shows only a slight tendency to moderation in his rhetoric compared to his roll call behavior.

Not too much should be made of the percentage differences between presidential rhetorical and roll call liberalism, however. Although the aggregation process creates percentage figures for both series, they are created from different data. The most important point here is the strong relative positioning of the presidents across the two series. Liberals are liberals in both series. The only positional difference is that Carter appears more liberal than Eisenhower in the roll call series, while the reverse was true in the rhetoric series. More importantly, both occupy moderate positions in both series.

Visually, there appears to be no consistent pattern between presidential roll call liberalism and public opinion. At times the two series seem to covary together. For instance, both series seem to indicate increases in liberalism from the late 1950s into the middle 1960s. Then both series head in a conservative direction. But at times the two series seem to head in different directions. By the Carter administration, the presidential series is moving left, while the public opinion series is moving right. Then when Reagan becomes president, the presidential series shifts to the right, while the public opinion series shifts to the left. One cannot discern the causal direction, from public to president or vice versa, or even if a strong causality exists, from visual inspection. The next section tests for the causal relationship between presidential roll call positions and public opinion more systematically and rigorously.

Presidential Roll Call Responsiveness to Public Opinion

In the introduction to this chapter, I developed two views of the possible relationship between presidential positions on roll calls and public opinion. The first, derived from the theory being tested here, argues that presidents will not be responsive to public opinion. Thus, we will not observe presidents getting more or less liberal as the public gets more or less liberal. The second perspective, derived from the idea that presidents need public opinion to persuade Congress, suggests that presidents will be at least somewhat responsive to public opinion.

To determine the causal relationship between presidential rhetoric and public opinion, I lagged public opinion. I will follow the same procedure to isolate the causality between presidential roll call positions and public opinion. There is one important difference here, however. We were able to specify exactly the timing of the State of the Union Address. The Address comes early in each calendar year, never later than March. Both the roll call and public opinion series are based on aggregating observations (roll calls, public opinion polls). Thus, they represent annual averages. The lack of timing precision may attenuate the relationship between public opinion and presidential roll call behavior. Thus, not finding a relationship between lagged public opinion and presidential roll call positions may be a function of either nonresponsiveness, as the theory of limited responsiveness suggests, or this attenuation problem. To help control for this possibility, I will also check the relationship between presidential roll call positions and nonlagged public opinion. Only if both the lagged and nonlagged tests show no relationship can we be confident in accepting the nonresponsiveness hypothesis.[9]

TABLE 6.2. The Impact of Public Opinion Liberalism on Presidential Roll Call Liberalism, 1956–89

Coefficients	Public Opinion (Lagged)	Public Opinion (Nonlagged)
Constant		
b	43.25	43.49
SE	19.47	17.52
t	2.22	2.48
Public opinion		
b	−.13	.92
SE	.29	1.02
t	−.45	.92
R^2/Adj. R^2/Rho	.29/.27/.73	.36/.34/.72

Initial Analysis

Simple correlations begin the analysis. The nonlagged Pearson's correlation between presidential roll call liberalism and public opinion is .23. For an n of 34, this is not significant at the .05 level. The relation between lagged public opinion and roll calls is even weaker at .14.[10] Correlations cannot test causality, nor can they account for time-dependent serialities. Thus, I turn to regression. I first regress presidential roll call liberalism on public opinion liberalism, lagging the public opinion series by one year. Table 6.2 presents the results. First order autocorrelation was detected. A Cochrane-Orcutt correction was applied. Table 6.2 also presents the results for the nonlagged regression.

The results of both estimations support the limited responsiveness theory, not the public opinion resource theory. Presidential roll call positioning displays no responsiveness to public opinion. The coefficient is small and its t value is quite weak in both the lagged and nonlagged estimations. These results continue the thrust of findings reported in chapters 3, 4, and 5.

This bivariate test is open to the same type of challenges as the results of the bivariate relationship between public opinion and presidential ideology. The impact of public opinion on roll call positions may be masked, may be conditional, and/or may be specific to certain policy areas. I will not be able to treat the policy areas critique; there are not enough votes in the ADA index to disaggregate by policy area in any meaningful way. The other challenges, however, can be tested.

Presidents, Public Opinion, and Alternative Sources
of Presidential Roll Call Liberalism

The relationship between presidential roll call liberalism and public opinion may be masked or suppressed because of missing variables in the equation. Controlling for other variables that affect roll call liberalism may help reveal a relationship, if it in fact exists. Three sets of variables may be pertinent here: party, president, and objective conditions. The logic for the party and president variables here is essentially the same as the logic used in chapter 5 when we looked at the impact of party and president on presidential rhetoric. Also, like chapter 5, international, economic, and political conditions may affect the roll call positions that presidents take.

Chapter 5 detected a strong impact of party on presidential ideology. Party may similarly affect the positions that presidents take on roll calls before Congress. Table 6.1, for instance, shows a strong relationship between party and presidential roll call liberalism. Democrats are significantly more liberal on average than Republicans (88.2 to 27.4). Moreover, each Democratic president is more liberal than each Republican president. Even the rhetorically moderate Carter is here more liberal than Eisenhower (72.5 to 61.0) The spread between the parties on roll calls is even greater than it is on rhetoric (61 percent on roll calls to 33 percent on rhetoric), which perhaps is due to the extremism bias that Snyder (1992) details. In any event, we expect party to strongly affect presidential roll call positioning.

Within the parties, however, considerable variance in presidential roll call positions still exists. Eisenhower, for instance, is positioned to the left of center, in contrast to the other Republican presidents who all stand right of center (that is, have less than 50 percent liberal scores). And among the conservative Republicans, a twenty-point spread exists from Nixon (22.5) to Reagan (3.6). Similarly, on the Democratic side, Carter scored about twenty-five percentage points less liberal than his Democratic predecessors, Kennedy and Johnson. These intraparty differences may result from presidential preferences, ideology, or other factors idiosyncratic to particular presidents, as discussed in chapter 5.

It is easy to demonstrate the joint effects of party and president on roll call positions. As party and all the presidential dummy variables cannot be entered into the same equation simultaneously, I had to experiment with combinations of the party and dummy variables. (As no autocorrelation problem was detected, OLS was used to estimate the equation.) The results of that analysis suggest that party, plus three presidential variables—Eisenhower, Carter, and Reagan—account for approximately 90 percent of the variance in presidential roll call positions. The signs for each variable point in the ex-

TABLE 6.3.   **Impact of Party and President on Presidential Roll Call Liberalism, 1953–89**

Variable	b	SE	t
Constant	18.41	3.30	5.58
Party (1 = Democrat)	77.01	5.78	13.31
Eisenhower	43.29	4.83	8.94
Carter	−21.57	6.90	−3.13
Reagan	−14.12	4.83	−2.92
R^2/Adj. R^2/DW d	.91	.90	1.84

pected direction, and all are strongly significant statistically. Table 6.3 presents the results of that analysis.

Presidents may also respond to objective conditions. Throughout this study, we have found the international context to be important in conditioning presidential behavior. Again we may find the presence of war affecting presidential behavior. The two major wars of the period, Korea and Vietnam, both pitted the United States against a communist adversary. To build and maintain support for their war policies, presidents would often stake out anticommunist positions. Doing so pushes them to the right.

Economic conditions may also affect the policies that presidents support and pursue. Throughout, I have focused on the twin macroeconomic problems of inflation and unemployment. Here I suggest that presidents who pursue anti-inflationary policies will generally adopt positions that conservatives support. Liberals are less strongly opposed to inflation than conservatives, and they are even less likely to support anti-inflationary policies, which often hurt the lower and working classes more than the upper classes. In contrast, liberals are more likely than conservatives to push for economic stimulation policies to deal with high unemployment and low economic growth. The stagflation of the 1970s, when both inflation and high unemployment occurred simultaneously, provides a crucial test for the policymaker and helps us identify their "economic ideological" stripes quite clearly. Conservatives should emphasize the inflationary aspects of stagflation; liberals should emphasize unemployment. Inasmuch as presidents are driven to deal with these twin economic ills, they may pursue policies to deal with these problems. Everything else being equal, when faced with inflation, presidents should adopt more conservative, anti-inflationary policies. When faced with unemployment, they may support more liberal, stimulative policies.

I begin this analysis by regressing party, presidential dummy variables, war, inflation, unemployment, and the time point dummies on presidential roll call liberalism. No autocorrelation problem was detected. OLS was used to estimate the equation. As we mentioned in previous analyses, one cannot enter all these variables into the equation at one time. There are too many such variables, and the combination of the party and president variables produces a singular matrix. Thus, considerable experimentation was used to arrive at a reduced form equation, which is shown in table 6.4. The reduced-form equation is highly stable given this set of variables.

The results suggest that party, Eisenhower, Carter, and Nixon affect presidential roll call position taking. Over 90 percent of the variance is explained. As expected, results suggest that Democrats are more liberal than Republicans; that, once controlling for party, Eisenhower is more liberal than the average president; and that the more liberal the president's rhetoric, the more liberal his roll call positions. Similarly, Carter is found to be more conservative, controlling for party, and Nixon is mildly more liberal than other Republicans. Each of these effects is quite pronounced.

Next I add public opinion liberalism (both lagged and unlagged) to the equation. I only display results for the reduced-form equation. The results, also presented in table 6.4, are quite clear—public opinion liberalism has no impact on presidential roll call liberalism. Presidents do not seem to respond *directly* to public opinion when expressing a position on a roll call before Congress. This finding is consistent with the theory I have developed, not the public opinion resource idea.

Still, we can make the case that public opinion indirectly affects presidential roll call positions. Recall that public opinion had an effect on presidential ideology. Public opinion effects may be filtered through this variable. If presidential roll call positions follow from what they publicly offered, and if those public offerings were in part a function of public opinion, then an indirect influence path of public opinion to presidential roll call positions may exist. Table 6.4 presents results of this analysis, which enters the presidential ideology variable into the basic reduced-form equation.

Here we find that presidential rhetorical ideology affects presidential roll call positions, but marginally so. Although significant, the variable suggests that each one-point change in rhetorical ideology leads to a .32 percent change in roll call liberalism. Furthermore, the equation shows no boost in predictive power by adding this variable; it draws down the predictive power of most of the other variables in the equation. A few, notably party and Eisenhower, show large increases in their standard errors, indicating that inclusion of the rhetorical ideology variable is collinear with them, a finding that makes sense in that both were found to be strong predictors of rhetorical liberalism. Adding public opinion to this new equation has no effect on these results. The important

TABLE 6.4. Impact of Public Opinion, Party, President, and Context on Presidential Roll Call Liberalism Model, 1956–89

	1			2			3			4		
	b	SE	t	b	SE	t	b	SE	t	b	SE	t
Constant	5.70	3.44	1.66	16.34	25.11	.65	16.19	32.01	.51	.92	3.84	.24
Party	90.41	5.29	17.08	92.14	5.14	17.93	91.49	6.30	14.53	71.47	9.73	7.34
Ike	50.26	6.15	8.18	46.15	6.13	7.52	51.60	7.45	6.93	33.99	9.21	3.69
Nixon	16.83	5.78	2.91	19.18	4.69	4.09	17.25	6.01	2.88	10.48	6.10	1.72
Carter	-23.64	6.98	-3.39	-26.27	7.84	-3.35	-25.99	10.05	-2.59	-17.84	7.02	-2.54
Public opinion $(t-1)$				-.12	.26	-.44						
Public opinion							-.11	.33	-.33			
President's ideology										.32	.14	2.26
R^2	.92			.94			.92			.93		
Adj. R_2	.91			.93			.91			.92		
DW d (Rho)	2.03			(-.27)			2.08			2.04		
Lagrange multiplier	.85			.80			.96			.66		
Equation type	OLS			AR1			OLS			OLS		

point, again, is that this lends support to the limited responsiveness idea I am promoting in this study.

One last possibility exists: that the contexts under which presidents govern may condition how much they need public support. Under the proper conditions, presidents may be responsive to public opinion in the policy legitimation process. The next section turns to that question.

Context and Presidential Roll Call Responsiveness to Public Opinion

Presidents may need public support at some times more than at others. They are more likely to need public support when they are politically weak and vulnerable and when other avenues to legislative influence are closed to them. Seeking public support becomes a fallback strategy when all else fails or is not a viable option. Ironically, such weak presidents are not likely to possess high popularity levels or strong public backing. Responding to public opinion becomes the one possible option for weak presidents to build political capital and influence. It is not a guaranteed road to influence because weak presidents have a hard time rallying and sustaining public support, but it may be the only option open to them.

There are two major sources of political weakness and vulnerability. The first is rooted in the bad political choices that presidents make. They may have damaged relations with key members of Congress through ignorance, neglect, or stupidity. They make have taken unviable positions. They may have made strategic or tactical mistakes. These kinds of problems may be peculiar to a particular president or a particular issue before Congress.

The other major source of vulnerability concerns the context that the president faces. Economic and political contexts may systematically heighten vulnerability across presidents. This is the source of vulnerability that I will treat in this section. In particular, vulnerability increases when the economy is not performing well, when the president is not popular, when his party does not control Congress, and when the president is in dire need of popular support. Presidents running for reelection or those who attained the presidency without being elected may be in greater need of public support than other presidents at other times. I expect that when these vulnerability-causing contexts exist, presidents will display greater responsiveness to public opinion than when these contexts do not exist. When they do not exist the logic of limited responsiveness takes hold, and presidents pursue the policy choices they deem best.

The public places great pressures on the president to ensure a healthy economy. Presidents who are not able to do this often find their popularity levels sinking and their chances for reelection fading. To partially divert public anger away from them, the president may follow public opinion when the economy is in a downturn. During the recession that plagued his tenure George Bush may be faulted for not following such a path. Public suspicion that Bush did not care about the average person's economic woes mounted, and he lost his reelection bid.

Political contexts also affect the president's ability to bargain with Congress and, hence, his need for public support. Bond and Fleisher (1990) and Edwards (1989) demonstrate the impact of political contexts on presidential support in Congress. Party distributions in the legislature clearly affect congressional support of the president. Presidents may be more responsive to public opinion when their party does not control Congress because they hope to use public opinion to pressure Congress to accede to the president's point of view.

The president's own position with the public may affect his responsiveness to public opinion. Presidents who are not very popular or were elected with slim margins may not feel they can stray too far from public opinion. Instead, they must prove that they can build public support, that they speak for the public. Presidents with wide victory margins or high popularity levels enjoy a larger comfort zone. They do not have to flatter every public whim. If they oppose public opinion on an issue, they may feel they can move the public to their position. And even if they cannot convert the public to their stand, popular presidents may feel that they will be able to regenerate public support some time in the future.

Nonelected presidents may be the most vulnerable of all to public opinion. Lacking the legitimacy of being the voter's choice, even by a narrow margin, nonelected presidents may not be able to stray far from the public's pulse, lest their weak position erode further. Thus, Gerald Ford may have made a major mistake when he pardoned Richard Nixon. He never seemed to recover the fragile public support that he had upon taking office; because of the pardon he was unable to legitimate his leadership.

Lastly, the cycle of elections may condition presidents to respond to the public. Two streams of research suggest that as the election nears, presidents may come to pay greater attention to public opinion and may shift to appear closer to public opinion. First, Brody and Sigelman (1983) demonstrate that one can predict election outcomes with presidential approval ratings. Popular presidents are more likely to be reelected than unpopular presidents. Second, literature on legislative responsiveness finds that as elections near, especially for legislators with long terms like senators, legislators will moderate their positions, closing the gap between public preferences and the roll call choices that legislators make (Bernstein 1988; Elling 1982; Kuklinski 1978; Thomas 1985; Wright and Berkman 1986, 1988). Thus, we can hypothesize that presidential responsiveness to public opinion will peak in reelection years in order

TABLE 6.5. Impact of Context on Presidential Responsiveness to Public Opinion, 1956–89

Variable	b	SE	t	Rho	R^2
High unemployment * Public opinion	−.13	1.11	−.12	.72	.29
High inflation * Public opinion	−.14	1.63	−.09	.73	.28
Low popularity * Public opinion	.008	.02	.39	.72	.31
Low popular vote * Public opinion	.02	.02	.88	.72	.36
Year 4 * Public opinion	.31	.29	1.07	.72	.34
Not elected * Public opinion	1.90	1.80	1.05	.68	.33
Minority control * Public opinion	1.84	1.17	1.57	.74	.39

to boost presidential popularity and enhance the incumbent's reelection chances.[11]

To test these ideas I create an interaction term between the context variables and public opinion liberalism. In each case, when the vulnerable condition does not hold, the variable is set to zero. Otherwise, it takes on the value of the public opinion variable. This is the same process I used in chapter 5, although on a different set of criterion variables. The results are displayed in table 6.5. Each line of the table is based on a different estimation, seven in all, one for each context-public opinion interaction.

The results give no support to the hypothesis that vulnerable conditions motivate presidents to respond to public opinion. Not one of the seven interaction terms proved to be statistically significant. This finding holds whether we use lagged or nonlagged public opinion and whether we control for the standard set of variables being used here: party, president, time point dummies, and the international and economic contexts.

Without controls, one variable or context begins to look promising: the interaction between chamber control of Congress and public opinion. When the president's party does not control both houses of Congress, presidents are nearly 2 percent more responsive to public opinion than when the president's party holds majorities in both chambers, but the variable does not reach comfortable levels of statistical significance ($t = 1.57$), and the practical impact may be trivial. It is unlikely that either the public or political elites will notice a shift of 2 percent.

The picture changes when controls are applied to this variable. Now, when the president's party does not control Congress, presidents become .89 percent less liberal for each one-point liberal increase in public opinion. As the public is getting more liberal, the president is getting less liberal.[12] This finding counters the presidential responsiveness hypothesis, though it is not necessarily contrary to the limited responsiveness theory. Opposition party control of Congress may pull presidents away from public opinion, as they must bargain with the congressional opposition.

The main finding, however, is that context does not seem to affect presidential responsiveness to public opinion. No matter the context, the logic of policy control moves the president to adopt policies that he prefers even if the public dislikes that position.

Conclusions

In this chapter I looked at presidential responsiveness to public opinion in the policy legitimation process. Findings were consistent with the theory of limited responsiveness—presidents were not found to be responsive to public opinion when taking positions on roll call votes before Congress. This finding was not upset when control variables were added, nor did it change when we looked at the economic and political context.

This set of findings repeated those found in chapters 3, 4, and 5, where we looked at presidential substantive rhetoric and policy formulation. Policy concerns, party preferences, and objective conditions affect presidential decisions in each of these substantively focused policy-making processes. The only time when presidents will display responsiveness to public opinion is when they can do so symbolically and when symbolic implications and opportunities for manipulation outweigh substantive implications. However, we all know of cases in which presidents seemingly caved in to public pressures. The next two chapters present case studies that allow us to peer more closely into the process of presidential responsiveness and nonresponsiveness to public opinion.

An Addendum on "Dynamic Representation"

As I was completing this book, an article by James Stimson, Michael MacKuen, and Robert Erikson was published in *American Political Science Review* (1995). Titled "Dynamic Representation," the paper has special relevance to my study because it explicitly deals with presidential responsiveness to public opinion.

Stimson, MacKuen, and Erikson create a measure of presidential liberalism that combines information on presidential supporters in Congress, presidential stands on key votes that the ADA has classified as tests of liberalism, and solicitor general amicus briefs. Using a dimensional analysis, they extract a latent variable that they call presidential liberalism. Importantly, one component of their measure, the ADA key votes, closely resembles my measure of presidential roll call liberalism (cf. fig. 6.1 with their fig. 4C, 553).

Their pertinent finding for my present purposes is that their latent presidential liberalism variable seems responsive to public opinion, specifically the public mood liberalism indicator, properly lagged. This result seems to fly against my finding, reported in this chapter, that presidential roll call liberalism is unresponsive to public opinion. Who is right? Can we reconcile these differences?

First the difference in findings is not attributable to different models. Although it is improper to do so, for reasons that Stimson, MacKuen, and Erikson give, I regress their latent liberalism variable on party, Eisenhower, unemployment, and public opinion, the variables found to affect presidential roll call liberalism in this chapter. This regression estimation finds latent presidential liberalism to be responsive to public opinion (simple OLS was used; no autocorrelation was detected.)

Latent Presidential Liberalism $= 25.95(3.84)$ Constant
$+\ 32.94(1.75)$ Party Dummy
$+\ 14.30\ (2.58)$ Eisenhower Dummy
$+\ .006(.57)$ Unemployment
$+\ .32(.009)$ Public Opinion$(t-1)$

$R^2 = .94$ Adjusted $R^2 = .93$ DW d $= 1.58$

In another regression estimation, using a different model and a different measure of latent liberalism, Stimson, MacKuen, and Erikson repeat the finding of presidential responsiveness.

I argue that the relationship between the latent variable and my roll call indicator of presidential liberalism is similar to that between the overall measure of presidential ideology and the policy-specific ones that were the focus of chapters 4 and 5.[13] Recall that in that chapter we found presidents to be responsive to public opinion for overall ideology but not policy-specific ideology.

In other words, latent presidential liberalism has extracted the liberal tendency of presidential behavior from several specific presidential behaviors. Viewing the variable from the perspective of the mix of symbolism and substance, the process of creating the latent variable, like the process of aggregation of the overall ideology measure, moves a step away from the substantive details of policy-making, highlighting the variable's symbolic aspects. The latent variable is a very good symbolic indicator, but its own aggregation or averaging process mutes the substantive implications of each policy decision or type of policy decision that constitutes it.

This argument reconciles the Stimson, MacKuen, Erikson finding of presidential responsiveness with my finding of nonresponsiveness. The difference is a function of the substantive-symbolic nature of the variables when compared. The process of aggregation extracts the symbolic component while muting substantive details. All the aggregate measures (overall ideology, latent liberalism) have substantive import, but when compared to their constituent elements, the symbolic element is pronounced. Thus, there is no necessary contradiction between Stimson, MacKuen, and Erikson and me.

The next two chapters will present case studies that highlight even further how disaggregation toward the policy itself leads us and presidents to focus more on substantive details of policy-making than when considering aggregate indicators. The case studies also provide us with another test of presidential responsiveness to public opinion.

CHAPTER 7

Presidential Policy Decisions and Responsiveness to Public Opinion I: Eisenhower, Kennedy, and Nixon

The previous chapters found only limited presidential responsiveness to public opinion. For the most part, presidential responsiveness to public opinion in the policy-making process seems more apparent when presidential activities are strongly symbolic and when such symbolism seems to override substance. Thus, presidents display some responsiveness to public concerns, such that when the public is concerned about foreign affairs or economic conditions presidents react by increasing their attention to those policy concerns. Also, presidential ideology, as measured through liberal and conservative statements in their State of the Union Addresses, is responsive to public opinion. Both of these presidential activities, attention to policy areas and general ideological stance, I argued, have strong symbolic components; the former is almost pure symbolism, while the latter ranks symbolism highly important.

But presidential responsiveness seems to ebb at this point. Presidents do not seem to construct policies with any systematic attention to the public in mind. When we consider the ideological leanings of presidents on specific policy areas, little responsiveness to the public is noted, nor do we find much direct responsiveness when looking at the positions that presidents take on roll calls before Congress. These findings of nonresponsiveness, while consistent with the theoretical argument being advanced here, are still curious. Almost any casual observer of presidential behavior can point to instances in which presidents seemingly caved in to public opinion and changed their course of action because of public pressures.

Although the analysis in the previous chapters has attempted to disaggregate to specific policy areas, that analysis is still essentially aggregate, focusing on sets of related policies, not individual policy decisions. This aggregation may mask whatever responsive tendencies presidents exhibit. It may mask all sorts of circumstances that may affect presidential responsiveness on particular policy decisions. Hypothetically, presidents may be highly responsive to public opinion, but only under certain conditions. Aggregating across many policy decisions, as I did in the previous chapters, may indiscriminately lump together policies that possess these responsive conditions with those that do not, thereby statistically weakening any presidential responsiveness to the public.

In this chapter, I disaggregate the analysis to the specific case level. Can we detect presidential responsiveness to public opinion on specific decisions? What factors at the decision level are associated with presidential responsiveness to public opinion?

This case analysis has another goal. The statistical analysis is generally unable to tease out the processes and mechanisms that promote or inhibit presidential responsiveness. Even within policy areas, presidents may be responsive to the public sometimes, but not responsive at other times. Moreover, the statistical finding of lack of responsiveness should be interpreted to mean that sometimes presidents are responsive, other times they are not, and at still other times they may be counterresponsive. All possibilities can exist at the specific policy decision level but become obscured when aggregating, as the quantitative analysis did. All the nonresponsiveness finding means is that there is no *systematic aggregate pattern* of presidential responsiveness.

The case analysis should help us peer more deeply into the factors that promote or inhibit presidential responsiveness. In the end, while overall responsiveness is important, it is the actions of presidents with regard to specific policies that we are interested in. The quantitative analysis is important for setting some theoretical boundaries or expectations for the case analysis, making that analysis more theoretically focused and efficient (King, Keohane, and Verba 1994).

Case Selection and the Logic of Comparative Case Analysis

There are limits to case studies as theory generators and hypothesis testers. Single case studies provide no comparative framework, and thus the research cannot separate the unique from the general, a necessary step in theory building. Moreover, single case studies are plagued by the overdetermination problem; there are more available explanations than cases. Comparative case analysis can help, but special attention must be given to case selection. One must be sensitive to the population from which one is sampling and the similarity of population and sample characteristics. A nonrepresentative set of cases, one that may over- or underrepresent certain characteristics found in the population, can still be useful as long as one knows how the selected cases differ from the population. Also, selecting cases to highlight certain expected theoretical relationships may be a useful way of boosting the theoretical power of comparative case studies while retaining the richness and insight that case studies offer (see the discussion in King, Keohane, and Verba 1994 for more on these points).

The theoretical question at hand is whether presidents are responsive to public opinion. In selecting cases, I begin by holding one variable constant—public opinion. Each case or issue must be very visible to the public. Quite likely, pressures for responsiveness decline as the issue becomes less visible to the public. As we have not yet unearthed much strong presidential respon-siveness to public opinion in substantive policy-making activities, it is theoret-ically important to build a set of circumstances that would maximize public pressures on the president. If the president is still nonresponsive, then the argument suggested in the previous chapters, that of nonresponsiveness, is bolstered. In other words, how responsive are presidents to public opinion when the issue is visible to the public? This also means that the selected cases are likely to be historically well known.

Second, the cases focus on actual policy choice, not on the early agenda-setting processes or other symbolic activities, though the symbolic aspects of policy choice will be duly noted. The quantitative results of the earlier chap-ters discerned presidential responsiveness to public concern in agenda setting when activities are highly symbolically driven. It is redundant to follow up on that with the case analysis. Not much new may be learned.

Moreover, the limitation of polling data constrain the time frame of the case selection. Polling data are necessary in testing the responsiveness hypothesis. Reliance on elite, journalistic, or historical assumptions about the public is just too crude a method for us to test the responsiveness hypothesis. Ideally, we want to compare presidential actions to public preferences on a policy area over the life history of that decision, not just at any one point in time. Only through such detailed resolutions over time can we distinguish the responsiveness from the leadership hypothesis. Detailed resolutions allow us to establish who changed first, the president or public opinion, and if the other changed in the same direction. If presidents changed, followed by the public, we can make a case for leadership effects. Determining who changed first will give us one important piece of information that will help us make causal statements of responsiveness versus leadership effects.

Thus, as in the quantitative analysis, I focus on the Eisenhower to Bush era, adding cases from the Clinton years as well. I can therefore say little about the impact of public pressures in the earlier era when polls were not so readily available (and consequently public opinion pressures may not have been as strong).

I also attempted to select as many cases as possible to assure as much variance in presidential response and other factors, given limitations of time and documentation. Eight cases were chosen:

1. Eisenhower and *Sputnik*
2. Kennedy and civil rights
3. Kennedy and the tax cut
4. Nixon and wage and price controls
5. Reagan and Social Security cuts
6. Bush and the extension of unemployment benefits
7. Clinton and gays in the military
8. Clinton and NAFTA

These cases vary in one important respect—sometimes presidents seem to cave in to public pressures (Reagan and Social Security, Nixon and controls); other times they seem resistant to public pressures (Clinton and NAFTA); and other cases are more ambiguous. This gives us considerable variance on the dependent variable, presidential responsiveness. Thus, with public opinion held somewhat constant, why do presidents sometimes respond to it but other times do not?

The reader will note that the quality of the case studies changes with the availability of material. In particular, the earlier cases (Eisenhower, Kennedy) contain sparser public opinion records, though the historical documentation of these events is quite thorough and rich. In contrast, the later cases suffer from less well-developed histories and documentation. In their place, I often had to rely on journalistic accounts, which can be unreliable and thin. But, these later cases presented me with a wealth of public opinion documentation because of the proliferation of polling that has occurred in the past decade or so. The Roper Center at the University of Connecticut, which houses the complete record of known polls, has made the task of tracking down polls much easier. Moreover, the availability of on-line access to this archive through the Lexis system has been invaluable. Because of the length and number of case studies, the material is presented in two chapters, divided historically: the Eisenhower, Kennedy, and Nixon cases presented in this chapter and the Reagan, Bush, and Clinton cases in the following chapter.

Eisenhower and *Sputnik*

In October 1957 the Soviet Union launched the world's first satellite, *Sputnik,* into earth orbit. It repeated that accomplishment one month later with an even larger satellite. These feats rocked the United States and the Eisenhower administration, and they provide us with a good case with which to study presidential reactions to public opinion.

First, the *Sputnik*s served as focusing events for the mass public, raising fears about U.S. security. Focusing events are often important in catalyzing attention to a problem. The literature on agenda building suggests that major focusing events may be irresistible, requiring that political leaders act to assuage public concerns (Edelman 1964; Kingdon 1984; Walker 1977). Moreover, such theories suggests that focusing events serve as opportunities for policy entrepreneurs to get their issues onto the agenda. The *Sputnik* crisis had all the earmarks of a major focusing event.

The public seemed unsettled and concerned about U.S. security and the ability of the educational system to provide the scientists and brainpower that a strong U.S. defense would require. Democrats with presidential ambitions fueled these fears, seeing an opportunity to blame Eisenhower for the Soviet lead in space and rocketry and for letting the United States fall behind. Much as the Democrats had been blamed for letting China fall to the Communists, they now had an issue with which to attack the Republicans and demonstrate to the American people that they were not soft on Communism nor too weak hearted to provide for a strong defense (Divine 1993, 77).

Second, the *Sputnik* crisis is a good one by which to examine presidential responsiveness to public opinion because Eisenhower was less impressed and worried about the Soviet "lead" in space than the average American and many in Congress. He preferred a less extreme course of action. How well did Eisenhower resist these public pressures for strong, swift action? How able was he to bend the public to his vision and policy prescriptions, thereby leading the public in a direction that he felt was better for the nation?

Public Opinion and *Sputnik*

It is somewhat difficult to assess with existing survey data the exact nature of public reactions to *Sputnik*. *Sputnik* itself is not an issue, but it had ramifications for other policy areas, including defense, education, and the federal budget. During late 1957 and 1958, other issues, including the economy, which was slipping into recession, attracted more direct public attention. Yet through part of 1957 and 1958, a small but measurable segment of the population saw *Sputnik* as the "most important problem" facing the nation, as reported in Gallup polls, though it is quite hard to ascertain exactly what these respondents meant.

In the weeks immediately following the first *Sputnik* launch, 6 percent of the public cited *Sputnik* at the most important problem facing the nation (Gallup poll, October 10–15, 1957). In early January 1958, after the Soviets had successfully launched their second satellite and several U.S. attempts to launch a satellite into orbit had failed, the number climbed to 11 percent (Gallup poll, January 2–7, 1958). But by March 1958 it dropped to 7 percent, and by early 1959 it had dipped further, to 2 percent, by which time the United States had shot one satellite into earth orbit (Gallup poll, March 6–11, 1958; February, 4–9, 1959).[1]

Although these numbers may seem small, they need to be put into perspective. First of all, the Gallup question allowed the respondent only one answer. Had the question been posed so that respondents were asked to name all important problems, it is likely that a larger number would have cited *Sputnik*. Second, considering the overriding importance of defense and the economy to public opinion, that any other problem could get identified as the most important problem indicates *Sputnik's* relative importance. More important, however, is how *Sputnik* affected American attitudes about other related policy issues, especially defense.

The *Sputniks* seemed to have weakened American's sense of defense security. Americans expressed a broad feeling that U.S. defense policies needed to be reviewed. In a November 1957 Gallup poll, 53 percent of respondents were dissatisfied with U.S. defense policies, saying it was time to take a new look at them. Only 26 percent professed satisfaction, and 21 percent held no opinion (Gallup poll, November 7–12, 1957).

Given the public's high regard for Eisenhower, a regard built primarily on his military background, reputation, and handling of the Korean conflict, these figures portended major problems for the Eisenhower administration. The foundation upon which his public support was built was being questioned. This opened an entry for the Democratic attack on Eisenhower and the Republicans, and the public's concerns about U.S. security could then be used as a campaign issue in the upcoming midterm elections and perhaps the 1960 presidential contest. Thus, Eisenhower had strong reasons to try to blunt the effect of *Sputnik* on his administration and counter the Democratic threat. One option open to him was to respond swiftly and forcefully, in effect caving in to public fears. This was not the course he took.

Eisenhower's Policy Reactions to *Sputnik*

Two factors determined much of Eisenhower's reactions. First, he was diametrically opposed to allowing the federal budget deficit to grow. Second, his own intelligence information indicated that the Soviets were not as advanced in rocketry as the nation thought, but he refused to air that information for national security reasons. Not doing so allowed public pressure on him to mount and persist; he withstood that pressure as much as possible.

Perhaps most central to Eisenhower's belief system was that he should not let the budget run into deficit. Throughout his presidential tenure he fought to restrain all types of spending, including that for defense, arguing that too much federal spending would harm the economy, which was the foundation for all defense efforts. To Eisenhower, a bankrupt nation could not pay for defense. Thus, he often sided with his treasury secretary, George Humphrey, in restraining spending of all types (Divine 1993, 19).

A second factor led Eisenhower to a cautious reaction to *Sputnik:* based on the best available evidence, he did not believe that the Soviets were as advanced in rocketry as their spectacular successes suggested. This belief was rooted in two facts. First, the United States had a long-standing commitment to rocket and missile development dating to the Truman administration, and all indications were that the programs were coming along. The United States maintained two missile programs, one run by the military under the director-ship of Wernher von Braun, the other run by civilians, with science as its main goal. Thus, Eisenhower felt that the United States already possessed the programs necessary for missile development.

More important, direct information, gathered by the U-2 spy planes that had flown over the USSR, revealed that the Soviet missile capability was not as far along as many had assumed and feared. That data, which Eisenhower kept secret from the public, showed that the Soviets were only in the early stages of testing Intercontinental Ballistic Missiles (ICBMs) and had not deployed any as of late 1957 (Divine 1993, 41–43). Without such a capability, the Soviet threat to U. S. defenses was not altered much by *Sputnik* alone.

Eisenhower refused to reveal these data to the public, thus "robbing him of his most telling response to his critics" (Divine 1993, 41). His refusal to do so was based on the need to continue the U-2 flights until a space satellite capable of replacing the valuable U-2s was available. Also, he wanted to avoid increasing tensions with the Soviets who objected to such flights over their airspace, although the United States publicly denied they took place.[2]

Despite these two bulwarks against overreacting to *Sputnik,* Eisenhower found that his exhortations to the nation that there was little to worry about had little effect on the mass public or his critics (Divine 1993, 68). He decided on several measured responses. They included increases in defense spending for missile programs, a reorganization of the Defense Department, the creation of a civilian space agency to prepare for a space launch to match and surpass *Sputnik,* and reforms in federal support for education. In each case Eisenhower resisted hasty action, yet in each case he finally moved further than he had first wanted to.

Across the defense budgets of 1958 and 1959, Eisenhower allowed in-creases in defense spending, especially for missile programs. In each exer-cise, he fought to hold down growth in such spending, but the public mood, plus the massive Republican defeats in the 1958 midterm elections, weak-ened his position with Congress immensely. He reasoned that if he fought with the military too hard, they would appeal to Congress. Thus, he accepted modest increases, hoping to satisfy them and keep them from seeking higher requests from what he felt was a fiscally irresponsible Congress (Divine 1993, 199–203).

Eisenhower did seek a reorganization of the Department of Defense, however. He wanted to end interservice rivalry over missile development, feeling that such competition lead to too much duplication and was wasteful (Divine 1993, 123–43). He wanted to upgrade the power of the secretary of defense to control, centralize, and run the missile programs. In this case, Eisenhower's actions were not a reaction to *Sputnik*. Rather, *Sputnik* created the conditions for him to seek a policy goal that he had long advocated. Defense reorganization came, and while he did not get everything he wanted, he was able to secure the creation of the post of director of defense research and engineering. This effectively centralized missile development programs, reducing the degree of interservice competition, so that the three branches would not go on developing their own missile programs without any sense of an "integrated national effort" (Divine 1993, 142).

A third major policy response to *Sputnik* was the establishment of a civilian space agency. Originally, Eisenhower opposed having both a military and a civilian missile program. His option was to develop only the former, with a reconnaissance satellite that could photograph the Soviet Union as the major goal (Divine 1993, 100). Public pressure for a dramatic space effort like the Soviet *Sputnik* intensified, however, with the final goal being manned space exploration. Scientists debated the manned effort but also lobbied for a scientifically based space effort. In the end, public and scientific pressure won out.

Eisenhower seemed to have a change of heart, and enthusiastically supported a civilian space agency, once his trusted adviser, James Killian, president of MIT, came up with a proposal that he liked. It is not clear why this change occurred. The scientists, like Killian, may have made a convincing case for science to Eisenhower. Furthermore, Killian convinced Eisenhower that duplication between the military and civilian programs could be overcome if the civilian agency were given "the dominating position with respect to space activities" (Divine 1992, 104).

Second, Eisenhower seemed to want to move quickly on this proposal because Democrats in Congress, especially Lyndon Johnson, were bent on a civilian space effort. By doing so, Eisenhower would perhaps be able to control the structure of the agency, the relationship between the military and civilian programs, and the overall cost, about which he was greatly concerned.

Lastly, public pressure for such an effort was intense. Once the United States launched a successful space satellite, public demand mounted to take away the Soviet lead. Eisenhower seemed to sense that neither he nor the nation could absorb another blow to national prestige, and thus the United States had to compete with the Soviets in space (Divine 1993, 109–10). But even behind this reasoning was the national security rationale, for Eisenhower believed the space effort could help the United States develop a reconnaissance satellite to replace the U-2, one of his top priorities (Divine 1993, 110).

The last policy front on which Eisenhower took some action in the aftermath of *Sputnik* concerned federal aid for education. Again, Eisenhower's fiscal stripes showed through quite clearly. He opposed any massive effort by the federal government, and he refused to allow the federal government to become a major source of school funding, which he felt was a local responsibility. But he recognized a need for federal help, too.

Like many in the nation, Eisenhower recognized that the United States would require more scientists and engineers than it was then producing to support the nation's defense and economic development, but he also held more general educational values, pointing out that it was important to educate young Americans so they would be "equipped to live in an age of intercontinental ballistic missiles" (Divine 1993, 55).

Thus, Eisenhower supported increased funding for the National Science Foundation (NSF) for basic research and to the Department of Health, Education, and Welfare (HEW) for college scholarships and fellowships and for high school and college equipment and supplies, mostly aimed at science and engineering. But he opposed a broad-based school construction program, and he stressed that he did not support a permanent federal role, promoting these as temporary measures (Divine 1993, 91). He signed the bill creating the National Defense Education Act, which authorized federal expenditures of about $1 billion, spread across four years, and by doing so effectively blocked for the time being "the attempt to set up a large-scale college scholarship program that could mark the beginning of a permanent federal role in higher education" (Divine 1993, 165).

How responsive was Eisenhower to public opinion? A definitive answer is impossible, yet Eisenhower showed some responsiveness to public opinion, especially with regard to a civilian space effort. And while each of the policies that he finally signed off on may have been more than he wanted, he did forestall even larger responses, such as those that Democrats in Congress advocated. With declining popularity and a national recession, as well as strong Democratic challenges, Eisenhower was in no position to resist public opinion completely. These factors, as well as his unwillingness to use the U-2 data, frustrated his ability to lead public opinion as successfully as he might have. That he succumbed to some public pressure was probably inevitable; that he resisted such pressure under these circumstances, never fully caving into it, may be the more important part of this story.

Kennedy and Civil Rights

When John Kennedy entered office in 1961, neither he nor the public placed civil rights very high on the agenda. The lack of public concern with civil rights in part explains the low priority that Kennedy gave to that issue, but the context of Kennedy's election and his strategic position in Congress are also part of the story. Furthermore, Kennedy himself was not personally very committed to civil rights upon assuming the presidency.

About the only issue that engaged Kennedy was the Soviet challenge. He was rabidly anticommunist and scored points in the 1960 presidential election campaign by charging the Eisenhower administration with permitting a missile gap to develop. His view of civil rights focused on its possible impact on the international competition between the United States and the U.S.S.R., not as a domestic issue of value in itself. His inaugural address omitted any reference to civil rights until advisor Harrison Wofford convinced him to put one in. He then proceeded to insert two words concerning domestic civil rights within a reference to global human rights (Reeves 1993, 39). Kennedy did not think that civil rights was his biggest problem early on. As he saw them, his biggest political troubles "centered on whether he was tough enough with the Russians and their friends in Cuba" (Reeves 1993, 271).

Kennedy's narrow election and the position of Southern Democrats in Congress also influenced the low place he gave civil rights. His slim election victory increased his worries about reelection in 1964; he felt he could not afford to alienate any major constituency. Civil rights, however, pitted two elements of the Democratic Party against each other, southerners and liberal civil rights advocates. Taking a strong stand would only cost him the support of either or both. Thus, he tried to steer a course between the two, showing some support for civil rights expansion, but not so much or so ardently that he would alienate southerners. At bottom, Kennedy feared that his personal involvement in civil rights would lead to defeat in 1964 (Reeves 1993, 467–68).

Southern Democratic support in Congress was critical to his legislative program. The faction was a potent force within the Democratic Party, holding many key committee posts, including the House Rules Committee. In the 1950s, southern Senators had not been adverse to using the filibuster to derail civil rights legislation or to hold other legislation hostage so they might kill civil rights proposals. Kennedy rightfully feared the same fate for his legislative program. In 1963, after he introduced a major civil rights bill, his fears became reality.

Without a large electoral mandate and with the strategic position held by Southern Democrats in Congress, Kennedy would require strong public support before he would push on civil rights. Throughout the first two and one-half years of his tenure, however, public concern with civil rights was minimal. On Gallup's "Most Important Problem" question, the percentage citing civil rights as the nation's most important problem usually hovered at less than ten percent. The 10 percent barrier was broken in October 1962, during the period of controversy and publicity surrounding James Meredith's attempt to enroll at the University of Mississippi. At this peak, only 11 percent cited civil rights as the nation's preeminent problem. The summer before, while the Freedom Rides were going on, public opinion was more concerned with other problems, especially the international situation and competition with the Soviets. As Burke Marshall, a Kennedy advisor heavily active in the civil rights events of the period, remarked, "the Negro and his problems were still pretty invisible to the country as a whole," in 1962 (quoted in Bernstein 1991, 102). It was not until summer 1963 that civil rights became a top public concern.

Given this context, Kennedy was not active on the civil rights front. For the most part, he reacted to events while trying to steer a course between civil rights advocates and southern resisters to those efforts. Kennedy viewed the job of president as reactive, responding to unpredictable forces and events (Reeves 1993, 480). He aimed to postpone political action on civil rights, but events, like the Freedom Rides and the Birmingham riots, among others, tended to force his hand (Reeves 1993, 353).

Time and again Kennedy said that the time was not right for action on civil rights (Reeves 1993, 357). He seemed very in tune with the public mood on this. In response to criticism from civil rights liberals like Senator Hubert Humphrey (D-MN), who were disappointed that after two years the only legislation Kennedy had offered Congress was a mild voting rights bill, Kennedy answered that the country was not ready, "When I feel that there's a necessity for a congressional action with a chance of getting that congressional action, then I will recommend it to the Congress" (Reeves 1993, 468). Even as late as mid-1963, after the Birmingham riots, he was "determined not to move any further than he had to until the rest of America was ready to accept Negroes as part of America—or were so shamed by what they saw on television [the Birmingham riots] that they could not resist the Negroes' cause and still call themselves American" (Reeves 1993, 498).

Public support for civil rights was modest at best. For instance, a Gallup poll on public reactions to the Freedom Rides in 1961 found 63 percent disapproving (Reeves 1993, 133). Still, 70 percent thought that Kennedy did the right thing in sending marshals to Montgomery to deal with that situation, though only 50 percent of southerners felt that way compared to 77 percent of northerners (Gallup poll, May 28–June 2, 1961).

Kennedy, however, tried to mollify civil rights proponents through a combination of supportive rhetoric, symbolism, and administrative actions, the last of which came in the form of several executive orders. This approach, he hoped, would also avoid alienating Southern Democrats in Congress. Moreover, some of his actions were designed to placate southerners. Thus, his actions prior to the summer of 1963 were middle of the road.

According to Shull's (1993, 63) data, which are aggregated by administration and do not offer yearly breakdowns, Kennedy was on average less attentive to civil rights than Presidents Eisenhower through Bush. He issued fewer policy statements, and they were shorter than the average. Compared to other Democratic presidents, his attention to civil rights ranked last, far behind Johnson and Carter.

Still, Kennedy's rhetoric on civil rights often fueled expectations among blacks and liberal whites of forthcoming administration actions. In September 1963, Kennedy asked Louis Martin, a black newspaper publisher where blacks were getting their ideas about movement on civil rights. Martin replied, "From you! You're lifting the horizons of Negroes" (Reeves 1993, 357). He also offered symbolic gestures to civil rights supporters. Black leaders were invited to the White House for social occasions, and the administration refused to use segregated facilities.

Kennedy issued three major executive orders pertaining to civil rights: EO 10925 in March 1961, EO 11063 in November 1962, and EO 11114 in June 1963. The first established the President's Committee on Equal Employment Opportunity, which was charged with promoting nondiscrimination in federal hiring and among federal contractors. The second barred discrimination in federally assisted housing, while the third put the Grant-in-Aid Program of the federal government under nondiscrimination orders.

The first two orders were clearly limited. They could not extend to the private sector, except through federal grants. Importantly, the second order was issued only after the 1962 midterm elections, a move that ensured that Kennedy's civil rights actions did not become a major campaign issue. That his executive actions were so few and so modest given the limitations of a legislative strategy underscores the low priority of civil rights for Kennedy.

The only significant legislation that Kennedy offered before summer 1963 was a voting rights bill. He presented the bill on the right to vote because "Americans in the North were united on that" (Reeves 1993, 353). The bill allowed a sixth-grade education to constitute literacy to vote, thereby weakening, but not eliminating, southern use of literacy tests to bar black voting. School and neighborhood integration issues confronted greater division, and thus were more politically difficult and therefore not dealt with. Kennedy's strategy was for blacks to win their voting rights and use that power to obtain other legislation (Reeves 1993, 491).

Not all of Kennedy's pre-1963 civil rights actions leaned in a liberal direction, however. His most notorious appointment put William Howard Cox on the federal bench. Cox was an outrageous bigot who delayed pending civil rights litigation in his court and often refused to adhere to Supreme Court rulings. In one infamous incident, he called black voting applicants, " a bunch of niggers . . . acting like a bunch of chimpanzees" (Stern 1992, 48).

Kennedy's strongest civil rights actions came in the wake of events and crises that forced his hand. At least four times—to deal with the Freedom Riders in 1961, the integration of the University of Mississippi in 1962, the

Birmingham riots, and integration of the University of Alabama, also in summer 1963—Kennedy had to intervene either through negotiation, federal marshals and/or troops, and/or public speeches. In almost every case, administration intervention was not premised on gaining civil rights victories but restoring public order and the authority of the federal government, its courts, and also the presidency from the challenges of segregationists. Kennedy often sought at first quiet negotiation to defuse these situations, sometimes seeking a way to get civil rights activists to desist and go home.

Thus, Kennedy tried to steer a delicate course to hold together a fragile coalition. He was hesitant to submit legislation, his executive actions were modest in tone, and, in general, events pushed Kennedy to take action.

The Changing Agenda and Its Policy Consequences

From the spring to the fall of 1963 public attention turned toward civil rights: in September 48 percent of the public cited it as the nation's most important problem, compared to 4 percent in March. Within those months, several key events took place that plausibly focused public attention on civil rights. The first was the Birmingham, Alabama, riots of May 1963. Television and the media covered the crisis copiously, including the famous pictures of Birmingham police using police dogs and high-pressure hoses on demonstrators. On the heels of the Birmingham explosion was the confrontation with Alabama Governor George Wallace over integration of the University of Alabama in June, and throughout June public disturbances across the South were common. Then in late August the famous March on Washington was held in which several hundred thousand people peacefully attended and Martin Luther King gave his famous "I Have a Dream" speech.

Kennedy may also have helped focus public attention. He gave a major speech concerning civil rights before a national audience in late June 1963 in which he announced that he would be submitting legislation for congressional enactment. Soon after, the bill was introduced. The lack of poll data between March and September leaves unanswered the questions of when the climb in public interest began, how steeply it moved, and to what event the public responded. Thus, we cannot say with certainty that Kennedy responded to public opinion, as he may have led it. Moreover, changing public perceptions and Kennedy's policy evolution may have moved so closely together that it may not be possible to disentangle them.

The pressure of public opinion may not have motivated Kennedy's legislative initiative, which was a clear change in policy for the administration. The Birmingham riots and the other incidents of the summer may have been the determining factor. Attorney General Robert Kennedy, an important point man on civil rights, thought that the "racial situation was close to spinning out of control," citing the fact that there were 160 civil rights incidents during the first week of June 1962 alone (Reeves 1993, 515). Thus, he tried to convince his brother, the president, that legislative action was necessary to get blacks out of the streets and to restore public order. Existing policy seemed incapable of doing this. Even Republicans were attacking Kennedy for his cool approach to civil rights, but these were mostly liberal Republicans, like New York Governor Nelson Rockefeller, who had a large number of black constituents (Reeves 1993, 465–67) and whom Kennedy feared most as a challenger in 1964. Civil rights was becoming a political issue that could be used against Kennedy.

The bill that Kennedy introduced was broad, asking for voting rights and access to public accommodations and public facilities, but it was later watered down to secure necessary Republican support. This may indicate Kennedy's "pragmatic" approach to civil rights rather than a moral or ideological commitment.

Kennedy's civil rights bill cost him politically in Congress. For example, a routine funding bill for the Area Redevelopment Administration was narrowly defeated because of the defection of Southern Democrats, who, according to Majority Leader Carl Albert, the administration "would otherwise have had" had it not been for the civil rights legislation (Reeves 1993, 525). In response, Kennedy held up progress on civil rights legislation until after his tax cut proposal had cleared the House, fearing that the civil rights legislation might harm more of his legislative agenda (Bernstein 1991, 111).

The public was also growing dissatisfied with Kennedy's civil rights policies, not because he was doing too little too late, but because they thought he was moving too fast. Gallup polls show that between May and October 1962 the percentage of respondents offering the view that Kennedy was moving too fast on civil rights grew from 32 to 42 percent (see table 7.1). Kennedy's actions were modest in that period, but he still had to deploy U.S. marshals and troops to deal with Meredith's enrollment difficulties at the University of Mississippi. His executive order banning discrimination in federally assisted housing did not come until November 1962, after the midterm election results were in.

Between June and September 1963, the public assessment that Kennedy was moving too fast grew even further, to 50 percent. Through the entire period, no more than 10 percent ever said that Kennedy was moving too slowly. Again, in that period Governor Wallace of Alabama challenged the federal courts and the president over integration at the state's university, the March on Washington was held, and Kennedy submitted his legislative proposal.

That public opinion climbed in the direction it did for over a year suggests that the violence associated with the civil rights movement may have

TABLE 7.1.   Public Attitudes toward Kennedy Administration's Civil Rights Policies, 1962–63

Question: "Do you think the Kennedy administration is pushing racial integration too fast or not fast enough?"

	5/3– 6/62	10/19– 26/62	6/21– 26/63	8/15– 20/63	9/12– 17/63	10/11– 16/63
Too fast	32	42	41	50	50	46
Not fast enough	11	12	14	10	11	12
About right	35	31	31	40	27	31
No opinion	22	15	14		12	11

Source: Gallup poll.
Note: For August 15–20, 1963, "No opinion" was excluded from calculations.

been important in stimulating this public reaction, but at the same time, while the public might have supported mild civil rights actions like voting rights, there was little support for other reforms for which demonstrators were clamoring. For instance, 63 percent of those polled disapproved of the March on Washington, though this poll was taken before the march was held (Reeves 1993, 579).

Kennedy timed the legislative proposal in 1963 with the hope that it would be passed before the 1964 presidential election. He clearly did not want civil rights to become an election issue and understood that he would lose southern support. He decided on a trade-off, calculating that a loss in southern support would be acceptable if he could garner black support in key states like California, which he did not carry in 1960. California held enough electoral college votes to offset the loss of a handful of southern states (Reeves 1993, 626). Rather than play the public opinion game, Kennedy was playing the electoral college game, with eyes on the 1964 election. After his polls dropped from 76 percent approval to 59 percent in November 1963, an analysis by his pollster Richard Scammon chalked up the loss as being entirely due to civil rights (Reeves 1993, 655).

Kennedy's policies regarding civil rights changed from his initial lack of regard and attention to one of concern. Perhaps that concern was genuine. More importantly for these purposes, his policy evolution was motivated by a desire to control the civil rights agenda, to present an image of a president who was in control. The violence and disorder associated with the movement, especially in the south, undermined that image. However, this case does not clearly point to a president responding to public pressure. Plainly, civil rights rose on the public's agenda, as it did on Kennedy's, but the scanty public opinion data suggest that once Kennedy began to take action he was ahead of the public on the issue and perhaps moving in a direction counter to public preferences. Interactions between the president and the public over policy issues can be quite complex and hard to tease apart and understand, as this case demonstrates. Rival hypotheses concerning presidential motivations are presented in this case; they cannot be ruled out as motivations for presidential action.

Kennedy and the Tax Cut

Tax cuts always seem popular. Chronically, Americans seem to complain that their taxes are too high. The tax cuts that Kennedy offered in 1962–63 could follow the simple story of a president offering the public a policy that it wanted: the public felt that its taxes were too high, and feeling that pressure, with an eye on the upcoming presidential election, Kennedy tried to boost his popular support by proposing a tax cut.

As we will see, the Kennedy tax cuts do not follow that typical script. Kennedy was slow to offer tax cuts and had to fight against a public that initially opposed the cuts. Rather than the Kennedy tax cuts being a case of presidential responsiveness, they represent a president pushing against public opinion. Why would a president resist the public on an issue as visible and as politically charged as taxes?

Kennedy and Economic Policy

Kennedy entered the presidency relatively uninformed about economics, holding conservative economic positions but believing strongly in the impact of the economy on elections and politics. His knowledge of economics was minimal. In college, he took a standard economics course, but this was in the 1930s before the Keynesian revolution had hit the economics profession. As his biographer Reeves pithily observes about Kennedy (and all other presidents), "Kennedy had come to office in the great tradition of American presidents, more or less blissfully ignorant of economics" (Reeves 1993, 54). His ignorance of macroeconomics was so severe that he asked his economic advisor, Walter Heller, chair of the Council of Economic Advisers, "Now tell me again how do I distinguish between monetary and fiscal policy?" Heller replied, "Monetary policy is 'M,' like Martin [William McChesney Martin, chair of the Federal Reserve Board]." (Reeves 1993, 294). Later, when Martin's term was about to expire, Kennedy asked how he would remember the difference between fiscal and monetary policy without Martin on the Board. Heller had to remind him that another member of the FED was Mitchell, another "M" (Bernstein 1991, 118).

Though lacking much economic expertise, Kennedy still brought to office economic beliefs, most of which were conventionally conservative. He believed in balanced budgets, holding the classic belief that "deficits were bad because they led to inflation" (Reeves 1993, 278). Moreover, unlike other liberals, Kennedy "believed that it was inflation, not unemployment, that was politically dangerous" (Reeves 1993, 295). Thus, budgets were tied to inflation in Kennedy's estimation, and inflation was to be avoided because of the political damage that it could do. The most important economic goals that Kennedy brought with him to the office concerned the budget. "From day one of his presidency, one of Kennedy's most rigid political goals was to hold the yearly deficit below $12.8 billion, the high during Eisenhower's eight years" (Reeves 1993, 278). This would not only guard against inflation but would place him in a favorable light when compared to Eisenhower and defuse the standard charge aimed at Democrats that they were fiscally irresponsible.

Thus, despite his lack of knowledge, Kennedy understood the impact of a poor economy on his popularity and his reelection chances; he "was too good a politician to be bored by the economy" (Reeves 1993, 277). The recessions of 1958 and 1960 gave him the opportunity to win the presidency, and he clearly wanted to avoid a Kennedy recession, which he felt would undermine his election prospects in 1964. The fact that the economy was only stumbling along in 1961 and 1962 caused him great concern.

Kennedy surrounded himself with talented economic advisers, balancing liberals against conservatives. To the Treasury Department he appointed Republican Douglas Dillon, a former member of the Eisenhower administration and a banker with strong ties to Wall Street. This appointment was in part designed to help ease Wall Street's fears of a Democrat in the White House (Bernstein 1991, 123). But at the Council of Economic Advisers (CEA) he appointed liberals Walter Heller, James Tobin, and Kermit Gordon, all young academics strongly committed to Keynesianism.

The combination of Kennedy's lack of an economics background, the liberal proselytizing of his CEA advisers, and the troubled economy of 1961 and 1962 proved fateful. The Keynesian liberals made it their task to educate the president on this new approach to macroeconomic management. Slowly, Kennedy absorbed their lesson, but he still resisted their policy prescription, which was to cut taxes to stimulate the economy. He had a hard time abandoning his balanced budget biases, and though the economy showed some signs of recovery from the 1960 recession, the estimates were that it would again hit recession some time in 1963 or 1964 (Bernstein 1991, 129). The Kennedy prosperity of late 1961 and 1962 were assets that the president wanted to keep, especially going into the election in 1964. Thus, Kennedy began to warm to the tax cut proposal.

Other factors, however, provided counterweights against tax cuts. Several international crises, including those associated with Cuba, Berlin, and

Vietnam, had pressured increases in defense spending. To pay for such increases, Kennedy had to cut into domestic programs, and he further had to ask people to sacrifice for the sake of national security. This made it hard for him to simultaneously ask for a tax cut, which would undermine the sacrifice theme. Moreover, the logic of defense needs led to pushes for the tax increases to finance them, creating counterpressures on the president (Reeves 1993, 197).

Finally, in June 1962, Kennedy publicly announced that he would submit tax cut legislation to Congress in January 1963. Putting off the tax cuts indicates again Kennedy's ambivalence toward the cuts and his bias toward keeping the deficit small. In part, he hoped that the economic signals would vitiate the need for the cut. To help sell it, Kennedy decided to wrap it into a package with tax code reform, a special favorite of Treasury Secretary Dillon. But the tax code reforms would not offset the revenue losses of the tax cuts. Net taxes would still decline, and the deficit would grow. In selling his tax cut proposal, he became an ardent convert to Keynesian macroeconomic management.

Public Opinion, the Economy, and Taxes in the Early 1960s

Most often, the mass public readily accepts and supports cuts in its taxes. This was not the case in 1962 and 1963. Evidence of public resistance exists, and there is little indication of a public clamoring for reduced taxes. Ironically, Kennedy had to sell the tax cuts over stiff opposition from Congress and the public.

One way to gauge public opinion toward taxes is to use the Gallup/National Opinion Research Center (NORC) opinion poll series, which asks people if they feel that their federal income taxes are too high, about right, or too low. Page and Shapiro (1992, 160) reproduce the Gallup/NORC series from 1947, the first time the question was asked, through 1990. As they report, never do more than 2 percent feel that their taxes are too low. The more reasonable comparison is between those who feel their taxes are too high and those who feel they are about right. In February and June–July 1962, the "too high" category is only slightly larger than the "about right" category (see table 7.2). What is most interesting for my present purposes is that other than 1950, these figures are the low ebb for the "too high" category across the entire time period (Page and Shapiro 1992, 160). By the late 1960s, that category had grown to about 70 percent. What this tells us is that there was comparatively little public dissatisfaction with taxes, at least not enough to encourage politicians to lower tax rates. This does not indicate public pressure for Kennedy's proposal.

TABLE 7.2.   Public Attitudes toward Income Taxes, 1961–66

Question: "Do you consider the amount of federal income tax that you have to pay as too high, about right, or too low?"

	2/10–15/61	2/8–13/62	6/28–7/3/62	2/10–15/66
Too high	46	48	47	52
About right	45	43	45	39
Too low	1	0	1	0
Don't know/no opinion	8	9	7	9

Source: Gallup poll.

Moreover, economics overall does not seem to be at the top of people's concerns between 1961 and 1962. In each reading of the Gallup Most Important Problem question, foreign affairs easily tops economics as the public's prime concern. And while significant proportions of the public still cited economics, the proportion dropped from the high point of 23 percent in June 1962 to 9 percent in November. In December 1962, shortly before Kennedy submitted his tax legislation, only 12 percent cited economics as the most important problem compared to 61 percent who cited foreign affairs. Of interest in these data is that public concern with the economy dived just as Kennedy began to push his program.

Neither of these data suggest public opposition to tax cuts. Kennedy could still be responding to public pressure for lower taxes, but other public opinion data from the period point to public resistance to tax cuts. In response to a Gallup poll question in late June 1962, after Kennedy announced his tax cut plans, 72 percent of the public opposed "a cut in income taxes at this time if a cut meant that the government would go further into debt." Only 19 percent favored the cut, and the poll data indicate no difference in the positions of Democrats and Republicans. The public seemed to hold more strongly to the traditional value of balanced budgets than to the increases in disposable income they would receive from cutting taxes. Louis Harris, Kennedy adviser and pollster, actually worried that tax cuts would become a political problem, even though he agreed with liberal economists that they would be a good thing economically (Bernstein 1991, 151).

Kennedy's proposal also met with opposition from liberal quarters in his own party. Liberals feared that tax cuts would harm programs. Senator Albert Gore told the president, "Once taxes are cut, they are not likely to be reimposed. The cut would kill exactly the kind of social programs Franklin Roosevelt created" (Reeves 1993, 434). Wilbur Mills, chairman of the Ways and Means Committee, who would have to shepherd the program through Congress, resisted tax cuts, told Kennedy to wait, and further instructed the president to educate the public on their need if he was to get support from Congress (Bernstein 1991, 152).

Kennedy took his case to the public in June 1962, when he announced the plan. He tried to instruct the public on the whys and ways of Keynesianism, suggesting that the tax system was too burdensome to the economy, that a tax cut would stimulate growth, and that growth would lead to higher future tax takes for the government. Deficit increases would only be short term.

Again in August he went public to make his case for the tax cuts after noticing public opposition in the poll just referred to. In his speech, he claimed that the tax cut was not urgent but would be vital next year (Reeves 1993, 334–35). Kennedy was walking a fine line between informing the public that the economy was not as strong as it seemed, something for which he could be blamed, and also trying to tell them that he was in control of the situation, that it was not an urgent problem, but that as the economy declined as a result of the business cycle tax cuts would be needed to stimulate it back to health.

Congress passed the Kennedy tax cut plan after his assassination. The story is not one of a president caving in to public pressure for lower taxes, the common story of tax cuts. Rather it is a story of a president pushing for tax cuts that ran up against another, more strongly held belief—balanced budgets.

Nixon and Wage and Price Controls

Richard Nixon's economic policies veered more sharply than any other president's. Coming into office with basically conservative economic views and advisors, and after initially following a conservative economic policy path, on August 15, 1971, Nixon made a radical departure by announcing a policy of wage and price controls for the next ninety days. How is it that a president who had publicly spoken against such federal intrusions would use them? As we will see, public pressure is part of the story. More of the story, however, should be credited to Nixon's reelection hopes and his anticipation of the harm that a sour economy could do to those aspirations; as an anticipated reaction to the public this constitutes an indirect form of public pressure.

Nixon's Economic Philosophy

When Nixon became president in 1969, he was opposed to too much government intervention into the economy, especially in the form of the wage and price controls he would later use. He based this not on a well-developed theory but on his own experience with controls during the Second World War. As Reichley (1981, 205) quotes Nixon concerning his experience with the Office of Price Administration during that war, "Mandatory controls can never be administered equitably and are not compatible with a free economy." Nor did Nixon support government intervention into the economy, believing that market devices were better and that government intervention would make matters worse.

Still, Nixon was neither ideological nor committed to conservative economic goals. First, economics bored him. For instance, in 1969 after devoting much time to preparing for the upcoming fiscal-year budget, Nixon decided that he did not want to spend so much time on the budget in the future. Presidential advisor John Ehrlichman and Budget Director Robert Mayo were instructed to do the legwork, which Nixon would then sign off on (Reichley 1981, 212).

Perhaps most important to Nixon's flexibility on economic policy was "his fear that strict adherence to the conservative approach would lead to political disaster" (Reichley 1981, 206). Most critical here was his experience running for the presidency in 1960. The economy was then in a mild recession, but Eisenhower refused to stimulate it. Given that the election results in 1960 were quite close, Nixon had always believed that Eisenhower's lack of action had cost him the election. He was determined not to let himself become such a victim again (Reichley 1981, 206). Thus, it is fair to say that while Nixon had preferences about governmental intervention in the economy that leaned in a conservative direction, he gave a higher priority to politics.

Leading Up to Controls

By current standards, the inflation of the early Nixon years appears modest, but by the standards of the time inflation seemed almost out of control. His first year in office saw inflation running at an annual rate of 5.4 percent. This climbed to 5.9 in 1970, despite efforts to curb it, and rates prior to the wage-price freeze in 1971 did not seem to abate much. These were the highest inflation rates in twenty years. One had to go back to the few years after the Second World War to find inflation rates as high or higher, and the cause of the inflation of the middle-to-late 1940s was the removal of wartime price controls. In comparison, inflation averaged just 1.4 percent across the Eisenhower years and 2.3 percent during the Kennedy-Johnson period. Even during the last year of the Johnson presidency, 1968, inflation ran at only 4.2 percent. In a comparative context, Nixon had a problem on his hands.

Nixon's initial economic policy was based on "gradualism." This meant that Nixon wanted to avoid leading the country into a recession, which might harm him politically, but he also wanted to keep the economy from overheating with inflation. The gradualism policy was based on relatively tight monetary policy because Nixon and his advisers had little faith in fiscal instruments, which they felt could not be well timed nor fully insulated from political pressures. For instance, during his first year in office, while he pursued a policy of budget cutting, Nixon gave in to some politically popular programs, such as Saturday mail delivery and the infant food stamp program, and he even decided to go ahead with the supersonic transport (SST), though his budget director objected to the project's cost (Reichley 1981, 211).

At first, the gradualist economic policy seemed to have some impact slowing the economy. Unemployment inched up, but no apparent effects on inflation were noted (Reichley 1981, 209). Throughout 1970 and into 1971, however, inflation continued to roll, and unemployment was also turning into a problem.

Within his administration, support for some kind of wage and price policy was also being articulated, while Democrats in Congress began to clamor for such a policy. First, Assistant Secretary for the Treasury Murray Weidenbaum, in testimony before the Joint Economic Committee in June 1970, stated, "I think the time has come to give some serious consideration to some form of incomes policy" (Reichley 1981, 213–14). In December of that year, Arthur Burns, who Nixon greatly admired (Nixon 1987, 643–44) and who now served as the chair of the Federal Reserve Board, also publicly advocated an incomes policy (Reichley 1981, 217).

Democrats had already adopted such an approach. In 1970 Congress gave the president sweeping powers to use wage and price controls. This may have been a political ploy to hand the president both the responsibility and the tools to manage the economic situation, but Nixon opposed the bill and refused to use the full extent of the powers granted. Still, he felt compelled to take some positive actions (Nixon 1978, 639–40). He created a National Commission on Productivity, instructed the Council on Economic Advisers to issue periodic inflation alerts, and established an interagency Regulations and Purchasing Review Board, to look at how federal practices affected inflation. None of these "symbolic" attempts at moderating inflation seemed to be effective.

Somewhat more forcefully, in February, Nixon, through an executive order, suspended the Davis-Bacon Act, which required the federal government to pay workers the local prevailing wage for all federally funded projects. A month later he issued another executive order requiring "constraints" on construction industry wages, an action that drew heat from labor and congressional Democrats.

Making matters worse was that labor in some of the nation's largest industries was able to extract new contracts with large wage increases. This included the auto, aluminum, steel, and telephone industries. A few successes were registered, such as the rollback in steel prices in early 1971, but there were not enough successes to stem inflation's tide.

Finally, the factor that seemed to tip Nixon into controls was a request by

Great Britain for gold to pay for the U.S. trade imbalance. The United States was on a gold standard, and the administration decided to cut the United Sates from that standard, effectively devaluing the dollar. Devaluation could add to inflationary pressures by making U.S. goods more affordable overseas, thus stimulating the economy. This action also gave the Nixon team cover for the wage-price action.

The timing of the wage-price policy in August 1971 was not only a function of international markets but also of the upcoming election. Nixon knew that the economy could not be turned around overnight. The election was only 14 months or so away. If he waited much longer, there might not be enough time for the policy to set in, work, and gain public support. Moreover, action close to the election might look too political, thereby neutralizing any ability to generate public support. And he also needed time to undo public criticism of his existing economic policies. If such criticism was still fresh in the public's mind, he would not reap all of the public support that he sought.

The Public and the Economy

Throughout 1969 and 1970, there are glimmers in poll data that the economy was becoming an issue that could hurt Nixon and his reelection prospects. Even though the Vietnam War was still running hot, public concern with the economy, as measured by the Gallup Most Important Problem item, began to climb. Upon taking office in January 1969, only 10 percent of the public called economic problems the nation's most important, compared to 36 percent citing Vietnam alone and 54 percent citing any type of foreign policy problem. This pattern of mild attention to economic problems continued until February 1971, when 22 percent claimed the economy as the most important problem. By June the number receded to 12 percent, about average across the Nixon years, but by August 1971 the figure had climbed to 35 percent, no doubt because the poll was taken shortly after Nixon's announcement, thus probably overstating the scope of the problem as a result of such intense presidential focus. Still, these data are limited. They are infrequent and do not discriminate very well among economic problems, such as unemployment versus inflation.

Other, more focused data reveal a more severe problem for Nixon. A November–December 1970 poll showed that inflation was beginning to take its toll on the public. That survey, by Opinion Research Corporation, found that 23 percent claimed to have been seriously hurt by inflation, another 56 percent claimed to be hurt a little, and only 19 percent did not feel hurt at all.

In 1971, Richard Nixon commissioned a series of polls concerning, among other things, the economy. The first of these polls, conducted in late March, gave poor grades to Nixon and his handling of inflation. Of those surveyed, 41 percent marked him poor and 38 percent fair, while much smaller numbers gave him good (16 percent) or excellent (2 percent) ratings. Nearly identical results were found using the same question in an early May survey. These numbers clearly revealed a weakness that his rivals could politically exploit. Another poll in mid-May found that 56 percent felt that not enough progress was being made on inflation, with unemployment receiving a similar judgment at 51 percent. Only crime and solving air and water pollution problems were able to command such numbers from the public (60 and 57 percent, respectively). Not only did the May poll find widespread feelings that more needed to be done about inflation, but 82 percent called it a very important problem. A later May poll found 18 percent citing the nation's economy as a major failure of the Nixon administration, while another 12 percent cited inflation directly. Only the continuation of the Vietnam War was cited more often, at 41 percent.

Polls indicated relatively strong public support for wage and price controls. A January 1971 Harris poll found that 62 percent of the public favored wage and price controls to deal with inflation, with only 25 percent opposed to such action. An Opinion Research Corporation poll in November–December 1970 found that 40 percent thought price and wage controls were needed to help bring down inflation. Only ending the Vietnam War (51 percent) received more support. Complicating matters were the results of a June 1971 survey, also commissioned by Nixon. The public was not sure whether inflation or unemployment should be given the highest priority, with 33 percent citing inflation, 31 percent pointing to unemployment, and 30 percent mentioning both.

Public and Political Reactions

Nixon's incomes policy proved quite popular with the public but received a mixed reaction from Capitol Hill. Democrats had long called for such an action. Nixon's wage-price policy took some wind out of those political sails, and the Democrats countered mostly with the critique that the policy was too late, a point especially emphasized by those running for the presidency.

The public tended to applaud the action, however. A week after the announcement, the Opinion Research Corporation found 77 percent approving of the action, with only 10 percent dissenting. Similar results were unearthed in a Nixon-commissioned poll of similar timing, with 73 percent in support and only 16 percent in opposition. But public optimism about the effectiveness of such measures was more guarded, as Harris surveys found in September, October, and late December. Although pluralities thought that the plans would work, the numbers in September and October were 46 percent; in December they were 43 percent. The September survey found 29 percent saying it would not work, with 28 percent in October and 32 percent in

December. All surveys found about one-quarter of respondents unsure about the effectiveness of the freeze.

Nixon's policy did not squelch inflation. It only hid it until the controls were lifted. This in part led to the stagflation problems of the mid and late 1970s and thus may have been consequential in killing liberal, interventionist economic policies in the late 1980s and 1990s. Still, this is one of the strongest cases of a president responding to public pressure, though Nixon seemed more concerned about public anticipations around election time than opinion at the moment.

This case also reveals how complicated and difficult it is to sort out the mechanisms of presidential responsiveness to public opinion. If presidents move in response to anticipations, we may mistakenly view that movement as an attempt at leadership. Quantitative data of the sort used in the previous chapters cannot distinguish anticipated reactions behaviors very well, but the combination of that data with the type of case analysis presented in this chapter and the next helps us sort through the many causal mechanisms with greater sensitivity.

CHAPTER 8

Presidential Policy Decisions and Responsiveness to Public Opinion II: Reagan, Bush, and Clinton

In this chapter, we continue the case analysis of presidential decisions and responsiveness to public opinion. The previous chapter found one possible example of presidential responsiveness to public opinion, the Nixon wage and price controls policy. Eisenhower and *Sputnik* was a case of moderate responsiveness, while the Kennedy tax cut demonstrated a president resisting public opinion and, in fact, following a policy course contrary to public preferences. Lastly, the case of Kennedy and civil rights was the most complex, but it did not suggest simple presidential responsiveness to public opinion either. In this chapter, we focus on four more cases: Reagan and Social Security, Bush and unemployment benefits extensions, Clinton and gays in the military, and Clinton and NAFTA.

Reagan and Social Security Cuts

In 1981, the Social Security system was on the verge of a financial crisis. It was paying out more money than it was taking in at a rate of $10 to $15 billion per month (Light 1985, 89). The system required reform, even though only four years earlier, in 1977, massive increases in Social Security taxes were passed to avert another financial crisis, a reform in which then President Carter stated, "This legislation will guarantee that from 1980 to the year 2030, the social security funds will be secure" (quoted in Light 1985, 89).

This case is a good one with which to look for presidential responsiveness to public opinion. Something had to be done about the Social Security problem. Beside Social Security's financial plight, a budget problem, the deficit, plagued the Reagan administration. Ronald Reagan held strong political views in favor of cutting taxes and increasing spending on defense. These policies produced large budget deficits, stimulating a quest to find items to cut, and Social Security's size made it an attractive item for budget reductions.

But the public held different ideas about Social Security. Most of the solutions, such as reducing benefits or increasing taxes, were not very palatable to the mass public. Moreover, Social Security is arguably the most popular program that the federal government offers. The combination of its popularity and the number of people affected make it a potent political issue with weighty electoral implications.

Public Support for Social Security

The public is highly supportive of Social Security, perhaps more so than any other domestic federal program. As Page and Shapiro report, "according to the responses to some four dozen surveys by various organizations between 1961 and 1989, many more people always wanted to increase than wanted to decrease Social Security spending. Very large majorities, on the order of 80 to 90 percent, have opposed cuts; majorities (not just pluralities) said 'spend more' rather than the same amount or less, or said 'too little' was being spent, or said the government should 'do more' to improve Social Security benefits" (1992, 119). In a series of Trendex surveys from 1978 to 1981, between 60 and 70 percent always wanted to "do more" on Social Security, and from 1984 through 1990, those saying that "too little" was being spent hovered slightly above 50 percent, in contrast to 10 percent or less saying that "too much" was being spent (Page and Shapiro 1992, 120). No other program received such resounding support.

Several reasons are given for this broad appeal. First, it is a broad-based program. In 1980, some 112 million people were covered under Social Security programs and 35 million received benefits (Stanley and Niemi 1994, 390). Almost every family in America is touched by Social Security, either paying into it with the expectation of receiving benefits upon retirement or already receiving benefits. Few programs can compete with Social Security's penetration into the population.

Moreover, people do not see it as a welfare program but rather as a social insurance program, one that is compulsory but also one in which contributors get back what they put in. Also, people tend to think that the elderly, the major group of recipients, is in need of Social Security. Although the public overestimates the incidence of poverty and crime afflicting the aged, it is still true that Social Security is the major income source for many elderly. Light estimates that in 1981, Social Security accounted for about one-half of the income of two-thirds of the elderly and all the income for one-fifth (Light 1985, 89). Lastly, those who receive benefits are considered deserving because the conditions under which they get benefits are beyond their control, like aging and disability. As one study reports, people believe that Social Security benefits society as a whole because people are forced to save for their retirement, and it helps those with no other source of income (Cook and Barrett 1988).

The popularity, support, and electoral implications of Social Security limit the options available to politicians when the program runs into trouble, as it did in 1981. Its sheer size, however, as well as its popularity, also forces politicians to take action when a problem hits the program.

The options open to politicians for dealing with the financial problem like that of 1981 must steer between two shoals. On the one hand, the public does not want to reduce benefits. On the other, the public does not want to increase taxes. Polls in 1979 indicated that 75 percent opposed benefit reductions, and 49 percent opposed tax increases to fix Social Security. However, the public seemed more disposed toward tax increases than benefit cuts. "When asked to choose between the two options in 1979, 63 percent selected tax increases, whereas only 15 percent picked benefit cuts. Moreover, 52 percent strongly opposed lowering benefits instead of raising taxes" (Light 1985, 69–71). It was into this thicket that Reagan entered.

Reagan's Proposals to Deal with the 1981 Crisis

Early in 1981, the Reagan administration made two proposals relating to Social Security. Both amounted to benefit cuts, the policy direction the public was most strongly opposed to. By pursuing this course, Reagan suffered his earliest policy defeats and had to reverse himself in the face of what looked like strong public opposition.

The first Social Security proposal came in March 1981. This proposal did not directly come from the president, but from his budget director, David Stockman. Under pressure from Congress to do something about the huge looming deficit in his earlier budget proposal, Stockman sought a way to cut federal spending. Tax increases were out of the question, being a pillar of the Reagan economic program. After looking for cuts, Stockman kept coming back to the only federal program that could generate the kinds of savings he was looking for, Social Security (Light 1985, 119–20).

Stockman proposed cuts in benefits. The first would reduce benefits to early retirees, those who retired before age 65. Second, he sought to delay the Cost of Living Adjustment (COLA) for three months. Combined, these cuts would amount to something on the order of $24 billion, over half of the $45 billion package of cuts that also dug deeply into other programs such as Job Corps, Head Start, women and children's food programs, and the like (Light 1985, 119–20).

Three problems plagued the Stockman plan. First, it did not deal with the long-term financial problems of Social Security, though it helped the short-term problem. Second, his proposals affected large numbers of Social Security recipients. Light estimates that 36 million would lose benefits from the COLA delay, 7 million would lose benefits from the early retirement savings, and 18 million more would lose from a technical change in the basic formula. All told, perhaps 60 million would lose benefits (1985, 121–22). A huge amount of political pressure was put on the Reagan administration because the elderly were one of the most active groups politically, having about the highest turnout rate of any age cohort, and because so many were affected, not counting those indirectly affected because a family member's benefits were cut.

Reagan let the proposals go to Congress; there was little dissension among staffers, the president's polls were high, and leading proponents of the package felt that Congress would accept it. Once it arrived in Congress, however, Democrats made the cuts into a potent political issue, and a little over a week later the Reagan administration withdrew the package. During congressional debates on May 20, "not one Republican rose in defense of the cuts" (Light 1985, 125).

The next day Reagan killed his administration's proposals, but in an attempt to undo some of the damage that the proposal inflicted on him, he stressed three principles for Social Security: that the Trust Fund's integrity must be maintained, the burden on workers who pay into the system must be held down, and abuse must be eliminated from the system (Light 1985, 127). Seemingly, the administration caved into intense public pressure.

Soon after the benefit reduction debacle, the administration sent another benefit cut to Congress. Buried within the budget was an item that would eliminate the minimum Social Security payment. This item did not generate much savings but affected three million, mostly elderly women in the most precarious of economic circumstances, and again Congress refused to go along with the administration (Light 1985, 129–32).

One last proposal was discussed within the White House, the three-month COLA delay, which Stockman initially convinced the president to support, but as it generated only $3 billion in savings while generating great political heat political strategists persuaded Reagan to abandon that effort, which he ultimately did (Light 1985, 132).

Still, something had to be done about Social Security irrespective of the budget. Reagan proposed a national commission, though the system had been studied repeatedly over the past several years. The commission was seen as a way to undo the damage that had been done to Reagan by shifting the focus away from the administration. The commission was also thought of as a way to develop a policy proposal while simultaneously providing the president with political cover if the proposal turned out to be controversial.

Responsiveness to Public Pressures

Reagan suffered much public damage from the Social Security issue and the way the administration handled it in 1981. Into fall 1981, 65 percent disapproved of the way Reagan handled Social Security. One month later, in late October, 68 percent still disapproved, even though Reagan gave a national address in an attempt to calm public fears that he would harm the system and to build support for the commission idea. Another poll found that half the public did not trust Reagan "to make the right kind of decisions about Social Security" (Light 1985, 133). That his leadership attempt had so little effect tells us much about the public politics of Social Security and why he gave in to public pressure.

Finally, the administration tried to undo any lasting damage that Social Security might do to the Republicans in the upcoming 1982 midterm elections. Although no cuts had come about, over half the public in February 1982 believed that the program had been cut (Light 1985, 153), and in April, still only 25 percent approved of Reagan's handling of Social Security, compared to 72 percent who gave him fair or poor marks. Reagan's position with the public had hardly budged.

The Republicans ran a television ad campaign shortly after the June COLA of 7.4 percent was announced. The ad showed a postman delivering checks to Social Security recipients, extolling the virtue of the COLA adjustment, claiming it came from Reagan. The ad seemed to work magic for Reagan and the Republicans. Before the ad, 17 percent said Reagan had increased Social Security benefits, but 49 percent saw cuts, with 34 percent seeing no change. After the ad campaign, 37 percent now saw benefit increases, with 41 percent seeing decreases, and 17 percent seeing no change (Light 1985, 153–54). Although not on top of the issue, the Republicans had neutralized the early lopsided disadvantage.

Reagan may have responded to public pressure because he held no strong beliefs about what to do with Social Security. Social security was not a top priority for him, and Light suggests that Reagan's pragmatic side led him on Social Security (1985, 118). Without any firm beliefs or policy positions to which he might be wedded, Reagan had great maneuverability in approaching Social Security. Ideally, he probably would have liked to reform it with budget considerations in mind, but the political costs of such an action were too high, and the benefits not high enough to promote such a course of action. When political costs are high, they must be counterbalanced. One possible counterbalance might come from a president's beliefs about a policy.

For example, Reagan seemed to have weathered the political storms associated with the 1981–82 recession because of his firmly held beliefs about his economic policies, which have come to be labeled "Reaganomics." He believed that those policies would result in a stronger economy and that improved economic performance would regenerate the public support that was lost as a result of the recession, which many thought his policies induced. He seemed to be proved right in that instance.

But in the case of Social Security, the immediate losses of public support imposed a high cost, and the benefits to be derived from reform and cutbacks of Social Security might not be realized for many years. This, coupled with Reagan's lack of commitment to a Social Security reform policy, undermined the actions that Stockman wanted to follow, and to which Reagan initially assented, and also account for Reagan's swift about-face and abandonment of the Stockman approach. Moreover, the high costs that Reagan paid for his short-term association with the Stockman approach provided much of the reason for the adoption of the commission approach to dealing with the issue.

Still, Social Security had some long-lasting effects. Something had to be done, and the commission process stimulated a solution to the problem that only came in early 1983 with the behind-the-scenes work of the nation's most important political leaders. Social Security also helped frame the Democrats' "fairness" attack on the Republicans, which at times over the next decade would prove effective. Finally, the Reagan administration abandoned its attempt to balance the budget on Social Security, instead calling for a balanced budget amendment. When serious debate over the balanced budget amendment surfaced after the 1994 midterm elections, Social Security was still publicly off the table as a way to get to a balanced budget.

Bush and the Extension of Unemployment Benefits

George Bush did not have a reputation for holding to his political positions (Duffy and Goodgame 1992). Once a strong supporter of civil rights, he became an active opponent of affirmative action in the 1980s and 1990s. He also switched his position on abortion, adopting an antiabortion stance once he decided to run for the presidency in the late 1970s. After calling Reagan's brand of supply-side economics "voodoo economics" in the campaign for the Republican presidential nomination in 1980, he became a strong advocate of such policies as vice president and president. Most glaring was his reneging of his 1988 presidential election campaign pledge of "no new taxes," when in the 1990 budget debacle with Congress he acceded to new taxes.

Bush's record with regard to unemployment benefits is much the same. After a year of resisting congressional efforts to extend unemployment benefits, Bush relented, even becoming an advocate of extensions. His declining polls, his weakness with the public on the economic issue, and the upcoming presidential election appear to account for his switch in position. Like Nixon, anticipations of electoral consequences, rather than direct public preferences, motivate this story. As journalists Duffy and Goodgame (1992, 62) argue, "All of domestic policy was subordinated to the goal of getting Bush's reelection, and almost everything that didn't fit was thrown overboard."

Three factors are important in setting the context for the unemployment benefits extension saga. First, in 1990 Bush entered into the famous budget agreement with the Democrats. With that agreement, Bush reneged on his no-new-taxes pledge, but he also got important budget concessions from the Democrats. Specifically, any new spending had to be paid for either by cuts in existing programs or new taxes. Only if both the president and Congress designated spending as an emergency could the "pay as you go" provision be waived.

The second factor was the state of the economy. Bush inherited a healthy economy from the Reagan administration. Into Bush's first year in office, the economy had exhibited nearly six years of sustained growth with low-to-moderate inflation. Bush, once a critic of Reaganomics, was now a confirmed advocate, and he was not about to abandon what appeared to be a successful approach to steering the economy. However, in late 1990, his second year in office, the economy began to dive.[1] Again, Bush tried to repeat Reagan's performance, suggesting that the economy would revive if the nation adhered to his Reaganomics-styled economic course and recalling how Reagan urged patience during the severe recession of 1981–82. Bush's resistance to most any economic stimulus other than the capital gains tax cut helped to forge an image in the public mind that the president was out of touch with ordinary people, that he really did not care about their plight.[2] Democrats would make this a major theme in their attacks on him throughout the rest of his tenure and the upcoming presidential election campaign.

The third important factor was the upcoming presidential election. The election magnified public opinion pressures on the president, especially in the areas where he seemed most vulnerable: his handling of the economy and, most critically, the unemployment issue.

Extending Unemployment Benefits: A Bill, A Veto, and Two More Bills

The unemployment benefits extension issue unfolded across a two-year period. In that time, the president signed one bill, vetoed the next, and signed two more. The issue can be roughly divided into two periods: Bush's resistance to extending benefits and Bush's support of, almost activism for, benefit extensions. The combination of the state of the economy, his declining reelection position, and the upcoming election account for his change in position.

The recession of 1990–92 was different from previous downturns. First, it was not as severe in terms of the depth of unemployment and contraction. For example, at the bottom of the recession the economy contracted 4 percent in terms of real economic growth.[3] In contrast, the 1981–82 recession saw a 6 percent contraction, and a 10 percent contraction occurred in 1980. Unemployment was also comparatively mild in 1990–92. At its height in late 1991 early 1992, unemployment stood at about 7 percent. In the 1982 recession, unemployment peaked at nearly 11 percent. Thus, the Bush recession seemed comparatively mild.

But the Bush recession seemed long and the recovery anemic. Economic growth in 1992 and 1993 could only manage 2 to 3 percent, compared to the 8 to 11 percent for the Reagan recession. Also, unemployment hit the middle class, especially middle-management workers, as corporations began a massive downsizing. Although these workers did not display extraordinarily high rates of unemployment, once out of work they found it difficult to gain new jobs. Consequently, many saw their unemployment benefits expire. In late 1990, about 200,000 persons per month saw their benefits end. This number climbed throughout 1991, with the July 1991 figure standing at nearly 350,000 (Zuckman 1991c, 2693).

Into this context, in the summer of 1991, Democrats, spearheaded by Representative Tom Downey (D-NY) and Senator Lloyd Bentsen (D-TX), chair of the Finance Committee, began to enter bills that would extend unemployment benefits to those whose benefits had expired. The House bill was more generous and also contained a provision that would require the president, by signing the bill, to agree that an emergency existed, thereby allowing the Treasury to spend money without the necessary offsets. The Senate version would allow the president to sign the bill but would require him to take the added step of declaring an emergency (Zuckman 1991a, 2164–65; 1991b, 2628).

In a mid-August statement, Bush rejected the House version, holding firm to his commitment not to bust the budget. He would only sign a bill that included the offsets and was unwilling to declare an emergency. Unemployment figures showed some easing, and Bush stressed that the economy was beginning to rebound. Between June and July 1991, unemployment dipped from 6.8 to 6.7 percent, helping Bush with his case. Furthermore, his popularity was still quite lofty at 70-plus percent, down from his high of nearly 90 percent in February–March during the Gulf War, but still very strong.

Bush dickered with Democrats, threatening to veto the House bill. Congressional Democrats reached a compromise, sending Bush a bill styled more like the Senate version, without the requirement that signing the bill would automatically initiate an emergency. Bush signed this bill in late August and refused to call an emergency, and no added money was issued (Zuckman 1991b, 2628).

Upon the heels of this action, Democrats geared up for a second round with the president in September. They found that the issue played well with voters and clobbered the president for releasing money to help war victims in the Middle East but not helping citizens at home.

In late September and early October, the House and Senate passed legislation to extend benefits, adding weeks of eligibility to unemployed workers seeking employment. This bill boxed Bush into a corner; his signature would automatically activate the emergency requirement. If he vetoed the bill and was overridden, the emergency would also go into effect.

OMB attacked the bill, charging that adding weeks of compensation to workers would discourage them from seeking work and also claiming that the recession was over (Zuckman 1991c, 2693). In an ill-considered remark, Bush called the bill "a bunch of garbage" (Zuckman 1991d, 2784). Democrats quickly pounced on the remark, seeing a way to further characterize Bush as insensitive to those struggling during the recession. Bush quickly backtracked, saying he would sign a bill that included budget offsets, one that did not add to the deficit (Zuckman 1991e, 2868), but he held firm to his threat to veto an unacceptable bill. Again, a small decline in unemployment of .1 percent and popularity hovering in the mid-60s emboldened the president. In a news conference he reiterated that the economy was on the upswing and that he preferred to stimulate it with a capital gains tax cut, that cut being a refrain he promoted throughout his presidency as one solution to the nation's long-term economic problems.

When the unacceptable bill turned up on his desk a week later, he vetoed it, claiming in his veto message of October 11 that the bill "would effectively destroy the integrity of the bipartisan budget agreement and put into place a poorly designed, unnecessarily expensive program that would significantly increase the federal deficit."[4] With the bill's passage by wide margins in both chambers, bill advocates felt they could override the president's veto. They were wrong.

Unemployment figures climbed the next month, and by early November the president's popularity had dipped below 60 percent. Since March, his popularity had lost about thirty points. Moreover, by November, 23 percent cited unemployment as the nation's most important problem, and another 32 percent cited the economy in general (see table 8.1). This compares with 8 percent citing unemployment in March and 24 percent citing the economy in general. Under this new context, in early November Bush publicly called for an unemployment bill that he could support (Zuckman 1991f, 3205).

Throughout the winter, legislators began working on a new bill, and serious attention was given to its financing. Many Democrats felt they could no longer play partisan politics with the president. His image was already weakened, and Democrats had to produce something for their constituents, lest they also begin to feel the political heat (Zuckman 1991g, 3282). Such a bill emerged from Congress and the President agreed to it (Zuckman 1991h, 3383–84; Zuckman 1991i, 3462), signing it in late November. The bill, like earlier ones, was only a temporary extension of benefits, but it did find ways to finance the extension through a combination of cuts, taxes, and the collection

TABLE 8.1. The Public's Most Important Problem and the Economy, 1991–92

Date	Percentage Citing Unemployment as the Most Important Problem	Percentage Citing the Economy in General as the Most Important Problem
January 3, 1991	4	15
January 30, 1991	5	16
March 7, 1991	8	24
April 25, 1991	8	20
May 23, 1991	9	21
July 14, 1991	8	16
September 5, 1991	11	16
November 21, 1991	23	32
March 26, 1992	25	42
August 28, 1992	27	37

Source: Gallup poll.

of money owed the federal government. By late November, however, the president's polls were edging near the 50 percent mark, matching the lowest he had seen in his tenure, and public concern had shifted decidedly to the economy. Planning for the primary season had already begun, adding to the political heat the president was feeling.

The temporary extension merely set the stage for another bill, which Democrats began proposing in January 1992. Unemployment had started creeping up, again hitting 7.1 percent by the new year. This was nearly .4 percent higher than the lowest figure of the past six months and almost a whole point higher than a year before.

By early February, another bill had been passed by Congress and signed by the president. Again the bill was only a temporary extension of benefits, with offsetting money to finance the bill. The president quickly signed the bill, after having urged quick action (Zuckman 1992b, 252).

The series of temporary extensions did not deal with the key problems that many cited. First, for benefit extensions to kick in, unemployment rates had to be quite high, higher than those recorded during most of the recession. Second, it took longer for people to find work during this recession than in previous ones. Fundamental reform was called for, something that Representative Tom Downey had been advocating for two years. After the February benefits extension, Congress began work on a permanent reform. Unlike the previous benefit extensions, this proved less controversial and found presidential cooperation.

Secretary of Labor Lynn Martin appeared before two congressional committees working on the legislation but refused to offer the administration's views, saying instead that the administration would only negotiate with Congress in closed session (Zuckman 1992d, 1164). Bush held to a line that opposed any permanent change in the unemployment compensation system, though he continued to support more extensions if money could be found (Zuckman 1992e, 1256; 1992f, 1449–50).

After negotiations between different House and Senate bills, a conference report emerged in July, which Congress accepted and sent to the president. The president's position continued to weaken as unemployment moved up. Although January 1992 figures stood at 7.1 percent, they reached 7.7 percent in July. Bush's polls continued to slide as well, dipping to under 40 percent by midsummer. Public concern with the economy continued to mount, with over 60 percent of the public citing either unemployment or the economy as the most important problem facing the nation (see table 8.1). Bush relented to the new, permanent legislation, feeling these political and election pressures. Still, he was able to exact some compromises from Congress (Zuckman 1992h, 1961–63).

The new changes would begin once current legislation expired in March 1993. The triggering mechanism to allow benefits extensions were eased, provisions to which Bush had long objected. An optional trigger device was allowed. States could adhere to the federal standard of basing extensions on the percentage of people receiving unemployment assistance, with its higher targets, or it could opt to use the trigger based on the total unemployment rates, which are based on all people who are looking for work, whether they had received benefits or not. The catch to the second option, which was easier to reach, was that states had to contribute one-half of the funding (Zuckman 1992h, 1961). Further, the legislation found several ways of financing the changes, while Bush and the Republicans were able to get Democrats to roll back the overall size of the changes.

Bush's reactions in this case closely resemble Nixon's. As long as his polls were high, he resisted public and Democratic pressures for increased unemployment benefits. But once his polls fell low enough to make him feel electorally vulnerable and as the economy, his source of public vulnerability, became the primary focus of public attention, he caved in and became an active supporter of policies to extend unemployment benefits.

Clinton and Gays in the Military

One of Bill Clinton's first actions as president was his announcement that he was going to end the ban on gays serving in the military. A leak that he was to issue such a policy forced him to announce it, perhaps before he wanted to go public. The announcement led to a political firestorm, coming shortly after he ended the abortion gag rule, which had prohibited federally funded clinics from telling clients about abortion services. These two actions helped forge an image in the public's mind of the new president as a left-leaning, McGovern-style Democrat, the type that had alienated so many Americans over the past two decades. As president, Clinton seemed to be far from the middle-of-the-road, new Democrat he portrayed himself as in the election campaign (Towell 1992).

The prohibition against gays serving in the military was a long-standing policy dating to 1943. Over the years, but especially during the 1980s, the policy was challenged in the courts. Time and again, the courts upheld the ban. This failure led Clinton to promise during the campaign to end the ban by executive order if elected. That promise did not gain widespread media attention during the campaign, but it did seem to secure the gay vote for Clinton.[5] Reports indicated that over 70 percent of gay voters cast their ballot for Clinton (Wilcox and Wolpert 1995, 3). Undercutting his position with the public was the feeling among many that Clinton took this position, not out of a matter of principle, but because he was responding to pressure from liberal and gay organizations.[6] Thus, initially the issue was politics as usual.

The announcement quickly ran into trouble. Conservatives found an issue with which to rally their opposition against the president, denying him much of the traditional honeymoon (Appelbome 1993, A1; Towell 1993a). Moreover, Clinton's top military advisers, including Joint Chiefs of Staff chair Admiral William Crowe and his successor, the highly respected General Colin Powell, publicly voiced their opposition. There was grumbling throughout the military ranks as well (Hackworth 1993, 24). President Clinton's leadership of the military was further hampered by his draft avoidance during the Vietnam War, which undermined the legitimacy of his pronouncements on military matters as well as his fulfillment of his constitutional role of commander in chief (Germond and Witcover 1993b, 1196).

Lastly, critically, and most damagingly, Senator Sam Nunn of Georgia, chair of the Armed Services Committee, announced his opposition, challenging the president's proposed action with legislation to retain the ban (Towell 1993b). Clinton was not willing to alienate Nunn, whose vote he needed on the budget and who was among the most highly respected members of the Senate. The president then announced that he would wait six months before making a final decision.

The six-month period led to gay activist criticism of Clinton (Berke 1993, E3) and reinforced in the public's mind the image of a president who would not stick to his policies or ideals. During the first budget battle, for instance, he compromised several positions with powerful legislators, notably backing away from his BTU tax proposal. The waiting period also opened up another window for conservative social critics to attack him (Germond and Witcover 1993a, 836).

Clinton instructed Secretary of Defense Les Aspin to work out a compromise with legislators, who had agreed not to push legislation during those six months. By mid-July a compromise had been worked out, called the "don't ask, don't tell" policy. The compromise restricted the military from asking recruits or actives about their sexual preferences and prevented recruits or actives from declaring their sexual preferences. Further, any homosexual act would constitute grounds for dismissal from the military. Both sides of the controversy were displeased with the results. Gays felt that their rights were sold out; conservatives were unable to restrict homosexual access to the military.

The President, the Public, and Gays in the Military

There were many political risks associated with the gays and the military service issue. Public antipathy toward homosexuals has been consistently high. Page and Shapiro's (1992, 98–100) collection of evidence indicates that throughout the 1970s and 1980s, upwards of 80 percent thought that homosexuality was always or almost always wrong. Still, there was less support for making homosexuality illegal, with only about half of the public feeling that way, a still sizable percentage, however. This was the context in which Clinton would make policy.

Still, public reaction to Clinton and the gays in the military issue was decidedly mixed but not the complete fiasco that some observers suggested. Nor does it seem to be the case that Clinton's compromise "don't ask, don't tell" policy was a result solely of public pressures, but public pressure surely played a part in his backing away from cleanly ending the ban.

First, Clinton's polls suffered during the first year of his administration while the ban debate was going on, and though Wilcox and Wolpert (1995) find that public attitudes on the issue affected assessments of Clinton, attitudes toward the economy and foreign affairs had a much larger impact.

Second, there was some movement to Clinton's side of the issue, but most polls are sketchy because of inconsistent question wording. For instance, before the "don't ask, don't tell" policy was announced, several polling organizations asked questions, with variations in wording, on the theme of support or opposition to allowing gays to serve in the military. As table 8.2 indicates, disapproval was generally more common than approval. It also appears that as the debate progressed from the initial announcement of Clinton's intention to revoke the ban through to mid-spring, support for gay military service eroded and opposition picked up.

Those types of questions were not asked once the compromise policy was announced. Questions turned to support or opposition for the compromise, a different issue. Now, public support appeared behind the president and

TABLE 8.2.   Public Attitudes about Gays in the Military and Clinton's Policies on That Issue

Date	Agree	Disagree	Don't Know	Pollster
1. Public Attitudes about Letting Gays Serve in the Military				
December 12, 1992	46	49	5	NBC-*Wall Street Journal*
January 23, 1993	41	50	9	NBC-*Wall Street Journal*
January 26, 1993	44	42	13	ABC-*Washington Post*
April 22, 1993	42	51	7	*Newsweek*
May 12, 1993	36	55	9	*Time*-CNN
2. Public Attitudes about the "Don't Ask, Don't Tell" Policy				
July 19, 1993	58	37	5	CNN-*USA Today*
January 15, 1994	50	47	3	Gallup
3. Public Attitudes about Clinton's Handling of Gay Rights				
November 4, 1993	37	55	6	Gallup-CNN
April 22, 1994	41	51	8	CNN-*USA Today*

the compromise by a hefty 58–37 margin in July, at about the time of the announcement. But by the cusp of the new year, support had dwindled to 50 percent, with opposition rising to 47. Still, this differs from the plurality opposition to gay service in the military during the first half of 1993.

The best data on hand to study the issue is the panel conducted as part of the American National Election Study, conducted by the University of Michigan's Survey Research Center, the core of the Wilcox and Wolpert (1995) analysis. Using more finely honed categories, they find that weak and strong opposition to gay service in the military stayed essentially stable from late 1992 until fall 1993, when the second wave of the panel was interviewed. About 8 percent of respondents were weakly opposed and nearly 30 percent strongly opposed.

Movement was detected in the weak and strongly supportive categories, however, with a strengthening of support across the two waves of the panel. In the 1992 wave, 29 and 33 percent weakly and strongly supported gay military service, respectively. The percentage of weak supporters declined to 16.5 percent by the fall 1993 wave, while the strong supporter category rose to nearly 46 percent.

The net result is not an across-the-board surge in support for the president's position but a strengthening of support among those most likely to be influenced by the president. Thus, there is some indication of presidential leadership effects in this case, much as we have seen in the Kennedy tax cut case.

Wilcox and Wolpert (1995) speculate about the source of this opinion change. The argument that they offer suggests that the way the issue was dealt with by Clinton shifted, that the issue was redefined. Initially, public reactions were based on their feelings toward homosexuals, which were, in varying degrees, negative. Clinton began to speak about the issue in terms of equality and civil rights, and this resonated among those who were weak supporters of the policy. Among those antagonistic toward military service by gays, attitudes toward gays created a barrier to their thinking about the issue in civil rights terms. But those mildly supportive were open to this issue redefinition, and consequently, their support for gay service increased.

Clinton did not buckle to public and political pressure about allowing gays to serve in the military. Still, like Eisenhower and *Sputnik,* he compromised. The guts of the compromise maintained the basic thrust of his policy, much as Eisenhower's compromises did not alter his basic stance toward military spending and budgetary priorities. Providing a bulwark against these public pressures was Clinton's commitment to this policy, which distinguishes Clinton's behavior in this case from Reagan's in the Social Security episode.

Ironically, here we have two presidents acting against type. Clinton is more known for his indecisiveness in decision making, for endlessly changing his mind. Woodward (1995) outlines how Clinton was of two minds about his macroeconomic policy, on the one hand being concerned about growth and populist issues, on the other wanting to do something about the budget deficit. Throughout, his economic policy has seemed to waver between these two poles. In contrast, as discussed earlier, Reagan had more of the reputation of one who stuck to his policies, especially his economic and foreign policies. Only after the Soviets seemed to be crushed under the weight of Reagan's military buildup did Reagan's foreign policy become less militaristic toward the Soviets. That process took six years.

This seems to suggest that presidential commitment to a policy is instrumental to keeping presidents on course and insulating them from pressures of all types, including public opinion. Of course, the number and depth of those commitments tells us much about presidential style in office. An interesting question becomes why the policy commitment of presidents varies in number and depth.

Clinton and NAFTA

The North American Free Trade Agreement (NAFTA) had it origins in the development of the European trading bloc and the decline of American competitiveness in foreign markets. NAFTA was an attempt to create a trade bloc in which the United States was a member, along with Mexico and Canada, the two top U.S. trading partners. The hope was that this would ensure U.S.

access to other markets while also retaliating against the European bloc, which was erecting barriers against imports from nations that were not members, the United States included. The controversy for Clinton was Mexico's membership in NAFTA and the fact that the NAFTA deal began as a Bush initiative, against whom he was running in 1992. The negotiations were nearing their end during the midst of the presidential election campaign in 1992, and opposition to the agreement within the Democratic Party was turning it into a campaign issue. Moreover, populist independent presidential candidate H. Ross Perot was challenging the proposed treaty, using the colorful image of Mexico as a huge sucking machine pulling jobs away from the United States.

During the campaign, Clinton was coy about NAFTA. His campaign "wants to support free trade, to protect itself against charges of protectionism that have plagued Democratic candidates. But the Clinton camp also wants to raise enough questions to maintain the loyalty of labor and environmental groups that generally oppose the pact" (Stokes 1993, 1901). Thus, Clinton straddled the issue, saying he would sign a good pact but not a bad one.

Clinton's public coyness belied his private support for free trade and NAFTA, however. According to Woodward (1995, 49), "Clinton believed in free trade, and as governor he had run personal campaigns to attract foreign investors to Arkansas. In addition, the New Democrats generally favored the agreement."[7]

For the Democrats, two major issues were key in their opposition to NAFTA. The first was the fear that American manufacturers and businesses would leave the United States for Mexico in search of lower wage costs. Labor was especially adamant about pushing this issue. Environmentalists also opposed the pact because Mexico's environmental laws and enforcement were much less stringent than those in the United States. Both groups were important constituencies within the Democratic Party that Clinton had to pay attention to and appease if he was to get elected.

To deal with these criticisms and not appear that he was accepting a Bush policy, which would undermine his campaign theme attacking Bush's economic policies, Clinton initiated a series of supplemental negotiations with the Mexican government upon attaining office. Those side agreements would focus on environmental, labor, and import surges issues (Stokes 1993, 1160).

Still, NAFTA was not high on the agenda early in the administration because of the paramount importance of the first budget and because Clinton's own personal agenda ranked health care reform a higher priority. But by late fall 1993, the treaty was to come up on the congressional agenda for approval and thus required presidential attention. Moreover, the negotiated side agreements with Mexico made NAFTA a Clinton policy, one that he could no longer back away from. Securing its passage was now thought to be another test of the administration, an administration that seemed to be repeatedly facing such "tests."

In August, Clinton began his campaign to secure passage of NAFTA. As it was placed on the "fast track," both the House and Senate had to vote on its adoption. Although passage in the Senate seemed a sure thing, opposition from House Democrats, such as Majority Leader Richard Gephardt (Missouri) and Whip David Bonior (Michigan), created a specter of possible defeat. Perot's opposition also appeared to dim prospects of passage.

Yet there was broad support for the plan in the so-called Establishment. In one publicity stunt, Clinton gathered all the ex-presidents from both parties, each of whom publicly endorsed the pact. Most businesses and economists were also supporters.

The public was not so sanguine about the idea, however. Two facts stand out about public opinion. First, opposition and support was fairly even, with a slight edge for the opponents. But, second, an even larger group was uninformed and/or had not framed an opinion about the issue.

The president seemed unable to capture public attention, either, as table 8.3 indicates. Several factors seem to account for this. One, the issue was complicated and could be viewed from several different vantage points. One tack that Clinton tried was to shift the debate away from jobs to foreign policy and thereby mobilize support behind the presidency (R. Cohen 1993, 2259). This did not seem to hold because of a second problem: the president was not campaigning very actively for the proposal. More effort was going into health care reform. This raised doubts about his commitment to NAFTA (Stokes 1993, 2472).

Finally, in October, a strong and coordinated presidential effort com-

TABLE 8.3. Public Support and Opposition to NAFTA

Question: "Do you favor or oppose the North American Free Trade Agreement with Mexico and Canada that eliminates nearly all restrictions on imports, exports, and business investment between the United States, Mexico, and Canada? If you feel you have not heard enough about this issue to have an opinion, please just say so."

Date	Support	Oppose	Don't know, No opinion
September 12, 1992	27	34	40
October 20, 1992	21	36	43
January 23, 1993	28	31	41
April 17, 1993	27	25	48
July 24, 1993	31	29	40
September 10, 1993	25	36	39
October 22, 1993	29	33	38
November 14, 1993	36	31	33

Source: NBC-*Wall Street Journal.*

menced, with a team of 20 White House people working full time on gaining NAFTA's passage. This mobilization and activity underscored Clinton's commitment to the policy and silenced those who thought he was uncommitted to it. The president worked with pro-NAFTA business lobbies, which also stepped up activity. And the president began to cut side deals with opponents, like citrus and sugar growers. The last tactic, while picking up some votes, also hurt Clinton's reputation, as charges flew that he would sell out to any interest seeking special treatment. Such action also undercut his attempt to sell NAFTA as being good for the nation.

Labor opposition intensified when movement leaders threatened to cut off political support in the 1994 midterm congressional elections to those who supported the deal. Perot's visibility and tirades against the agreement also intensified.

With the prospects of a loss in the House looming, the administration decided on a risky gamble—to debate Ross Perot. The debate was held on November 9, just a week before the scheduled House vote. Vice President Albert Gore was called in to do the debate honors. The gamble seemed to pay off for the administration. Gore was prepared for the debate with facts, figures, and rationale. Perot, meanwhile, appeared uninformed, unable to marshall evidence to support his claims. This public relations coup reinvigorated the administration's position.

Movement toward the administration's position is evident in the available public opinion data. NBC–*Wall Street Journal* polls show a surge of seven points in support of the agreement, from 29 to 36 percent in polls between late October and just prior to the vote (see table 8.3). Opposition saw only a small decline of two points. Gains seemingly came from the previously undecided. CBS–*New York Times* polls tell a similar story. Support moved from 33 to 37 percent between mid-September and mid-November, opposition was stable, and undecideds declined about five points. Although these movements might seem small, in Washington politics they were read as momentum in the president's direction.

NAFTA is not a case of presidential responsiveness to public opinion. Too many people had no opinion, and the rest were almost evenly divided. Moreover, opposition was stronger within the president's party than among Republicans. NAFTA represents a case of a president trying to mobilize support for his position. Although modest movement did occur, it happened at a strategic time, helping passage of the treaty. After passage, stronger support for the treaty emerged, as polls by Times-Mirror (December 2, 1993), Harris (December 20, 1993), and Gallup (January 1, 1994) all found majority support for NAFTA. Still opposition sentiment in those polls remained as it had before, around 35 to 40 percent. It was among the undecideds that numbers dropped, to around 10 percent, from 40 percent in October.

Conclusions

The eight cases reviewed in these two chapters present us with three types of presidential reactions to public opinion. First, presidents may directly and strongly respond to public opinion or to the anticipation of public opinion effects. Thus, Reagan abandoned any effort to cut or modify Social Security. Nixon imposed wage and price controls, and after about a year of resistance Bush accepted unemployment benefits extensions and increases. On the other extreme are examples of presidents resisting public opinion and at times moving in the opposite direction. This is clearest in the case of the Kennedy tax cut and, to a lesser extent, Clinton with NAFTA and Kennedy with civil rights. Lastly, there is a middle category where presidents concede somewhat to public pressures but not completely. A compromise is offered, one that they hope will appeal to the public, but one that does not undermine the president's basic policy thrust. Eisenhower and *Sputnik a*nd Clinton and gays in the military are examples of this middling response.

What accounts for these types of responses to public opinion? Two variables seem to stand out. First, the stronger the president's commitment to a policy, the more resistant he appears to be to public opinion when a policy difference exists. Second, when presidents lose control of the policy agenda, their resistance to public pressures may subside.

In two cases, and perhaps a third, presidents seemed uncommitted to the policy, and in each such case we witness presidential responsiveness to public opinion. First, take the case of Nixon and his wages and prices policy. Nixon was not committed to any definite economic program, though he leaned in a conservative direction. His defeat for the presidency in 1960, which he blamed in part on Eisenhower's refusal to boost the then flagging economy, limited how economically orthodox Nixon would be. He saw economics as a political issue, and thus when the economy soured, affecting his reelection prospects, and as the 1972 election neared he abandoned his preferred traditional Republican economic approach for the most radical peacetime economic policy on record.

Similarly, Reagan abandoned any attempt to cut Social Security benefits because such a course was not critical to his primary goals of cutting taxes, quelling inflation, restoring the economy, and building up the military. Social security was tangential, not central, to the policy that he had built and submitted to Congress. This made it easy for Reagan to abandon the effort to modify Social Security, especially when the political costs of pursuing retractions in Social Security were added to the equation.

Bush is the most complicated character of the three presidents who display some responsiveness to public pressure. After almost a year of wrangling with Congress over the issue of unemployment extensions, he finally relented to public and political pressures. Bush is often characterized as a president without policy commitment, one who would easily shift his policy stance with changes in the political winds. He altered his abortion position once he decided to enter the race for the presidency in the late 1970s. He broke his no-new-taxes promise. There are numerous other policy twists and turns throughout his career. About the only policy that he steadfastly stood by during his presidential tenure was the capital gains tax cut.

On unemployment benefits extensions, he seemed to reexhibit his propensity to shift position. Although his popularity was riding high and he had time until the next election, he maintained a relatively conservative economic posture and refused to further burden the budget deficit or increase federal programs. Once his polls plummeted and the reelection contest neared, he noticed his reelection vulnerability and shifted position on the unemployment benefits issue. Now he had to attend to his public image. The public viewed Bush as one who did not care about the economic plight of Americans, like an earlier Republican president, Hoover. In this context, like Nixon, the electoral pragmatist won out over the economic conservative, and Bush not only relented but pushed for extensions and increases in unemployment benefits. Although the story on Bush is not complete, it appears that he was not wedded or committed to a policy course on unemployment benefits. At least, this is how I read him in this case.

When presidents are, in contrast, committed to a policy goal, they are more likely to resist public pressures and sometimes even move policy in an opposite direction. Clinton, for example, became a strong proponent of free trade and NAFTA. His support for the pact waffled during the election campaign because of Bush's imprimatur on it, but once he negotiated side agreements with the Mexicans over environmental and other issues, Clinton strongly pushed the policy in spite of strong opposition from his own party and a mixed public reception.

Kennedy also illustrates the boldness of presidents once they have committed to a policy course. Having been successfully indoctrinated into Keynesian economic thinking, Kennedy pushed his stimulative tax cuts despite polls that reported public opposition. Although the public tends to readily agree to tax cuts, in this instance concern over the budget weighed more heavily. Keynesianism had not yet become the public philosophy. This forced Kennedy into a major public relations campaign to build support for the program, which Congress finally adopted.

Both of these examples illustrate some reasons why presidents will persist, even in the face of public opposition. First, presidents may calculate that they can bend public opinion to their side. Although public opinion reports are ambiguous on this point, for Clinton we find that after the passage of NAFTA increased public support for the policy is evident.

Second, presidents may feel a responsibility for the quality of public policy and at times will take chances for policies that they believe in. Short-term political calculations may be discounted in the face of expected future gains. The presidential policy calculus is not simple, nor focused merely on public opinion. It is more complex and includes short-term and longer-term factors, a concern for policy effectiveness and legacy, as well as political gain. Presidents may even surmise that political gain can be acquired through the implementation of effective policies.

Two other cases, Eisenhower and *Sputnik* and Clinton and gays in the military, show presidents compromising in the face of public pressure. In both cases, the president believed strongly in his course of action. These compromises resulted from losing control of the agenda. Compromise, a tactical retreat, became the only way for the presidents to salvage their preferred policy course.

Several factors may pull the agenda out of presidential control. Unexpected events, like *Sputnik,* provide one type of agenda-destabilizing factor. Neither the administration nor the public was fully prepared to deal with *Sputnik,* which burst onto the political scene. A leak activated the gays-and-the-military issue, which meant that the president could not control the timing or the presentation of the issue to the public. Both presidents engaged in a rearguard action against more radical critics and finally forged compromises that maintained the essence of the policy that they preferred while somewhat defusing the opposition. In both cases, these presidents were criticized for their actions, especially their compromises. That they accepted these politically costly compromises attests to the power of presidential commitment to a policy.

These two cases also raise another point related to responsiveness. How much responsiveness must there be for a presidential action to be considered responsive? Compromises must be understood in their context before one can suggest that the president sold out to public or other types of pressures. In these cases, my judgment is that they did not sell out in wholesale fashion. The story of these cases revolves around presidential attempts to salvage a policy to which they were committed. The quantitative evidence reported in the earlier chapters will have a hard time with this type of nuanced, but theoretically crucial, point.

The case of Kennedy and civil rights is perhaps the most difficult to sort through. Like the cases of clear presidential responsiveness, Kennedy did not possess a strong feeling or policy direction early in his presidential tenure. Civil rights was a nuisance and he had to sail between two positions, lest he fracture his already fragile and limited political base. But as time progressed, Kennedy became convinced that he needed a civil rights policy, one that was more than what southern resisters would accept but one that was also less than satisfactory to advocates. Rather than appeal to these groups or to public opinion, Kennedy needed a way to control the issue. Importantly, with his 1963 legislation, Kennedy began to pull away from public opinion, going beyond and perhaps faster than general public opinion felt desirable.

The president offered civil rights legislation because he was no longer able to control the civil rights agenda. Much like Eisenhower and *Sputnik* and Clinton and the gays-in-the-military issue, events were propelling the issue. The president was forced into a policy of trying to keep the issue from spinning further out of his control. Presenting new legislation, under his sponsorship, and presumably under his control, was the road that Kennedy took to deal with this issue. But this also required a compromise on his part. He could no longer passively sit back, nor could he solely wait for public signals about what to do. He had to make the issue his, defining it in a way that would suit his needs.

Thus, Kennedy developed a commitment to his version of civil rights, and this commitment, while sensitive to public pressures, was more concerned with public reactions in the future if he could not control the issue. Short-term political losses would be accepted for longer-term gains; he hoped that an effective policy, one that would take civil rights politics off the streets and into the chambers of Congress, would rally the public to his side, generating the support he needed for the next election. Again, the variables of agenda control and commitment are instrumental for understanding the relationship between the president and public opinion. Both may affect the short-term responsiveness to public opinion.

In previous chapters, I discussed how ideology and party can act as resources for the president to draw upon and can help insulate presidents from excessive public pressure. Commitment to a policy, as discussed in this chapter, is quite close in meaning to the way I used the term *ideology* in previous chapters. Commitment is a resource that motivates presidents to lead, not merely follow, public opinion. When presidents lack commitment to a specific policy, the likelihood that they will follow public pressure, rather than resist that pressure, increases.

In this chapter we also see starkly the impact on the president of losing control of the policy-making process. When presidents lose control of that process, they become exposed to all kinds of political pressures, including public opinion. Commitment, however, motivates presidents to try to retain as much control as possible. Thus, tactical compromise often results.

CHAPTER 9

Conclusions

In this final chapter I offer some conclusions concerning contradictory public expectations and the president's pattern of responsiveness to those expectations. I begin this chapter by restating the argument and reviewing the findings, and I then place these results into perspective. I conclude with some thoughts on the implications of this study and its findings for theories of the presidency.

Contradictory Expectations and Presidential Responsiveness to Public Opinion

The public has many contradictory expectations about the presidency. One set of contradictions that strikes at the core of the presidency is that the public expects the president to provide policy leadership while it also expects him to respond to public opinion—it expects him to *lead* and to *follow.* The aim of this book has been to understand the implication of these contradictory expectations on the presidency and on presidential behavior.

The need for public support as well as these public expectations about the office create an incentive for presidents to be responsive to public opinion. At the same time, the alternative public expectation, that presidents provide leadership, together with the responsibility that the public places on them for the conduct of public policy and their own policy agendas create another set of incentives. This other set impels presidents to try to control the policy-making process. By controlling that process, presidents are better able to ensure that policies to their liking get implemented. Responsiveness to public opinion in the process of making policy, however, may result in presidents losing some of that control, in effect giving it to the public.

There are other costs of responsiveness. If following the public leads to the implementation of ineffective policies, the president will be judged harshly by the public; the public will blame him for those policy failures. However, if he resists public pressures and implements policies that prove effective, a president may be able to rebuild public support. Thus, the public support that he might lose by not being responsive to the public may be restored by implementing effective policies. In effect, what we have here is a trade-off between prestige and reputation, a point that we will address more fully later.

These incentives thus restrict presidential responsiveness to public opinion. Fundamentally, when substantive decisions about policy are at stake presidential responsiveness to the public should weaken. When there are no such important substantive implications, presidential responsiveness to the public should strengthen.

How can presidents be responsive to the public without losing control of the policy process, without affecting substantive decisions about policy, like timing, size, scope, implementing agency, and the like? Presidents can be responsive symbolically rather than substantively.

The distinction between symbolism and substance is not simple. One does not substitute symbols for substance because all substantive acts have symbolic components. But some symbols may be vague and/or ambiguous in their substantive implications, including policy symbols. Presidents can be responsive by employing these "substanceless" symbols, reserving decisions about the substantive details of a policy to themselves and their advisers and allies. For instance, a president may commiserate with the public about the state of the economy without detailing what policies he will offer to deal with it. In this way he is responding to a public concern about a policy without being specific about the substantive direction or details of that policy.

In contrast to this type of symbolic responsiveness, once decisions and actions have greater implications for the substance of the policy, we should see less of a responsive reaction of the president to public opinion. Rather, presidential attention turns toward control of those aspects of the policy-making process that will affect the substance of the policy. One ultimate goal of presidents is to implement effective policies. This requires some measure of presidential control over the policy-making process to ensure the outcomes that the president thinks will be most effective and to his liking.

The president has at least two reasons to produce desirable or effective policy outcomes. First, desirable policy outcomes boost the confidence of the public, which leads to greater levels of approval and popularity. This may translate into reelection victory, greater influence with Congress, and greater leeway in future policy decisions. Second, desirable policy outcomes will enhance the president's standing in the history books. Desirable policy outcomes become one basis of his legacy to the nation.

At each stage of the policy-making process, presidents have opportunities to offer symbolic gestures to the public to demonstrate their responsiveness. Great opportunities for such symbolic demonstrations occur in the early stages of the policy-making process, that is, in the process of problem identification, but all subsequent stages also provide such opportunities. However, as a policy moves from these earliest stages of policy-making to policy formulation, legitimation, and implementation, the substantive aspect of the policy grows in importance to the president. Presidents still have opportunities to create symbols to offer the mass public, but decisions about the substance and design of the policy become increasingly important.

The bulk of this book was an empirical test of this major hypothesis, that presidents will be more symbolically than substantively responsive to the mass public in policy-making. Special attention was paid to the symbolic and substantive nature of each policy indicator that I developed. Generally, results support the responsiveness hypothesis. The next section reviews the results of that analysis.

Reviewing the Results: Symbolic Responsiveness but Substantive Nonresponsiveness

To test the theory, I created quantitative indicators of presidential behavior on four policy-making processes—problem identification, substantive rhetoric, policy formulation, and policy legitimation—as well as offered detailed case studies of specific policy decisions. Throughout the analysis, I discussed the symbolic-substantive mix of each indicator, noting that different indicators mix these attributes in different measure.

Problem Identification

An important process of agenda building is identifying those problems that are considered important enough to be candidates for public actions. In chapter 2 I looked at the interaction between the public's and the president's problem agendas. The theory suggests that presidents are likely to be responsive to the public in this process because of the highly symbolic nature of problem identification and the fact that problem identification can occur without strong implications for future policy-making.

Using data on the public's Most Important Problem and a comparable measure using presidential State of the Union Addresses, my analysis found that the president both responds to and leads public opinion in the problem identification process. Thus, when the public thinks that a problem is important, the president follows suit in his speech and increases his attentiveness to that problem area. Similarly, when the president emphasizes a problem, public attention to that problem also increases.

These processes were more fully specified by noting that not all problems are alike. Some are required and easily reach the problem agenda, others are more discretionary and move onto or off the problem agenda of the president and the public. International affairs and macroeconomics (inflation and unemployment) were identified as required policy problems. Civil rights and domestic policy were termed discretionary policy problems. This distinction between required and discretionary policy problems led to an important asymmetry in presidential leadership and responsiveness to public opinion. The differing incentive structures of required versus discretionary policy problems led to this asymmetric pattern.

Specifically, presidents were more likely to be responsive to the public on required, as opposed to discretionary, policy problems. The incentives toward presidential responsiveness are stronger for required than discretionary policy problems. The strength of the incentives for responsiveness to required policy problems derive from their persistence on the public's agenda and the number of people who are affected or feel that the policy problem is important. Required policy problems persist on the agenda because of their profound implications for the lives of ordinary people and because of the responsibility that people give the government, especially the president, to manage these problems. Discretionary problems may be important but usually not to as many people. Thus, their electoral and popularity implications for presidents do not match the implications of required policy problems. Furthermore, the public does not assign the president as much responsibility for discretionary policy problems as it does for required policy problems. Lastly, required policy problems may crowd discretionary ones off the public's agenda. Either objective factors or presidential leadership may create this crowding-out effect. Thus, presidents are not likely to be highly responsive to the public on discretionary policy problems but are highly likely to be responsive to the public on required policy problems.

Substantive Rhetoric

Rhetoric need not be void of substance. Though often general and lacking in detail, presidents do take stands on issues when they speak. Doing so provides some information about their policy choices and directions. In this sense, presidential rhetoric may have substantive implications, and thus, according to the theory being tested, presidents will be less responsive to public opinion when making substantive pronouncements and statements than when those statements are void of substance, when they are purely symbolic.

From the State of the Union Addresses I created indicators of policy substance in presidential rhetoric. The analysis looked at the substantiveness of the president's Address overall and broken down by four issue areas: international affairs, economic policy, civil rights, and domestic policy. I found that the greater the public's concern with foreign policy, the more substantive the president's State of the Union Address is overall. This does not, however, imply presidential responsiveness because presidents could offer substantive proposals on other issues in an attempt to divert the public away from its major concerns. Thus, while the public may be concerned about foreign affairs, presidential substantiveness might be increasing for domestic policy.

Lacking a global indicator of overall public concern and the degree to which the public wants government to address problems limits our ability to say if the overall substantive tone of the president's Address was responsive to the public or not. However, relating public concern about specific policy areas with presidential statements on those same policy areas does allow a test of presidential responsiveness. As substantive statements on particular policies have a clear implication for policy-making and control of the policy-making process, we did not expect to find much presidential responsiveness here.

Disaggregating the analysis into the four policy areas revealed a mixed pattern of presidential responsiveness. Mostly, presidents demonstrated little responsiveness. This was especially the case for economic and foreign policy. And presidents demonstrated some counterresponsiveness for domestic policy. Only for civil rights policy was there a clear indication of presidential responsiveness. The moral implications of civil rights distinguishes it from most other types of policies, and this might serve as the motivation for presidential responsiveness to the public. Civil rights, when a major public concern, is not politics as usual and thus is treated differently in the polity.

The analysis also unearthed some important presidential leadership effects on public opinion. In particular, I found that substantiveness in presidential rhetoric did not enhance presidential leadership of public opinion. To capture public attention, all a president has to do is mention a policy problem. Increases in public attention will follow. Presidents do not have to offer positions to rally the public. This leadership effect, however, decays quite quickly for all policy areas except international affairs. Presidents do not have much trouble directing public attention to an issue of their choice, but they have to consistently readdress that issue to keep it high among the public's concerns.

This finding tells why presidents can afford to be resistant to the public at times. Presidents do not have to do much to influence public opinion, at least in the short run. With such a resource, presidents can close the "policy gap" between themselves and the public, not by moving to the public's position, but by moving the public toward their own. This leadership potential, like other resources identified in this study, helps insulate presidents from public opinion. When presidents lack these resources, they feel public pressures more intensely and often find that they must respond. Thus, we may understand why presidents seem so keen on developing resources that are independent of the public. It helps them resist public pressures and maintain their control over the policy-making process and its outcomes.

Policy Formulation

The substantive implications of formulating policy proposals are easily evident, while the symbolic may be easily overlooked. When presidents formulate policy proposals they make decisions about the policies' timing, size, scope, and other factors, all of which are important substantive decisions. This, and the fact that the public is a poor guide to building policy alternatives reduces presidential incentives to be responsive to public opinion. But presidents also present their policy ideas to the public. Moreover, they package their policy ideas when presenting them to the public. This packaging enables presidents to foster an image of what they want to do. This is an important symbolic aspect of policy formulation.

Again, I used the president's State of the Union Address to create an indicator of presidential policy formulation. Here I coded whether or not the president took a liberal or conservative stance on issues when he took a position. I used a liberal-conservative public opinion series to test whether presidential policy formulation decisions responded to public opinion.

The analysis supported the basics of the theory of presidential responsiveness. Presidents displayed no responsiveness to public opinion when we look at specific policy areas, but when we look at the entirety of their comments, there is a responsive reaction. And this is as we would suggest, because the global indicator, the one that cuts across all policy areas, is one step removed from the specific policies, therefore its symbolic aspect is stronger than the policy-specific indicators. Presidents may manipulate their comments across policy areas to create an impression or image that is more consistent with the public than is the case for any specific policy area. Thus, if a president finds himself out of step with the public in one policy area, say, economic policy, he may compensate by accenting how similar his policies are to the public's in another policy area, say, domestic or civil rights policy. This ability to manipulate the overall image of his Address through the relative frequency and direction of statements within policy areas enables a president to be out of step with the public on specific policy areas, while appearing more responsive and closer to the public overall.

There is even a hint of counterresponsiveness when we look at economic policy, though the overall message of the Address remains responsive to the public. When the public got more liberal (or conservative), the president moved in the opposite direction. Presidents may be trying to modulate public pressures here, indicating that they will not be able to deliver perfectly what the public desires, that in other words all economic policy-making involves trade-offs. This counterresponsive finding fits well with the overall theme: presidents are likely to be more symbolically responsive than substantively responsive.

Policy Legitimation

The policy legitimation process, which involves the passage of bills into laws, is a highly substantive one, and thus the theory hypothesizes that presidents will not be very responsive to public opinion. This contrasts with a theory that emphasizes the importance of public opinion as a bargaining resource for presidents. The implication of the resources theory is that presidents will follow public opinion to use it to influence Congress in the legitimation process. I used presidential positions on roll call before Congress to test these competing notions.

I constructed an indicator of presidential positions on roll calls before Congress that the ADA defined as tests of liberalism and conservatism. Analysis detected no evidence of presidential responsiveness to public opinion. Rather, party, president, unemployment, and the tenor of presidential rhetoric determined presidential roll call positions. This is as we would expect given the importance of substantive considerations to the construction of this indicator.

Case Analysis

Much of the quantitative work presented in the study is aggregate in nature, though in varying degrees. Thus, all the quantitative measures are at least one step removed from actual policy decisions. Case studies of actual policy decisions, eight in all, were used to further test the theory of presidential responsiveness. The case studies are all the more important because the substantive aspect of policy-making looms so large the closer we get to the actual policy. Symbolism without strong substantive implications is more likely the further away we get from the actual policy decision. Thus, the case studies become a strong test of the ideas being put forth here.

That analysis proved quite useful. Several instances of presidential responsiveness were detected as well as several cases of presidents resisting public pressures. The difference in the two responses seems to be one of policy commitment. When presidents lack commitment to a policy course, they are likely to give in to public pressures. When presidents are, in contrast, committed to a policy action, they are more likely not only to resist public pressures but to try to convert the public to their view, that is, to lead. This is one consequence of presidents trying to control the outcome of the policy-making process. This finding is also reminiscent of early quantitative results on presidential leadership of public opinion. Commitment to a policy, like leadership resources, helps insulate presidents from strong public pressure.

Commitment is important for understanding presidential behavior in policy-making. We found that Reagan, a president noted for the persistence and stability of his policy initiatives, caved in to public pressures on Social Security, while Clinton, usually thought of as a waffler who cannot decide on what policy direction to pursue, resisted public pressures on NAFTA. Here, these presidents were behaving against type because Reagan was not committed to Social Security reform, while Clinton was committed to NAFTA.

Several cases were found in which presidents partially responded to public opinion, what I termed a tactical retreat or compromise. These presidents did not give in completely to public pressures because they were committed to a policy, but they were forced to compromise because they had lost control over some aspect of the policy-making process. In these cases that loss of control seemed to be at the agenda stage, but loss of control can happen at other stages too.

In all, analysis was generally supportive of the theory. Presidents were responsive to public opinion when the response could be symbolic and when it held few direct implications for substantive decisions about public policy-making. In contrast, when presidential decisions have important substantive implications, presidents display less inclination to respond to public opinion and at times even exhibit counterresponsiveness, making decisions counter to public concerns and the public mood. Further, important intervening variables in this process are the degree of presidential commitment to a policy and the president's ability to maintain control of the policy-making process.

The Irony of the Presidency: Democratization with Policy Nonresponsiveness

The presidency is now arguably the most democratic of the three branches of government. Ironically, it may be the least policy responsive. The democratization of the presidency began soon after the establishment of the office. The first democratizing move came with changes in the election of the president, a consequence of the Jacksonian party-building and reform movement. The democratizing trend accelerated with the Progressive Era reforms of the early twentieth century. The Progressives altered the conception of the presidency and introduced a new method for nominating party candidates. Technological developments in the twentieth century enhanced the trend toward democratization.

The Progressives' conception of the presidency viewed the office as a policy leadership post. The president was to use his premier position to move the policy-making process and to take his views directly to the people, mobilizing public opinion in his behalf. Theodore Roosevelt was the great innovator here, in what Tulis labels the "rhetorical presidency" (Tulis 1987). Roosevelt would use the "bully pulpit" of the presidency to lead the nation. Woodrow Wilson expanded on the Roosevelt policy leadership model, but it was under Theodore's cousin, Franklin, that the process of policy leadership would institutionalize.

To institutionalize policy leadership, presidents required a way to communicate to the people directly, without political interpretation mediating their message. The creation and diffusion of the electronic media gave them such a method for communicating to the people. Now they could speak directly and personally to the public. Institutionalizing policy leadership also required a rationale for presidential action. The Great Depression provided that rationale. Lastly, the institutionalization process required a president willing to take the means (radio) and the opportunity (the Depression) to mold public expectations in that direction. That president was FDR.

The second great Progressive legacy related to the method of nominating candidates for the presidency, the primary, which replaced the Jacksonian party-leader nomination system. The primary spread across the states during the first two decades of the twentieth century until about twenty states utilized the primary to select delegates to the party conventions by 1916. After this experiment in popular nomination control, use of the primary receded. By 1940 only thirteen states used it. Whereas over 50 percent of delegates to the conventions were selected by primaries in 1916, only slightly more than one-third were so selected by 1940 (Reiter 1985, 3). By the 1950s, primaries had become beauty contests, a way to demonstrate the voter appeal of candidates, not a way to gain delegates. This move away from the primary was not so much a political as a technological decision.

The transportation infrastructure did not exist that could support large numbers of primaries across the huge American territorial expanse. Woodrow Wilson's national campaign to secure the Treaty of Versailles exposed the great weakness of the transportation system. Wilson traveled from coast to coast on the trains, speaking in every town through which he passed. The heavy schedule taxed him dearly. Some feel it caused his physical breakdown, stroke, and death soon after leaving the presidency. The rail system just took too long and imposed too heavy a physical burden on candidates to enable them to travel across the nation to battle in numerous primary fights within a short time frame.

This changed with the introduction of the airplane, and in the 1960s the jet. That, plus the twin strains of race and Vietnam in the Democratic Party, provided the political motivation to reintroduce nomination through primaries (Polsby 1983). By the 1970s the primary had replaced the party-leader model for nominating candidates in most states.

Another technological development reinforced the democratizing trend: the public opinion poll. The public opinion poll institutionalized itself into the fabric of American politics. Lyndon Johnson carried the latest poll results around in his pocket to display to his critics his popularity and demonstrate public support for his performance as president. The public opinion poll exposed presidents even more to the tide of public opinion and the need for public support. In Lowi's (1985) terms, a "plebiscitary presidency" arose, whereby presidents graded themselves by the support they received from the public. They also engaged in campaigns to manipulate public opinion to ensure a good grading from other poll watchers. The latest poll results became the benchmark for political observers trying to assess how well the president was doing. Curiously, the quality of the actions the president was taking diminished as indicators of presidential job performance.

The result of democratizing the presidency was that as ties to the public were forged and strengthened, presidential ties to other political institutions weakened. This is most evident with the breakdown of the parties, which had important implications for presidential leadership of Congress. Party follower-ship of the president was less predictable, and the president often had to build bipartisan coalitions, surely a harder task than relying on his own party for support. Compounding this problem was the increased incidence of divided government, the decentralization of power in Congress in the 1970s, and the growing incumbency advantage, the latter insulating many legislators from presidential coattails and other forms of influence.

Thus, the policy presidency developed along with the democratization of the office. Ironically, as the office assumed policy-making and leadership responsibilities, policy responsiveness to the public declined, though pres-sures to appear responsive remained, if not actually intensifying. Democratiz-ing the presidency did not create a responsive presidency. Instead it created the logic of responsiveness—substantive policy-making and symbolic politics were separated. The gap between symbol and substance, and the occasional incidence of counterresponsiveness that we have noted, may be one cause of the high degree of public cynicism toward government during the past three decades.

Mechanisms of Presidential Responsiveness

The findings of this study tell us much about the mechanisms of presidential responsiveness to the public. Political and policy change comes about through two major mechanisms, replacement of personnel, basically through elections, or changes in the policies of incumbents while in office. Both seem important for understanding responsiveness in the presidency, but the former seems a better route for ensuring substantive policy change than the latter.

We see this, for instance, in the impact of party and person on presiden-tial policy actions. These factors were especially critical in the policy formula-tion and legitimation processes. Changing the person in office, rather than changing the person *while* in office, seems a surer route to policy change. Changing the person while in office may not lead to much in the way of policy change, may not promote presidential policy responsiveness to the public. Changing the person while in office may affect the symbolic relationship between the president and the public without necessitating substantive policy change. Moreover, if substantive policy change and responsiveness do occur, it may be at the expense of presidential commitment to policy, that is, at the expense of presidential leadership.

Responsiveness to the public may also be generated through personnel change. The cost of this form of responsiveness is that it may be slow. Policy change to promote responsiveness may occur at most only every four years. In the interim between elections, policy stability, and thus nonresponsiveness, is to be expected. But we may also expect there to be high levels of presidential commitment to policies, that is, strong presidential leadership. Ironically, if the public can desist from strong demands for too much policy change while presidents are in office, it can have committed presidents who provide strong leadership while also ensuring *responsiveness in the institution of the presidency rather than in the person of the president.*

In a sense, our current political culture may have overdemocratized the office, asking for responsiveness within terms. This may motivate presidents to play the symbolic responsiveness game, which may lead to public cynicism when it is noted that presidential actions do not follow the sense that the president tried to convey to the public through symbols and images. Another consequence of this demand is that responsiveness is most likely to occur when policy commitment is lacking. In other words, the quality of presidential leadership erodes.

Presidential leadership and responsiveness may be maintained if we view them from an institutional perspective rather than a person-in-office perspective. Although responsiveness may be slower, occurring at most every four years, leadership will maintain a consistent level throughout the term. Asking for more frequent responsiveness by the president to the public may not only undermine the quality of that responsiveness, rendering it mostly symbolic, but also undercut presidential leadership and diminish incentives toward presidential commitment to policy as well.

Another benefit of the institutional perspective is that people can use the conduct and effectiveness of implemented policies as a standard for judging whether or not to keep the president (or his party) and thus his policies. Of course, this removes the public one step from the actual process of policy-making, though ironically public impact on policy-making may surge. Public participation in the policy-making process to promote presidential within-term responsiveness does not necessarily entail change and responsiveness in the actual output of government policy, though it surely affects the quality of political and policy symbols offered to the nation.

Although it might be thought that increased public participation in policy should improve the process, making it more responsive—if not capable of affecting the quality of government policy output—the results of this study suggest otherwise. Making presidents more responsive to the public in the policy-making process may only mean that the president tries harder to insulate himself from public pressures through the accumulation of resources independent of the public and symbolic manipulation. Part of the motivation to centralize and politicize resources in the presidency may be reflected in this dynamic. Ironically, while the democratization of the office has increased the power, resources, and responsibilities of the presidency, these accumulations have come at a price, the greater permeability of the office to the whims of public opinion. Modern presidents do much to resist these pressures. One implication may be the alienation and cynicism of the public from the political process because its expectations are not met in reality.

Symbolic Responsiveness, Substantive Nonresponsiveness, and Theories of the Presidency

This study speaks to several important theoretical issues confronting scholars of the presidency. These include whether we should view the office from a president-centered or a presidency-centered perspective. Another important but less discussed issue is the relationship between the politics of prestige and the politics of reputation, the twin pillars of presidential power that Neustadt (1960) identified in his seminal work of nearly four decades ago.

A very important debate has animated much research on the presidency: whether it is more fruitful to conceptualize the office in terms of the individual president or in terms of the presidency. President-centered theories of the office have a long history. These theories suggest that we should focus on the individual in office, his beliefs, personality (Barber 1972), and other individual traits. Scholars who follow in this tradition often focus their research on one occupant of the office at a time, providing us with a very rich description of many presidencies. One time-honored aspect of this tradition is to look at the impact of the person on the office, to detail how presidents have altered and shaped the office and the political system over time. Assumed in this approach is that while institutional structures and constraints on the presidency are important, personal factors are more important and powerful.

Thus, while the Depression was a necessary ingredient for understanding the creation of the modern presidency, that development also required a leader willing and able to take up that mantle. Such a leader was found in Franklin Roosevelt. But the Depression was into its third year by the time FDR assumed office. Hoover was not the leader up to the task of reforming the office into the modern office that we now recognize. The person in office makes a difference, a profound difference.

The contrasting view focuses instead on the office itself, the constraints that it imposes on the occupant, and similarities in behavior across presidencies. The argument of this school is that theory building is founded on being able to make general statements and that by looking at the institutional context of presidential behavior, one will note the similarity in presidential behavior. Thus, modern presidents seem prone to centralize power and resources in the White House and to politicize operations around them (Moe 1985), to take just one such theoretical insight. The peculiar behaviors of presidents are only understandable within their contexts, or so proponents of this view would suggest (King and Ragsdale 1988). Focusing exclusively on the unique and the person in office obscures the similar tendencies across presidents.

The motivation for this study began from the latter, presidency-centered perspective. For instance, the model of symbolic responsiveness and substantive nonresponsiveness is rooted in public expectations and the resources available to the office. No mention is made here of presidents as individuals with different traits, skills, preferences. Rarely did I mention a particular president in developing the model, other than by way of example or illustration. Presidents were treated as a generic type facing a common problem and possessing comparable resources and motivations.

But as the study unfolded, the insights to be gained from the president-centered perspective also became apparent. Although an understanding of the symbolic responsiveness-substantive nonresponsiveness problem is rooted in the presidency perspective, the details of presidential behavior across the policy-making process were often heavily influenced by personal attributes. Thus, party, person, and commitment were important variables in explaining presidential behavior across various stages of the policy-making process. In another study, Brace and Hinckley (1992) argue that a full statistical model of presidential behavior must take into account person differences, modeled as presidential dummies.

I not only followed that lead but at times pushed one step beyond, arguing that there may be substantive interest in the impact of the presidential dummies. Thus, there is substantive import in noting that Eisenhower was more liberal than other Republican presidents and Carter more conservative than other Democrats, that Johnson was more substantive, Reagan more temporally stable in his conservatism, or Nixon more volatile. The increase in the statistical power of the equations that were estimated not only enhanced our understanding of presidential behavior across the policy process, but also improved our substantive understanding of presidents and helped to spell out when president differences made a difference.

Presidency and president are both important for understanding the behavior of presidents and for developing powerful theories of presidential behavior. Each, however, has a different role to play in understanding presidential behavior. Presidency-centered models seem most powerful when delimiting the institutional and structural constraints that all presidents face. Moreover, presidency models seem useful for understanding presidential behavior once an optimal or satisfactory accommodation or solution to a constraint or problem has been found and that response has been institutionalized. When presidents follow the lead of previous occupants in solving a problem, presidency-centered models seem very appropriate. Presidency models seem most useful for understanding continuities of the presidency over time.

When looking at dynamics or changes in the office, president models may be more useful, though they should not be taken as the sole explanation for changes in the office. Environmental pressures and changes may also stimulate changes in the office. But so will presidents. A president may land upon a novel solution to a problem. A president-centered model is probably best at explaining why a president landed upon a specific solution or behavior. The presidency model will take over in explaining why succeeding presidents follow that lead. A president model is probably quite useful for understanding why a president opens the office into a new direction, such as FDR did with the modern presidency. A presidency model is better suited to explaining the continuation of the modern office as a pattern of expected behavior.

President models are also appropriate when looking at situations in which presidents have a degree of choice, some discretion or latitude. President models may thus be useful in explaining why presidents vary in their commitment to policy and their policy leanings. Other than innovative changes in the office, which may be felt as the innovation becomes a part of the office, president models may be more useful in understanding short-term aspects of the office, while presidency models will be more useful in understanding long-term continuities. And president models will be important in understanding some dynamic processes of the presidency. The office may pull presidents to behave in certain ways; the person may try to alter the ways that presidents behave. A theory of the presidential *dynamics and continuities* will probably have to draw upon both explanations.

A second important theoretical consideration relates to the politics of prestige versus the politics of reputation. Neustadt (1960), in his famous and seminal book, *Presidential Power,* noted the importance of both of these resources to presidential influence. Although Neustadt seems to suggest that presidents would like to have both of these resources, he spends little time discussing their interconnections. Based upon this study, I would like to suggest that while reputation may enhance prestige, at least in the long run, the pursuit of prestige may undermine a president's ability to build a reputation. Furthermore, in the short run building a reputation may undermine presidential prestige. The relationship between reputation and prestige is quite complex.

The contrasting public expectations of leadership and followership closely parallel the distinction between reputation and prestige. Followership is one strategy for building public support, that is, a president's popularity and prestige. However, it is a fragile resource. Its fragility derives from the speed with which its moves from high to low and the seeming inability of presidents to find a way to build public support beyond the short term. Even George Bush's unmatched poll ratings during the Gulf War episode quickly evaporated. Further, it is not clear how much instrumental value popular support has. As I noted in earlier chapters, the body of evidence over the impact of presidential popularity on legislative support is mixed, with several studies finding effects (Brace and Hinckley 1992; Rivers and Rose 1985; Ostrom and Simon 1985) but just as many finding no effect (Bond and Fleisher 1990; Edwards 1989).

Also, as I have argued throughout this study, if presidents try to curry public favor by implementing policies that follow public wishes, and if those policies fail, it will be the president, not the public, that bears the brunt of the blame. At best, prestige can garner the president some short-term victories. But as this resource is rooted in an unstable environment and is so susceptible to change, it cannot provide a long-term foundation on which to build an administration.

This is part of the reason for the limited responsiveness syndrome that was detected in this study. It seems that presidents might intuitively understand the longer-term reliability of reputation. As I argued in this study, one way to build a reputation is to implement policies that prove effective. Controlling the policy process, especially insulating it as much as possible from public pressures, is one way to begin to build a reputation. One of the elements of what we may define as a "presidential reputation" is rooted in policymaking.

For example, Lyndon Johnson had a reputation for knowing how to manage the congressional policy-making process. Even after his polls slid and his Vietnam War policies began to take their toll on his administration, he still had that reputation. Ronald Reagan also built a reputation for accomplishment based on his supply-side economic policy and the long period of economic growth that some argue was the result of that policy. His anti-Soviet policies, which some say led to the arms reduction treaties, reinforced his reputation for accomplishing his goals. This reputation, I would argue, helped him weather the storms of the Iran-Contra scandal.

But reputation may also help build prestige and popularity, as I have argued in this study, though not in the short run. To build a reputation through the implementation of effective policies requires presidential resistance to public pressure. This may undermine his momentary popular support, as the public criticizes him for not paying attention to public concerns. Ironically, if the unpopular policy proves effective, the public is likely to forget its criticisms and rally behind the president. In this way, public support can be generated, but in the long run.

This type of popular support is likely to be quite stable and might provide the president with less resistance when he and the public seem to collide on other issues. When this happens the president can point to his successes, thereby defusing public criticism. With a reputation, the president is less likely to be obstructed by the public in future presidential policies because they are willing to give him a chance. Even though not necessarily popular, a president with a reputation for policy accomplishment may face a quiescent, docile, and/or impressionable public. And such a public will be more resistant to mobilization by the president's political adversaries. The whole political environment that a president faces will be less hostile if he possesses a reputation.

But in this media-saturated age, there are powerful pressures for presidents to follow public opinion, to play the politics of prestige, and to do so in a way that might undercut their ability to build a reputation. Still, the analysis just given suggests that presidents seem somewhat resistant to those public pressures, especially when they are committed to a policy. An important question for us to ask is whether presidents can stay committed to a policy with all of these pressures on them and whether the primary nomination process is conducive to recruiting committed presidents. For too long political scientists have forgotten this element of the presidency. Hopefully this study will redirect some attention in that direction.

Appendix: Data Used in the Study

On the following appendix tables, I present the original data I collected for this study. This is primarily the content analysis data from the presidential State of the Union Addresses, and they are presented in yearly breakdowns, as used in the analysis. These data are also presented graphically on the many figures throughout the text.

(see following page)

TABLE A.1. **Percentage of Sentences in the State of the Union Address Referring to Specific Policy Areas**

Year	Economic Policy	Foreign Policy	Civil Rights	Domestic Policy
1953	21.97	32.46	8.52	37.05
1954	20.46	38.61	6.56	34.36
1955	20.00	33.22	5.42	41.36
1956	22.22	30.12	10.53	37.13
1957	24.22	54.66	5.59	15.53
1958	9.81	85.98	0.00	4.21
1959	26.69	50.85	5.51	16.95
1960	19.47	58.41	5.31	16.81
1961	25.00	60.37	1.22	13.41
1962	11.90	64.29	3.17	20.63
1963	21.35	66.15	1.56	10.94
1964	33.33	24.32	10.81	31.53
1965	12.15	50.28	4.42	33.15
1966	14.80	65.92	4.04	15.25
1967	11.72	48.97	10.34	28.97
1968	23.74	34.34	15.66	26.26
1969	28.36	2.99	8.96	59.70
1970	19.70	21.21	12.88	46.21
1971	12.78	0.75	0.75	85.71
1972	26.51	49.40	2.41	21.69
1973	52.17	21.74	4.35	21.74
1974	10.71	27.98	7.74	53.57
1975	45.26	20.44	4.38	29.93
1976	29.63	25.93	14.29	30.16
1977	33.08	12.03	0.00	54.89
1978	33.16	34.74	2.63	29.47
1979	27.13	53.49	3.88	15.50
1980	4.73	78.38	0.00	16.89
1981	62.56	10.90	0.00	26.54
1982	36.76	21.57	3.43	38.24
1983	44.13	30.05	5.63	20.19
1984	43.52	32.12	7.77	16.58
1985	37.28	32.54	10.65	19.53
1986	33.07	37.80	2.36	26.77
1987	22.05	50.39	2.36	25.20
1988	32.14	40.48	10.71	16.67
1989	19.55	25.91	18.18	36.36

TABLE A.2. Percentage of Substantive Sentences in the State of the Union Address, Overall and by Policy Areas

Year	All	Economic Policy	Foreign Policy	Civil Rights	Domestic Policy
1953	43	49.25	27.27	57.69	37.41
1954	62	60.38	66.00	82.35	38.71
1955	34	30.51	11.22	68.75	36.88
1956	32	39.47	13.59	58.33	26.19
1957	32	38.46	20.45	55.56	20.97
1958	25	33.33	21.74	MD	11.54
1959	23	28.57	6.67	100.00	18.07
1960	24	40.91	12.12	83.33	13.58
1961	27	26.83	18.18	50.00	21.54
1962	22	40.00	9.26	100.00	21.28
1963	17	29.27	11.02	100.00	6.25
1964	63	64.86	37.04	100.00	30.77
1965	34	54.55	15.38	62.50	32.98
1966	52	48.48	52.38	66.67	24.00
1967	48	20.59	54.93	33.33	35.77
1968	45	34.04	38.24	54.84	31.91
1969	46	57.89	0.00	50.00	20.48
1970	33	53.85	21.43	17.65	22.47
1971	45	64.71	100.00	100.00	30.92
1972	24	27.27	19.51	50.00	8.33
1973	52	83.33	20.00	0.00	2.08
1974	22	11.11	21.28	0.00	18.80
1975	45	64.52	35.71	0.00	14.29
1976	40	50.00	28.57	40.74	23.00
1977	36	31.82	31.25	MD	25.00
1978	33	42.86	30.30	100.00	11.11
1979	36	54.29	26.09	80.00	7.94
1980	22	71.43	17.24	MD	10.29
1981	55	46.21	56.52	MD	41.41
1982	47	52.00	31.82	100.00	29.75
1983	32	40.43	17.19	66.67	13.95
1984	32	47.62	9.68	40.00	13.89
1985	48	53.97	49.09	44.44	16.00
1986	39	64.29	22.92	66.67	11.69
1987	38	42.86	35.94	0.00	17.33
1988	52	68.52	35.29	33.33	29.58
1989	26	25.58	24.56	15.00	23.01

Note: MD = Missing Data.

TABLE A.3. Liberalism of the President's State of the Union Address, Overall and by Policy Areas

Year	Rhetoric	Economic Policy	Foreign Policy	Civil Rights	Domestic Policy
1953	1.97	15.15	96.30	86.67	45.45
1954	20.55	62.50	90.91	71.43	52.08
1955	20.71	50.00	81.82	100.00	69.49
1956	29.09	43.33	100.00	100.00	86.36
1957	9.60	20.00	88.89	100.00	53.85
1958	30.00	14.29	97.50	MD	33.33
1959	10.71	16.67	100.00	100.00	53.33
1960	2.73	16.67	100.00	100.00	0.00
1961	41.34	81.82	88.89	100.00	100.00
1962	39.29	58.33	100.00	87.50	100.00
1963	18.57	16.67	92.86	100.00	100.00
1964	19.86	16.67	100.00	100.00	91.67
1965	42.42	66.67	100.00	100.00	96.77
1966	−3.28	100.00	15.58	100.00	100.00
1967	8.67	85.71	21.79	100.00	100.00
1968	32.22	87.50	46.15	100.00	100.00
1969	−30.95	9.09	MD	100.00	23.53
1970	−2.17	0.00	33.33	100.00	80.00
1971	−2.54	81.82	0.00	100.00	40.43
1972	0.00	50.00	37.50	100.00	60.00
1973	−44.12	0.00	0.00	MD	0.00
1974	−9.46	50.00	60.00	MD	32.00
1975	−18.75	30.00	60.00	MD	16.67
1976	−29.52	14.29	14.29	18.18	39.13
1977	3.19	42.86	100.00	MD	48.28
1978	−0.75	22.22	100.00	100.00	27.27
1979	5.10	10.53	94.44	100.00	60.00
1980	18.75	60.00	60.00	MD	100.00
1981	−41.23	3.28	15.38	MD	14.63
1982	−31.63	5.13	7.14	85.71	25.00
1983	−30.28	7.89	0.00	100.00	25.00
1984	−41.05	0.00	16.67	16.67	40.00
1985	−41.57	14.71	0.00	0.00	16.67
1986	−45.83	7.41	0.00	0.00	11.11
1987	−41.85	0.00	4.35	MD	23.08
1988	−50.00	0.00	0.00	0.00	0.00
1989	−12.71	0.00	0.00	83.33	61.54

Note: MD = Missing Data.

Notes

Chapter 1

1. For instance, it is commonly asserted that expectations of the president have grown, but there exists no series of surveys, presumably the best way of learning about public expectations, to test this proposition. At best, we have scattered questions across surveys that might be taken as indicators of public expectations, and only one full-scale survey of public expectations exists. See Edwards (1983) and Wayne (1982) who employ that survey.

2. Only if the outgoing president is concerned with his party's fortune in the upcoming election will lame ducks still feel the pressure of election and public opinion on their actions. Neither of the two modern lame ducks, Eisenhower and Reagan, evidenced much of this concern. Eisenhower seemed lukewarm about Richard Nixon's candidacy; neither did he seem pleased with any other prospect in the GOP for 1960 (see Ambrose 1990). Still, some semblance of electoral concern may have affected Eisenhower's behavior in that he felt "that the election [1960] was a vote of confidence and approval of his policies over the past seven and a half years" (Ambrose 1990, 519). Similarly, Reagan was quite inactive in George Bush's first presidential election campaign and like Eisenhower toward Nixon was slow to endorse Bush.

Chapter 2

1. There are a large number of other studies that find policy content in presidential speech. An early effort is Prothro 1956; also see Brunner and Livornese 1984; Calder 1982; Chang 1989; Chester 1980; Ingold and Windt 1984; Klingsberg 1952; Krukones 1980, 1985; Moen 1988; O'Loughlin and Grant 1990; and West 1982. The symbolic dimension can be found in Anderson 1988; Campbell and Jamieson 1985; R. Hart 1984; McDiarmid 1937; Miller and Stiles 1986; C. Smith and K. Smith 1985; M. Smith et al. 1966; Stuckey 1991; Tetlock 1981; Williams and McCall 1983; and Zernicke 1990.

2. The citation is from Ragsdale's dissertation (Lyn Ragsdale, "Presidents and Publics: The Dialogue of Presidential Leadership, 1949–1979," Ph.D. Dissertation, University of Wisconsin-Madison, 1982).

3. In several instances, presidents did not issue State of the Union Addresses. This was sometimes a problem of newly elected presidents. In those cases, I substituted with a major national address presented close to the time that the State of the Union Address would normally be given. There are four such cases across this series: 1969, 1977,

1981, 1989. In each case, the outgoing president gave the State of the Union Address. The replacement speeches are Nixon's April 14, 1969, "Plan for Domestic Legislation" speech; Carter's February 27, 1977, "Report to the American People" speech; Reagan's February 21, 1981, "Economic Proposal" speech; and Bush's February 9, 1989, "Address to Congress and the Nation." The dates of each speech used are as follows:

February 2, 1953	State of the Union Address
January 7, 1954	State of the Union Address
January 6, 1955	State of the Union Address
January 3, 1956	State of the Union Address
January 10, 1957	State of the Union Address
January 9, 1958	State of the Union Address
January 9, 1959	State of the Union Address
January 7, 1960	State of the Union Address
January 30, 1961	State of the Union Address
January 11, 1962	State of the Union Address
January 14, 1963	State of the Union Address
January 8, 1964	State of the Union Address
January 4, 1965	State of the Union Address
January 12, 1966	State of the Union Address
January 10, 1967	State of the Union Address
January 17, 1968	State of the Union Address
April 14, 1969	Plan for Domestic Legislation
January 22, 1970	State of the Union Address
January 22, 1971	State of the Union Address
January 20, 1972	State of the Union Address
February 2, 1973	State of the Union Address
January 30, 1974	State of the Union Address
January 15, 1975	State of the Union Address
January 19, 1976	State of the Union Address
February 27, 1977	Report to the American People
January 19, 1978	State of the Union Address
January 27, 1979	State of the Union Address
January 23, 1980	State of the Union Address
February 21, 1981	Economic Proposal Text
January 26, 1982	State of the Union Address
January 25, 1983	State of the Union Address
January 25, 1984	State of the Union Address
February 6, 1985	State of the Union Address
February 4, 1986	State of the Union Address
January 27, 1987	State of the Union Address
January 28, 1988	State of the Union Address
February 9, 1989	Address to Congress and the Nation

4. Walker's distinction is actually more finely drawn. He suggests that policies can range from those that are required (the permanently recurring problems) to those that are sporadically recurring to crises and pressing problems and finally to discretionary problems. The last group is chosen by policymakers to deal with (1977, 424–25).

5. In 1969, outgoing President Johnson gave the State of the Union Address rather than, following the customary practice, Nixon. However, it is also traditional for incoming presidents to give a State of the Union-like speech early in their administrations. Nixon did so on April 14, 1969, but that speech focused only on domestic affairs; foreign policy matters were not mentioned other than in passing.

In 1971, Nixon attempted to create a two-address system, one for the foreign policy area, the other for all other areas, but only the domestic speech was televised with the fanfare of the typical State of the Union Address.

Figure 1 does not reveal the missing data points for the foreign affairs series for aesthetic reasons; instead it connects the points straddling the missing years. Analysis deletes 1969 and 1971 from the discussion of foreign affairs. Experimentation found that deleting the missing points, interpolating to create data points, or using the series average for the missing data points makes little difference in statistical estimation. Including or excluding 1969 and 1971 in the economic and civil rights series does not seem to affect analyses of those series either.

One would expect that the exclusion of foreign policy concerns would inflate the impact of economics and civil rights on these two speeches (1969 and 1971), but inspection of the series indicates no such effect. In fact, both economics and civil rights are somewhat suppressed as other concerns, like welfare reform and the environment, absorb more attention.

6. In these domestic policy data, I deleted one data point, 1971, because of the impact of Nixon's dual-address system on the domestic policy numbers. That year, because of the exclusion of foreign policy, domestic policy totaled over 85 percent of all mentions. This created an extreme outlier for domestic policy, though it had little impact on civil rights and economic policy. Thus, this data point is dropped from the analysis for domestic policy.

7. Historical accounts of the modern presidents provide evidence of their penchant for foreign over domestic policy. Giglio (1991) asserts that Kennedy's "greatest interest remained foreign affairs" (14), a policy area that he wanted to control. He wanted to "be his own secretary [of state]" (20), and consequently chose Dean Rusk, a career diplomat without a constituency. During his first year in office, Kennedy "stayed away from most departmental activities to concentrate on foreign affairs" (34–35).

On Nixon, Genovese (1990) states that Nixon took a special pride in foreign affairs (61) and did not "have the driving interest in economic policy that he did for foreign affairs" (62). Even Carter displayed more interest in foreign policy. He was "far more detached from the formulation of domestic policy than of foreign policy" (Hargrove 1988, 26–27). Bush clearly concentrated his efforts on foreign policy. To Bush, "foreign policy and national security are the paramount tasks of a president" (Thompson and Scavo 1992, 150). The cost of this attention was that he responded slowly to the economic downturn, which resulted in the criticism that he was inattentive to matters at home (Barilleaux 1992, 21).

8. Brace and Hinckley conceptualize presidential behavior within a pooled cross-sectional time series framework, where time point dummies address the time element and presidential dummies the cross sections. However, when analyzing annual data, like that used here, they drop the presidential dummy component. I, similarly, do not provide a full cross-sectional treatment, dropping the presidential dummies but retaining the time point dummies. Retaining all the presidential dummies eats up too many degrees of freedom, which is a problem in this data series that never has more than thirty-seven data points. Moreover, adding the full complement of presidential dummies into the equations would disrupt the meaning of the intercept. As used here, it refers to the criterion year, in this case year one of the president's term. Adding all the presidential dummies would also require leaving one presidential dummy out, and the intercept would become a combination of president and year one. This complicates analysis of the dummies. Lastly, the time point dummies have substantively interesting referents, while the presidential ones do not in this case. Still, I treat the presidential dummies on an individual basis adding them to the equations singularly and in combinations to see what impact they have. When they emerge as important variables, I note that in the presentation.

9. The Lagrange multiplier test is computed by regressing the equation's residuals on the lagged residuals plus all the independent variables. Multiplying the resulting R^2 by the equation n produces a statistic that can be tested for significance on a chi-square distribution. The critical values of the chi-square with one degree of freedom are 3.85 at 0.05 and 6.635 at 0.01. For more on this test see Maddala (1988, 85–86, 137–38, 206–7).

10. My use of the term *distributive* is not meant to imply distributive as Lowi means it. All I am signifying here is that politicians offered to "distribute" policies or political benefits to certain identifiable groups

11. There is one important objection to the analysis presented earlier, that both the dependent variable and independent variable of interest, public opinion, are both measured as levels. The relationship found between them for the economic and foreign policy equations could be just a matter of both series being correlated to a time trend. The sharing of such a trend could produce the results, not a true causal relationship between the variables. To check for this possibility, I converted the presidential attention and public opinion variables into change variables. The presidential variables become annual changes in presidential attention. The public opinion variables use the last reading prior to the president's speech and the reading immediately after the last presidential address. This represents something less than a year's change. I also used all of the controls from the previous equations.

The results indicate that presidential attention to foreign policy is still responsive to public opinion, but now in changes ($b = .50$, SE $= .27$, $t = 1.87$) and at magnitudes similar to that found earlier. Economic policy, however, now displays no responsiveness ($b = 16$, SE $= .14$, $t = 1.19$). But civil rights policy now demonstrates presidential responsiveness ($b = .20$, SE $= .11$, $t = 1.82$), and as before domestic policy shows no responsiveness to public opinion ($b = .001$, SE $= .08$, $t = .01$). (The statistics reported are from equations using all the control variables reported in table 2.2). Thus, we find presidential responsiveness again for two of the four equations but not as the discretionary-required policy area distinction predicts. This analysis, however, does reduce degrees of freedom by losing cases associated with creating the change variables.

And though the discretionary-required hypothesis might now be undermined, the basic point of presidential responsiveness at this stage of the policy-making process is found. Overall, the major point is that while we detect some presidential responsiveness in this early stage of the agenda-setting process, what is also notable is the weakness of the presidential response. I pick up on this theme later in this book.

12. This curvilinear response to political stimuli in mass publics was first suggested by Converse (1962) and later refined and elaborated upon by Zaller (1992).

13. Sketchy and limited evidence suggests that the president is able to influence the media, thereby weakening this effect (Iyengar and Kinder 1987, 124; Behr and Iyengar 1985).

14. Mass media effects are missing from this analysis. A substantial literature has documented the impact of the mass media on the public agenda using this Gallup series (Funkhouser 1973; MacKuen 1981; Behr and Iyengar 1985; Iyengar and Kinder 1987). I do not include mass media for several reasons. The most important has to do with assessing causality. We expect the president's Address to affect media content, which then affects public opinion. Including a media variable would obscure this presidential effect, confusing it with media affects. Had we been concerned with the causal impact of the mass media, inclusion of such a variable would be important. But our concern is with the causal impact of the president.

15. The use of the prior public opinion variable in the equation is similar to using a lagged dependent variable as an independent one. Thus, the standard Durbin-Watson's d is not appropriate. In its place I used the Durbin-Watson h (Pindyck and Rubinfeld 1981, 193–95). A stronger test for the presence of serial correlation is the Lagrange multiplier, which I also calculated. All tests indicate absence of seriality after using first order autocorrelation corrections when appropriate. See table 2.3 for details on each equation.

16. It is likely that the effect of war is being mediated by the presidential variable here; there is some correlation between presidential attention to foreign affairs and war.

17. This finding should be qualified by the following fact: when I changed the analysis to look at changes, rather than levels, I found presidential responsiveness to foreign policy, a required area, but also civil rights, a discretionary one.

Chapter 3

1. Presidents may also take positions on valence issues, issues over which there is no debate. In the State of the Union Address, the lack of policy specificity often makes it hard to distinguish valence positions from the more purely symbolic mentioning of a policy area. Moreover, the policy areas under scrutiny usually raised ideological divisions.

2. The literature on the trade-off between military and nonmilitary spending is quite

large. Several important studies find no trade-off between the two; rather they both increase together, at least in the pre-Reagan era (Russett 1982; Domke, Eichenberg, Kellerher 1983; Mintz 1989) and in the short run (Mintz and Huang 1991). These budgetary findings are consistent with the agenda findings reported here.

3. The Lagrange multiplier test indicated that some seriality may still be present after the AR1 correction, but that test was only significant, and marginally so, at the .05 level. Using a higher standard of .01 suggests no seriality.

4. The regression results indicate a negative intercept, which properly is not possible in the real world. To check whether this is causing a disruption in the regression results, I reestimated the equation with a Tobit procedure, which can force the dependent variable to be bound within the logical limits of 0 and 100 percent. The substantive results of the regression analysis remain intact.

5. Another possibility is that in the mass of relationships, we are bound, just by chance, to find some presidential responsiveness somewhere.

6. As I did in the previous chapter, I computed change equations as a further test. Thus, I regressed the annual change in presidential substantiveness against the host of variables found significant plus the measure of change in public opinion concern for the policy area in question. The change equations reinforce the interpretation of the levels equations. Of the four public opinion change variables used in the overall substantiveness equation, only one, civil rights concern, reveals any significant association with change in presidential substantiveness, and that effect is modest and barely statistically significant ($b = .69$, SE $= .40$, $t = 1.72$). On the four equations that looked at each policy area separately, none of the public opinion variables reached statistical significance. In fact, not one t value moved above 1.00.

Chapter 4

1. It seems highly unlikely that Congress will defeat a policy with strong public backing, but examples exist, including congressional reluctance to regulate firearms. Strong special interests in Congress can sometimes thwart popular support.

2. The literature on presidential use of the polls indicates that presidents aim more to lead public opinion than follow it when formulating policy options. See Edwards 1983, 16–18, for a good overview.

3. Two other studies that look at public opinion from a long historical perspective include T. Smith (1990) and Page and Shapiro (1992). Smith discusses the rise in liberalism in the American mass public from the 1930s on, but he does not present his data in a manner that would enable me to use them here. Page and Shapiro discuss opinions on many types of policies, focusing on stability and change. As I discuss later, Stimson's methodology, which extracts the "liberal" mood of the public, is the most appropriate for my purposes. In addition, his year-by-year presentation of the data makes them readily available for use.

4. The ADA has published two periodicals, the *ADA World* and *ADA Today*. They serve as these sources.

5. There are numerous other studies that use or analyze the ADA scores. Daniels (1989) finds that the ADA rating anchors the liberal end of a liberal-conservative

continuum. Also see Poole (1981) and S. Smith (1981), who use ADA and other interest group ratings to understand the dimensional structure of congressional roll call voting.

6. The quantitative data indicate that during the first-term downturn, Eisenhower moved left. His 1954 and 1955 scores were 62 and 50. By 1957, his economic score was 20, the highest of his last four years. In the recession of 1958, he made no rhetorical attempt to deal with the mounting unemployment problem. Neither did he make any policy moves.

7. The quantitative data actually show a shift to the right for Kennedy. His 1961 economic policy score was 81, in 1962 it was 58, and in 1963 it was 17. The shift to the right is accounted for by two facts. One, his tax cut proposal did not initially appeal to liberals. They wanted to deal with the looming economic slowdown through increased spending. Kennedy's tax cut proposal, though Keynesian, looked conservative. Only later did liberals come to adopt that position. Moreover, after the steel crisis, Kennedy's rhetoric moved right to bridge the gulf created by his actions against the steel industry.

8. This is a very different interpretation than that found in Shaffer 1980a. Shaffer contends that there was not much ideological difference between Kennedy and Carter, but Shaffer relies only on ADA roll call positions. Looking ahead to similar data that I present in chapter 6, Kennedy and Carter do look quite alike. However, these rhetorical data establish the difference between Carter and the liberal wing of his party, the wing for whom Kennedy served as standard-bearer in the late 1970s.

9. The constant also indicates that the public is on the average more liberal than the president by about "one-half of a percent." More important is that the constant is clearly statistically significant ($t = 2.85$).

10. In an unpublished paper, Durr and Stimson (1991) perform a similar analysis with a different measure of presidential liberalism. That measure is based on congressional roll calls and the behavior of presidential supporters in Congress. Their analysis, which also employs a control for presidential party, finds a statistically significant impact of public opinion on their measure of presidential liberalism ($b = .28, t = 2.33$). This result is similar to that reported here.

11. The sentence unit is quite common in content analyses such as this. It provides a grammatically whole unit, but one that is not too long to combine too much information, nor too short (such as words or phrases) that may provide incomplete or ambiguous information. Other content analyses that employ sentence units include Kessel (1974, 1977) and Smith and Smith (1985). Other content analyses include Hart (1984), Hinckley (word counts, 1990), Miller and Stiles (1986), Moen (word counts, 1988), O'Loughlin and Grant (word counts, 1990), Prothro (paragraphs, 1956), and Tetlock (1981).

12. Studies of mass opinions find no relationship between abortion and ideological leanings, self-placement, or other traditional liberal-conservative issues (see Erikson, Luttbeg, and Tedin 1991 and Cohen and Barrilleaux 1993). However, the abortion debates seem to cleave elites along liberal-conservative lines (Tribe 1989).

13. Change over time in the meanings and attachments of symbols and words also requires that we employ an intentional content analytic methodology.

14. In these papers, John Gates and I used presidential statements on civil rights as

an indicator of presidential policy preferences and then related those preferences to the civil rights decisions of justices that they appointed to the Supreme Court. Presidential preferences were found to be strongly predictive of later judicial behavior.

Chapter 5

1. From a different perspective but with similar implications, Edelman (1964, 22–43) argues that leaders manipulate political symbols during periods of threat, like war or economic distress, to increase their policy-making options.

2. See Brace and Hinckley (1992) for the rationale for including time point dummies in the estimation.

3. I also converted these variables into change terms, as I have done throughout. None of the change equations showed any impact on change in presidential ideology either.

4. Again, equations that looked at change in these variables with changes in presidential ideology revealed no impact.

5. This result holds with controls for party, the presidential dummy, and the time point dummies and whether the model is specified as levels or changes.

6. I also ran the equation controlling for the time point dummies. None had any impact. The presentation shows results without the time point dummies.

7. Again, time point dummies were added into the equation, but demonstrated no effect.

8. In chapter 1 I discussed the several different types of constituencies that presidents may have and the potential for conflict among those multiple constituencies. This party-public opinion example is a specification of that general proposition.

9. I did not use the effects variables in this analysis because statistical misinterpretation can occur if only a subset of the presidents is being used, as is the case here. Thus, dummy variables are more appropriate.

10. Many different functional specifications of this variable were created. One interacted the variable with public opinion lagged one year. Another used public opinion of the same year. Further, I entered both lagged and unlagged forms of these variables in the estimation. All forms and trials point in the same direction: no impact.

11. The intercorrelations (Pearson's r) across the four policy areas and with the overall indicator of presidential ideology are as follows:

Pearson's r of Presidential Ideology by Policy Area and with Overall Ideology

	Economic Policy	Foreign Policy	Civil Rights	Domestic Policy
Economic Policy	—	—	—	—
Foreign Policy	.28	—	—	—
Civil Rights	.39	.58	—	—
Domestic Policy	.69	.39	.55	—
Overall Liberalism	.62	.81	.70	.78

12. I repeated the change analysis for these equations and again I was unable to find a significant relationship between changes in public opinion and changes in presidential ideology by policy area.

13. Recall that the public opinion series is not scaled in percentages like the presidential rhetoric series. Thus, I cannot properly talk about percentage shifts in the public opinion series as I can for the rhetoric series. Still, since there is a scaled metric to the public opinion series that meets the criterion necessary for an interval-level variable, I can talk about movements of x points. These point movements should not be confused with percentage point changes.

14. However, one must be cautious in interpreting this finding. When I convert the public opinion and presidential ideology variables into change variables, as I have done in each previous analysis, and reestimate the equation, no public opinion effect was found. Thus, it might be the case that presidents and public opinion are both similarly liberal or conservative, but movement in public opinion does not move the president. Perhaps a third factor, like a secular trend, is pushing both in the same direction, and the causal ties from public opinion to presidential ideology are more modest than the levels analysis suggests.

Chapter 6

1. Of course, policy legitimation may occur in administrative processes through, for instance, the rulemaking process of administrative and regulatory agencies.

2. Both the Rivers and Rose (1985) and Ostrom and Simon (1985) studies are subject to serious methodological debate and criticism. See Bond and Fleisher (1990, 24–26) for a well taken critique of these studies.

3. Recall that Ostrom and Simon (1985) found that legislative success leads to increases in popularity, a finding that Brace and Hinckley (1992) also report.

4. Recall that the correlation between the roll call measure and the rhetorical measure of overall ideology is .85 (Pearson's, significance $p = .001$).

5. Other important analyses of congressional roll call voting that use the ADA scores include Poole 1981; Poole and Daniels 1985; Schneider 1979; Shaffer 1980a, 1980b; and Smith 1981.

6. Zupan (1992) has presented similar data and provides another justification for using this type of series. Unfortunately, I did not come upon his completed data series until after I had collected my data and begun analysis.

7. Correlations suggest that the roll call indicator is very highly correlated with each policy-specific ideology indicator, as well as with overall ideology:

Pearson's r correlations between presidential ADA roll call liberalism and
1. Economic policy liberalism: .56
2. Civil rights liberalism: .62
3. International relations liberalism: .70
4. Domestic policy liberalism: .80

The very high domestic policy liberalism correlation is probably due to the fact that the

ADA roll call index usually contains more of these types of votes than for any other policy area.

8. I adjust the presidential roll call series by subtracting fifty from each data point.

9. Or if both show inverse relationships, signifying counterresponsiveness.

10. The Pearson's r between lagged roll calls and nonlagged opinion is a paltry .003.

11. This should also hold for lame-duck presidents who aim to help their party successor win the office (e.g., Eisenhower-Nixon, 1960, and Reagan-Bush, 1988). There is some indication that successful two-term presidents view the election of a successor from their party as a mandate on how well they governed the nation. See Ambrose (1990, 519).

12. The b, SE, and t value for the minority control-public opinion interaction with controls for party, Eisenhower, rhetorical liberalism, and unemployment are $b = -.89$, SE $= .33$, $t = -2.67$.

13. The latent presidential liberalism measure is correlated (Pearson's r) with overall presidential ideology at .80.

Chapter 7

1. The first successful U.S. rocket, *Explorer I,* was launched on January 28, 1958.

2. In 1960 the Eisenhower administration was greatly embarrassed when U-2 pilot Gary Powers was shot down over the Soviet Union, thus proving that the United States was engaged in activities that for years it had denied.

Chapter 8

1. A few critics charge that the tax increases that resulted from the 1990 budget agreement were a factor in the economic slowdown.

2. In one amusing incident, Bush toured a supermarket and was amazed to discover the price scanner, a device that had been installed in supermarkets for several years. This and his lack of carrying cash, widened the perceived barrier between him and the people.

3. These and the following figures are taken from *Congressional Quarterly Weekly Report,* January 25, 1992, 161.

4. The text of the message is in *Congressional Quarterly Weekly Report,* October 19, 1991, 3074.

5. A late January 1993 poll by CNN-*USA Today* found that 58 percent said they were aware of the campaign promise versus 42 percent who said they were not aware. What the actual level of awareness was during the campaign is unclear, for by the time of the poll the president was already talking about the issue and it was being covered in press reports.

6. A Gallup poll in January 1993 found that 52 percent said that Clinton was taking his position on gays and the military because of liberal and gay organization pressure. In contrast, only 39 percent saw it as a matter of principle to the president.

7. New Democrats were a group of moderate Democrats, heavily southern, who

tended to stand for stronger defense than did traditional liberals in the party. They were still liberal on social policy, but on economic policy they shied away from the tax-and-spend syndrome of which they accused traditional liberalism. In its place was their aim to tame government and make it more efficient, while retaining the populism so inherent among Democrats.

References

Aberbach, Joel D., and Bert A. Rockman. 1988. "Mandates or Mandarins? Control and Discretion in the Modern Administrative State." *Public Administration Review* 48:606–12.

Achen, Christopher H. 1978. "Measuring Representation." *American Journal of Political Science* 22:475–510.

Aldrich, John H. 1993. "Presidential Selection." In *Researching the Presidency: Vital Questions, New Approaches,* edited by George C. Edwards III, John H. Kessel, and Bert A. Rockman. Pp. 23–67. Pittsburgh: University of Pittsburgh Press.

Aldrich, John H., John L. Sullivan, and Eugene Borgida. 1989. "Foreign Affairs and Issue Voting: Do Presidential Candidates 'Waltz before a Blind Audience?'" *American Political Science Review* 83:123–42.

Altschuler, Bruce E. 1990. *LBJ and the Polls.* Gainesville: University of Florida Press.

Ambrose, Stephen E. 1990. *Eisenhower: Soldier and President.* New York: Simon and Schuster.

Anderson, Dwight G. 1988. "Power, Rhetoric, and the State: A Theory of Presidential Legitimacy." *Review of Politics* 50:198–214.

Appelbome, Peter. 1993. "Homosexual Issue Galvanizes Conservative Foes of Clinton." *New York Times,* 1 February.

Arnold, R. Douglas. 1990. *The Logic of Congressional Action.* New Haven: Yale University Press.

Arterton, F. Christopher. 1987. *Teledemocracy: Can Technology Protect Democracy?* Newbury Park, CA: Sage.

Barber, James David. 1972. *The Presidential Character: Predicting Performance in the White House.* Englewood Cliffs, NJ: Prentice-Hall.

Barilleaux, Ryan J. 1992. "George Bush and the Changing Context of Presidential Leadership." In *Leadership and the Bush Presidency: Prudence or Drift in an Era of Change?* edited by Ryan J. Barilleaux and Mary E. Stuckey. Pp. 3–23. Westport, CT: Praeger.

Baumgartner, Frank R., and Bryan D. Jones. 1993. *Agendas and Instability in American Politics.* Chicago: University of Chicago Press.

Beck, Paul Allen, and M. Kent Jennings. 1979. "Political Periods and Political Participation." *American Political Science Review* 73:737–50.

Behr, Roy L., and Shanto Iyengar. 1985. "Television News, Real-World Cues, and Changes in the Public Agenda." *Public Opinion Quarterly* 49:38–57.

Berke, Richard. 1993. "A Gay-Rights President Is at a Loss for Words." *New York Times,* 4 April.

Berman, Larry, and Bruce W. Jentleson. 1991. "Bush and the Post-Cold War World: New Challenges for American Leadership." In *The Bush Presidency: First Appraisals,* edited by Colin Campbell and Bert A. Rockman. Pp. 93–128. Chatham, NJ: Chatham House.

Bernstein, Irving, 1991. *Promises Kept: John F. Kennedy's New Frontier.* New York: Oxford University Press.

Bernstein, Robert A. 1988. "Do U. S. Senators Moderate Strategically?" *American Political Science Review* 82:237–41.

Bierce, William B. 1974. "A New Era in International Aviation: CAB Regulation, Rationalization and Restrictions on the North Atlantic." *New York University Journal of International Law and Politics* 7:317–60.

Bond, Jon R., and Richard Fleisher. 1990. *The President in the Legislative Arena.* Chicago: University of Chicago Press.

Brace, Paul, and Barbara Hinckley. 1992. *Follow the Leader: Opinion Polls and the Modern Presidency.* New York: Basic Books.

———. 1993. "Presidential Activities from Truman through Reagan: Timing and Impact." *Journal of Politics* 55:382–98.

Brock, Clifton. 1962. *Americans for Democratic Action: Its Role in National Politics.* Washington, DC: Public Affairs Press.

Brody, Richard A. 1991. *Assessing the President: The Media, Elite Opinion, and Public Support.* Stanford, CA: Stanford University Press.

Brody, Richard A., and Lee Sigelman. 1983. "Presidential Popularity and Presidential Elections: An Update and Extension." *Public Opinion Quarterly* 47:325–28.

Brunner, Ronald D., and Katherine M. Livornese. 1984. "The President's Annual Message." *Congress and the Presidency* 11:37–58.

Burke, John P. 1992. *The Institutional Presidency.* Baltimore: Johns Hopkins University Press.

Calder, James D. 1982. "Presidents and Crime Control: Kennedy, Johnson, and Nixon and the Influence of Ideology." *Presidential Studies Quarterly* 12 (fall):574–89.

Campbell, Colin. 1986. *Managing the Presidency: Carter, Reagan, and the Search for Administrative Harmony.* Pittsburgh: University of Pittsburgh Press.

Campbell, Karlyn Kohrs, and Kathleen Hall Jamieson. 1985. "Inaugurating the Presidency." *Presidential Studies Quarterly* 15:394–411.

Carmines, Edward G., and James A. Stimson. 1989. *Issue Evolution: Race and the Transformation of American Politics.* Princeton, NJ: Princeton University Press.

Carter, Jimmy. 1982. *Keeping Faith: Memoirs of a President.* New York: Bantam.

Ceaser, James W. 1985. "The Rhetorical Presidency Revisited." In *Modern Presidents and the Presidency,* edited by Marc Landy. Pp. 15–34. Lexington, MA: Lexington.

Ceaser, James W., Glen E. Thurow, Jeffrey Tulis, and Joseph M. Bessette. 1981. "The Rise of the Rhetorical Presidency." *Presidential Studies Quarterly* 11:158–71.

Champagne, Anthony, and Edward J. Harpham, eds. 1984. *The Attack on the Welfare State.* Prospect Heights, IL: Waveland.

Chang, Tsan-Kuo. 1989. "The Impact of Presidential Statements on Press Editorials

Regarding U. S. China Policy, 1950–1984." *Communication Research* 16:486–509.

Chester, Edward W. 1980. "Beyond the Rhetoric: A New Look at Presidential Inaugural Addresses." *Presidential Studies Quarterly* 10:571–82.

Citrin, Jack, and Donald Philip Green. 1986. "Presidential Leadership and the Resurgence of Trust in Government." *British Journal of Political Science* 16:431–53.

Clausen, Aage. 1973. *How Congressmen Decide.* New York: St. Martin's.

Cobb, Roger W., and Charles D. Elder. 1972. *Participation in American Politics: The Dynamics of Agenda-Building.* Baltimore: Johns Hopkins University Press.

Cobb, Roger W., Jeannie-Keith Ross, and Marc Howard Ross. 1976. "Agenda Building as a Comparative Political Process." *American Political Science Review* 70:126–38.

Cohen, Jeffrey E. 1980. "Presidential Personality and Political Behavior: Theoretical Issues and an Empirical Test." *Presidential Studies Quarterly* 10:588–99.

———. 1988. *The Politics of the U. S. Cabinet: Representation in the Executive Branch, 1789–1984.* Pittsburgh: University of Pittsburgh Press.

Cohen, Jeffrey E., and Charles Barrilleaux. 1993. "Public Opinion, Interest Groups, and Public Policy Making: Abortion Policy in the American States." In *Understanding the New Politics of Abortion,* edited by Malcolm L. Goggin. Pp. 203–21. Newbury Park, CA: Sage.

Cohen, Michael D., James G. March, and Johan P. Olsen. 1972. "A Garbage Can Model of Organizational Choice." *Administrative Science Quarterly* 17:1–25.

Cohen, Richard E. 1993. "Democratic Salvage Operation on Nafta." *National Journal,* 18 September, p. 2259.

———. 1993. "Clinton's Nafta Team Battling Uphill." *National Journal,* 11 November, p. 2674.

Converse, Philip E. 1962. "Information Flow and the Stability of Partisan Attitudes." *Public Opinion Quarterly* 26:578–99.

———. 1964. "The Nature of Belief Systems in Mass Publics." In *Ideology and Discontent,* edited by David E. Apter. New York: Free Press.

Cook, Fay Lomax, and Edith J. Barrett. 1988. "Public Support for Social Security." *Journal of Aging Studies* 2:339–56.

Covington, Cary R. 1987a. "Mobilizing Congressional Support for the President: Insights from the 1960s." *Legislative Studies Quarterly* 22:77–95.

———. 1987b. "'Staying Private': Gaining Congressional Support for Unpublicized Presidential Preferences on Roll Calls." *Journal of Politics* 49:737–55.

Cox, Gary W., and Mathew D. McCubbins. 1993. *Legislative Leviathan: Party Government in the House.* Berkeley: University of California Press.

Cronin, Thomas E. 1980. *The State of the Presidency.* 2d ed. Boston: Little Brown.

Dahl, Robert A. 1990. "Myth of the Presidential Mandate." *Political Science Quarterly* 103:355–72.

Daniels, R. Steven. 1989. "Rehabilitating the Raters: An Assessment of Interest Group Ratings of Congress." *Congress and the Presidency* 16:23–36.

Davidson, Roger H. 1969. *The Role of the Congressman.* New York: Pegasus.

Davidson, Roger H., and Walter J. Oleszek. 1990. *Congress and Its Members.* 3d ed. Washington, DC: Congressional Quarterly Press.

Derthick, Martha, and Paul J. Quirk. 1985. *The Politics of Deregulation.* Washington, DC: Brookings.

Destler, I. M. 1988. "Reagan and the World: An 'Awesome Stubbornness.'" In *The Reagan Legacy: Promise and Performance,* edited by Charles O. Jones. Pp. 241–61. Chatham, NJ: Chatham House.

Divine, Robert A. 1993. *The Sputnik Challenge.* New York: Oxford University Press.

Dixon, William J., and Stephen M. Gaarder. 1992. "Presidential Succession and the Cold War: An Analysis of Soviet-American Relations, 1948–1988." *Journal of Politics* 54:156–75.

Domke, William K., Richard C. Eichenberg, and Catherine M. Kelleher. 1983. "The Illusion of Choice: Defense and Welfare in Advanced Industrial Democracies, 1948–1978." *American Political Science Review* 77:19–35.

Downs, Anthony. 1972. "Up and Down with Ecology: The Issue Attention Cycle." *The Public Interest* 28:38–50.

Duffy, Michael, and Dan Goodgame. 1992. *Marching in Place: The Status Quo Presidency of George Bush.* New York: Simon and Schuster.

Durant, Robert F. 1992. *The Administrative Presidency Revisited: Public Lands, the BLM, and the Reagan Revolution.* Albany: State University of New York Press.

Durr, Robert H. 1993. "What Moves Policy Sentiment?" *American Political Science Review* 87:158–70.

Durr, Robert H., and James A. Stimson. 1991. "Public Policy and Public Mood." Paper presented at the 1991 American Political Science Association Meeting.

Edelman, Murray. 1964. *The Symbolic Uses of Politics.* Urbana: University of Illinois Press.

———. 1974. "The Politics of Persuasion." In *Choosing the President,* edited by James David Barber. Pp. 149–73. Englewood Cliffs, NJ: Prentice-Hall.

Edwards, George C., III. 1983. *The Public Presidency: The Pursuit of Popular Support.* New York: St. Martin's.

———. 1989. *At the Margins: Presidential Leadership of Congress.* New Haven: Yale University Press.

———. 1991. "George Bush and the Public Presidency: The Politics of Inclusion." In *The Bush Presidency: First Appraisals,* edited by Colin Campbell and Bert A. Rockman. Pp. 129–54. Chatham, NJ: Chatham House.

———. 1995. "Frustration and Folly: Bill Clinton and the Public Presidency." In *The Clinton Presidency: First Appraisals,* edited by Colin Campbell and Bert A. Rockman. Pp. 234–61. Chatham, NJ: Chatham House.

Edwards, George C., III, and Stephen J. Wayne. 1990. *Presidential Leadership: Politics and Policy Making.* 2d ed. New York: St. Martin's.

Elder, Charles D., and Roger W. Cobb. 1983. *The Political Uses of Symbols.* New York: Longman.

Elling, Richard C. 1982. "Ideological Change in the United States Senate: Time and Electoral Responsiveness." *Legislative Studies Quarterly* 7:75–92.

Erikson, Robert S., Norman R. Luttbeg, and Kent L. Tedin. 1991. *American Public Opinion: Its Origins, Content, and Impact.* 4th ed. New York: MacMillan.

Erikson, Robert S., and Kent L. Tedin. 1995. *American Public Opinion: Its Origins, Content, and Impact.* 5th ed. New York: MacMillan.

Fenno, Richard F. 1978. *Home Style: House Members in Their Districts.* Boston: Little, Brown.

Flash, Edward S. 1972. "Conversion of Kennedy from Economic Conservative to Economic Liberal." In *J. F. Kennedy and Presidential Power,* edited by Earl Latham. Pp. 76–81. Lexington, MA: D. C. Heath.

Fowler, Linda L. 1982. "How Interest Groups Select Issues for Rating Voting Records of Members of the U. S. Congress." *Legislative Studies Quarterly* 7:401–13.

Friedrich, Robert. 1982. "In Defense of Multiplicative Terms in Multiple Regression Equations." *American Journal of Political Science* 26:797–833.

Funkhouser, G. R. 1973. "The Issues of the Sixties: An Exploratory Study in the Dynamics of Public Opinion." *Public Opinion Quarterly* 37:62–75.

Gates, John B., and Jeffrey E. Cohen. 1988. "Presidents, Supreme Court Justices, and Racial Equality Cases: 1954–1984." *Political Behavior* 10:22–36.

———. 1989. "Presidential Policy Preferences and Supreme Court Appointment Success." *Policy Studies Review* 8:800–812.

Genovese, Michael A. 1990. *The Nixon Presidency: Power and Politics in Turbulent Times.* Westport, CT: Greenwood.

Germond, Jack, and Jules Witcover. 1993a. "Clinton's Gays-in-the-Military Snare." *National Journal,* 3 April, p. 836.

———. 1993b. "Draft Issue Is Still Haunting Clinton." *National Journal,* 15 May, p. 1196.

Giglio, James N. 1991. *The Presidency of John F. Kennedy.* Lawrence: University Press of Kansas.

Gillon, Steven M. 1987. *Politics and Vision: The ADA and American Liberalism, 1947–1985.* New York: Oxford University Press.

Goggin, Malcolm L. 1984. "The Ideological Content of Presidential Communications: The Message-Tailoring Hypothesis." *American Politics Quarterly* 12:361–84.

Gottschalk, Peter T. 1988. "Retrenchment in Antipoverty Programs in the United States: Lessons for the Future." In *The Reagan Revolution?* edited by B. B. Kymlicka and Jean V. Matthews. Pp. 131–45. Chicago: Dorsey.

Greenstein, Fred I. 1974. "What the President Means to Americans: Presidential 'Choice' Between Elections." In *Choosing the President,* edited by James David Barber. Pp. 121–47. Englewood Cliffs, NJ: Prentice-Hall.

———. 1982. *The Hidden-Hand Presidency: Eisenhower as Leader.* New York: Basic Books.

Greenstein, Fred I., ed. 1988. *Leadership in the Modern Presidency.* Cambridge, MA: Harvard University Press.

Grossman, Michael Baruch, and Martha Joynt Kumar. 1981. *Portraying the President: The White House and the News Media.* Baltimore: Johns Hopkins University Press.

Hackworth, David H. 1993. "Rancor in the Ranks: The Troops vs. the President." *Newsweek,* 28 June, 121:24.

Hager, Gregory, and Terry Sullivan. 1994. "President-centered and Presidency-centered Explanations of Presidential Public Activity." *American Journal of Political Science* 38:1079–1103.

Hargrove, Erwin C. 1988. *Jimmy Carter as President: Leadership and the Politics of the Public Good.* Baton Rouge: Louisiana State University Press.

Hargrove, Erwin C., and Michael Nelson. 1984. *Presidents, Politics, and Policy.* New York: Alfred A. Knopf.

Hart, Roderick P. 1984. "The Language of the Modern Presidency." *Presidential Studies Quarterly* 14:249–64.

———. 1987. *The Sound of Leadership: Presidential Communication in the Modern Age.* Chicago: University of Chicago Press.

Heclo, Hugh. 1974. *Modern Social Politics in Britain and Sweden.* New Haven: Yale University Press.

———. 1975. "OMB and the Presidency—The Problem of Neutral Competence." *The Public Interest* 38:80–98.

Herzik, Eric B., and Mary L. Dodson. 1982. "The President and Public Expectations: A Research Note." *Presidential Studies Quarterly* 13:168–73.

Hibbs, Douglas A., Jr. 1987. *The American Political Economy: Macroeconomics and Electoral Politics.* Cambridge, MA: Harvard University Press.

Hinckley, Barbara. 1990. *The Symbolic Presidency: How Presidents Portray Themselves.* New York: Routledge.

Hodges, Tony. 1976. "The Struggle for Angola: How the World Powers Entered a War in Africa." *Round Table* 66:173–84.

Hoxie, R. Gordon. 1983. "Eisenhower and Presidential Leadership." *Presidential Studies Quarterly* 13:589–612.

Huntington, Samuel C. 1968. *Political Order in Changing Societies.* New Haven: Yale University Press.

———. 1973. "Congressional Responses to the Twentieth Century." In *Congress and America's Future,* 2d ed., edited by David Truman. Pp. 6–38. Englewood Cliffs, NJ: Prentice-Hall.

Ignatius, David. 1988. "Reagan's Foreign Policy and the Rejection of Diplomacy." In *The Reagan Legacy,* edited by Sidney Blumenthal and Thomas Byrne Edsall. Pp. 173–212. New York: Pantheon Books.

Ingold, Beth A., and Theodore Otto Windt Jr. 1984. "Trying to "Stay the Course": President Reagan's Rhetoric during the 1982 Election." *Presidential Studies Quarterly* 14:87–97.

Iyengar, Shanto, and Donald R. Kinder. 1987. *News That Matters: Television and American Opinion.* Chicago: University of Chicago Press.

Jackson, John E., and John W. Kingdon. 1992. "Ideology, Interest Groups, and Legislative Votes." *American Journal of Political Science* 36:805–23.

Jacobs, Lawrence R., and Robert Y. Shapiro. 1994. "Issues, Candidate Image, and Priming: The Use of Private Polls in Kennedy's 1960 Presidential Campaign." *American Political Science Review* 88:527–40.

———. 1995a. "The Rise of Presidential Polling: The Nixon White House in Historical Perspective." *Public Opinion Quarterly* 59:163–95.

———. 1995b. "Public Opinion in President Clinton's First Year: Leadership and

Responsiveness." In *The Clinton Presidency: Campaigning, Governing, and the Psychology of Leadership,* edited by Stanley A. Renshon. Pp. 195–211. Boulder, CO: Westview Press.

Jones, Charles O. 1988. *The Trusteeship Presidency: Jimmy Carter and the United States Congress.* Baton Rouge: Louisiana State University Press.

———. 1991. "Meeting Low Expectations: Strategy and Prospects of the Bush Presidency." In *The Bush Presidency: First Appraisals,* edited by Colin Campbell and Bert A. Rockman. Pp. 37–67. Chatham, NJ: Chatham House.

Kallenbach, Joseph E. 1975. "The Presidency and the Constitution: A Look Ahead." In *The Presidency in Contemporary Context,* edited by Norman C. Thomas. Pp. 33–54. New York: Dodd, Mead.

Kahn, Michael A. 1992. "Shattering the Myth about President Eisenhower's Supreme Court Appointments." *Presidential Studies Quarterly* 22:47–56.

Kaufman, Burton I. 1993. *The Presidency of James Earl Carter.* Lawrence: University Press of Kansas.

Kearns, Doris. 1976. *Lyndon Johnson and the American Dream.* New York: Signet.

Keefe, William J., and Morris S. Ogul. 1989. *The American Legislative Process: Congress and the States.* 7th ed. Englewood Cliffs, NJ: Prentice-Hall.

Kelley, Stanley Jr. 1983. *Interpreting Elections.* Princeton, NJ: Princeton University Press.

Kemp, Kathleen. 1981. "Symbolic and Strict Regulation in the American States." *Social Science Quarterly* 62:516–26.

Kenski, Henry C. 1992. "A Man for All Seasons? The Guardian President and His Public." In *Leadership and the Bush Presidency: Prudence or Drift in an Era of Change?* edited by Ryan J. Barilleaux and Mary E. Stuckey. Pp. 91–114. Westport, CT: Praeger.

Kernell, Samuel. 1993. *Going Public: New Strategies of Presidential Leadership.* 2d ed. Washington, DC: Congressional Quarterly Press.

Kessel, John H. 1974. "Parameters of Presidential Politics." *Social Science Quarterly* 55:8–24.

———. 1977. "Seasons of Presidential Politics." *Social Science Quarterly* 58:418–35.

King, Gary, Robert O. Keohane, and Sidney Verba. 1994. *Designing Social Inquiry: Scientific Inference in Qualitative Research.* Princeton, NJ: Princeton University Press.

King, Gary, and Lyn Ragsdale. 1988. *The Elusive Executive: Discovering Statistical Patterns in the Presidency.* Washington, DC: Congressional Quarterly Press.

Kingdon, John W. 1984. *Agendas, Alternatives, and Public Policies.* Boston: Little, Brown.

Klingberg, F. L. 1952. "The Historical Alternation of Moods in American Foreign Policy." *World Politics* 4:239–73.

Krippendorf, Klaus. 1980. *Content Analysis: An Introduction to its Methodology.* Beverly Hills, CA: Sage.

Krukones, Michael. G. 1980. "Predicting Presidential Performance through Political Campaigns." *Presidential Studies Quarterly* 10:527–43

———. 1985. "The Campaign Promises of Jimmy Carter: Accomplishments and Failures." *Presidential Studies Quarterly* 15:136–44.

Kuklinski, James H. 1978. "Representativeness and Elections: A Policy Analysis." *American Political Science Review* 72:165–77.

Lammers, William W. 1981. "Presidential Press Conference Schedules: Who Hides and When." *Political Science Quarterly* 96:261–78.

Langston, Thomas S. 1992. *Ideologues and Presidents: From the New Deal to the Reagan Revolution.* Baltimore: Johns Hopkins University Press.

Lehne, Richard. 1993. *Industry and Politics: United States in Comparative Perspective.* Englewood Cliffs, NJ: Prentice-Hall.

Light, Paul C. 1982. *The President's Agenda: Domestic Policy Choice from Kennedy to Carter.* Baltimore: Johns Hopkins University Press.

———. 1985. *Artful Work: The Politics of Social Security Reform.* New York: Random House.

———. 1993. "Presidential Policy Making." In *Researching the Presidency: Vital Questions, New Approaches,* edited by George C. Edwards III, John H. Kessel, and Bert A. Rockman. Pp. 161–99. Pittsburgh: University of Pittsburgh Press.

Lipset, Seymour Martin, and William Schneider. 1983. *The Confidence Gap: Business, Labor, and Government in the Public Mind.* New York: Free Press.

———. 1987. "The Confidence Gap during the Reagan Years, 1981–1987." *Political Science Quarterly* 102:1–23.

Lowell, A. Lawrence. 1902. "The Influence of Party upon Legislation." *Annual Report of the American Historical Association for 1901* 1:321–545.

Lowi, Theodore J. 1985. *The Personal President: Power Invested, Promise Unfulfilled.* Ithaca, NY: Cornell University Press.

MacKuen, Michael B. 1981. "Social Communication and the Mass Policy Agenda." In *More Than News: Media Power in Public Affairs,* edited by Michael MacKuen and Steven Coombs. Pp. 19–44. Beverly Hills, CA: Sage.

———. 1983. "Political Drama, Economic Conditions, and the Dynamics of Presidential Popularity." *American Journal of Political Science* 27:165–92.

Maddala, G. S. 1988. *Introduction to Econometrics.* New York: MacMillan.

Malecha, Gary Lee, and Daniel J. Reagan. 1992. "George Bush and Congress: The Question of Leadership." In *Leadership and the Bush Presidency: Prudence or Drift in an Era of Change?* edited by Ryan J. Barilleaux and Mary E. Stuckey. Pp. 59–80. Westport, CT: Praeger.

Mannheim, Jarol B. 1979. "Presidential Leadership of Public Opinion: Does the Tail Wag the Dog?" Paper presented at the 1979 American Political Science Association Meeting.

Marshall, Thomas R. 1993. "Symbolic versus Policy Representation on the U.S. Supreme Court." *Journal of Politics* 55:140–50.

Mayer, William G. 1993. *The Changing American Mind.* Ann Arbor: University of Michigan Press.

Mayhew, David R. 1974. *Congress: The Electoral Connection.* New Haven: Yale University Press.

McClosky, Herbert. 1958. "Conservatism and Personality." *American Political Science Review* 52:27–45.

McClure, Charles E., Jr. 1990. "Reagan's Tax Policy." In *Looking Back on the Reagan*

Presidency, edited by Larry Berman. Pp. 156–71. Baltimore: Johns Hopkins University Press.

McCullough, David. 1992. *Truman.* New York: Simon and Schuster.

McDiarmid, J. 1937. "Presidential Inaugural Addresses—A Study in Verbal Symbols." *Public Opinion Quarterly* 1:79–82.

McDonald, Forrest. 1994. *The American Presidency.* Lawrence: University Press of Kansas.

McKay, David. 1989. *Domestic Policy and Ideology: Presidents and the American State, 1964–1987.* Cambridge: Cambridge University Press.

McNiven, James D. 1988. "'Ron, Reaganism, and Revolution.' The Rise of the New American Political Economy." In *The Reagan Revolution?* edited by B. B. Kymlicka and Jean V. Matthews. Pp. 54–64. Chicago: Dorsey.

Milkis, Sidney M. 1993. *The President and the Parties: The Transformation of the American Party System since the New Deal.* New York: Oxford University Press.

Miller, Lawrence, and Lee Sigelman. 1978. "Is the Audience the Message? A Note on LBJ's Vietnam Statements." *Public Opinion Quarterly* 42:71–80.

Miller, Nancy L., and William B. Stiles. 1986. "Verbal Familiarity in American Presidential Nomination Acceptance Speeches and Inaugural Addresses (1920–1981)." *Social Psychology Quarterly* 49:72–81.

Mintz, Alex. 1989. "'Guns' vs. 'Butter': A Disaggregated Analysis." *American Political Science Review* 83:1285–93.

Mintz, Alex, and Chi Huang. 1991. "Guns versus Butter: The Indirect Link." *American Journal of Political Science* 35:738–57.

Miroff, Bruce. 1982. "Monopolizing the Public Space: The President as a Problem for Democratic Politics." In *Rethinking the Presidency,* edited by Thomas Cronin. Pp. 218–32. Boston: Little, Brown.

———. 1990. "The Presidency and the Public: Leadership as Spectacle." In *The Presidency and the Political System,* 3d ed., edited by Michael Nelson. Pp. 289–313. Washington, DC: Congressional Quarterly Press.

Mishler, William, and Reginald S. Sheehan. 1993. "The Supreme Court as Countermajoritarian Institution? The Impact of Public Opinion on Supreme Court Decisions." *American Political Science Review* 87:87–101.

Moe, Terry M. 1985. "The Politicized Presidency." In *The New Direction in American Politics,* edited by John E. Chubb and Paul E. Peterson. Pp. 235–71. Washington, DC: Brookings.

Moen, Mathew C. 1988. "The Political Agenda of Ronald Reagan: A Content Analysis of the State of the Union Messages." *Presidential Studies Quarterly* 18:775–85.

Moen, Matthew C., and Kenneth T. Palmer. 1992. "'Poppy' and His Conservative Passengers." In *Leadership and the Bush Presidency: Prudence or Drift in an Era of Change?* edited by Ryan J. Barilleaux and Mary E. Stuckey. Pp. 133–46. Westport, CT: Praeger.

Mondak, Jeffrey J. 1993. "Source Cues and Policy Approval: The Cognitive Dynamics of Public Support for the Reagan Agenda." *American Journal of Political Science* 37:186–212.

Mueller, John. 1970. "Presidential Popularity from Truman to Johnson." *American Political Science Review* 64:18–34.

Nathan, Richard P. 1983. *The Administrative Presidency.* New York: John Wiley.

Neustadt, Richard E. 1955. "Presidency and Legislation: Planning the President's Program." *American Political Science Review* 49:980–1021.

———. 1960. *Presidential Power: The Politics of Leadership.* New York: John Wiley.

———. 1990. *Presidential Power and the Modern Presidents: The Politics of Leadership from Roosevelt to Reagan.* New York: Free Press.

Niskanen, William A. 1988. "Reflections on Reaganomics." In *The Reagan Revolution?* edited by B. B. Kymlicka and Jean V. Matthews. Pp. 104–8. Chicago: Dorsey.

Nixon, Richard M. 1978. *RN: The Memoirs of Richard Nixon.* Vol. 1. New York: Warner Books.

O'Loughin, John, and Richard Grant. 1990. "The Political Geography of Presidential Speeches, 1946–87." *Annals of the Association of American Geographers* 80:504–30.

Ostrom, Charles W., Jr., and Brian Job. 1986. "The President and the Political use of Force." *American Political Science Review* 80:541–66.

Ostrom, Charles W., Jr., and Dennis M. Simon. 1985. "Promise and Performance: A Dynamic Model of Presidential Popularity." *American Political Science Review* 79:334–58.

———. 1989. "The Man in the Teflon Suit: The Environmental Connection, Political Drama, and Popular Support in the Reagan Presidency." *Public Opinion Quarterly* 53:353–87.

———. 1988. "The President's Public." *American Journal of Political Science* 32:1096–119.

Page, Benjamin I. 1976. "The Theory of Political Ambiguity." *American Political Science Review* 70:742–52.

———. 1978. *Choices and Echoes in Presidential Elections: Rational Man and Electoral Democracy.* Chicago: University of Chicago Press.

Page, Benjamin I., and Robert Y. Shapiro. 1983. "Effects of Public Opinion on Policy." *American Political Science Review* 77:175–90.

———. 1984. "Presidents as Opinion Leaders: Some New Evidence." *Policy Studies Journal* 12:649–61.

———. 1985. "Presidential Leadership through Public Opinion." In *The Presidency and Public Policy Making,* edited by George C. Edwards III, Steven A. Shull, Norman C. Thomas. Pp. 22–36. Pittsburgh: University of Pittsburgh Press.

———. 1989. "Educating and Manipulating the Public." In *Manipulating Public Opinion: Essays on Public Opinion as a Dependent Variable,* edited by Michael Margolis and Gary A. Mauser. Pp. 294–320. Pacific Grove, CA: Brooks/Cole.

———. 1992. *The Rational Public: Fifty Years of Trends in Americans' Policy Preferences.* Chicago: University of Chicago Press.

Page, Benjamin I., Robert Y. Shapiro, and Glenn R. Dempsey. 1987. "What Moves Public Opinion?" *American Political Science Review* 81:23–43.

Parker, Glenn R. 1986. *Homeward Bound: Explaining Changes in Congressional Behavior.* Pittsburgh: University of Pittsburgh Press.

Pastor, Robert A. 1990. "The Centrality of Central America." In *Looking Back on the Reagan Presidency,* edited by Larry Berman. Pp. 33–49. Baltimore: Johns Hopkins University Press.

Peterson, Mark A. 1990. *Legislating Together: The White House and Capitol Hill from Eisenhower to Reagan.* Cambridge, MA: Harvard University Press.

———. 1992. "The Presidency and Organized Interests: White House Patterns of Interest Group Liaison." *American Political Science Review* 86:612–25.

Peterson, Mark A., and Jack L. Walker. 1986. "Interest Group Responses to Partisan Change: The Impact of the Reagan Administration upon the National Interest Group System." In *Interest Group Politics,* 2d ed., edited by Allan J. Cigler and Burdett A. Loomis. Pp. 162–82. Washington, DC: Congressional Quarterly Press.

Peterson, Paul E., and Mark Rom. 1988. "Lower Taxes, More Spending, and Budget Deficits." In *The Reagan Legacy: Promise and Performance,* edited by Charles O. Jones. Pp. 213–40. Chatham, NJ: Chatham House.

Pfiffner, James P. 1988. *The Strategic Presidency: Hitting the Ground Running.* Chicago: Dorsey.

Phelps, Glenn A. 1989. "George Washington: Precedent Setter." In *Inventing the American Presidency,* edited by Thomas Cronin. Pp. 259–81. Lawrence: University Press of Kansas.

Pika, Joseph A. 1991. "Opening the Doors for Kindred Souls: The White House Office of Public Liaison." In *Interest Group Politics,* 3d ed., edited by Allan J. Cigler and Burdett A. Loomis. Pp. 277–98. Washington, DC: Congressional Quarterly Press.

Pindyck, Robert S., and Daniel L. Rubinfeld. 1981. *Econometric Models and Econometric Forecasts.* 2d ed. New York: McGraw-Hill.

Polsby, Nelson W. 1983. *The Consequences of Party Reform.* New York: Oxford University Press.

Poole, Keith T. 1981. "Dimensions of Interest Group Evaluations of the U. S. Senate, 1969–1978." *American Journal of Political Science* 25:49–67.

Poole, Keith T., and R. Steven Daniels. 1985. "Ideology, Party, and Voting in the U. S. Congress, 1959–1980." *American Political Science Review* 79:373–99.

Prothro, James W. 1956. "Verbal Shifts in the American Presidency: A Content Analysis." *American Political Science Review* 50:726–50.

Putnam, Robert D. 1973. *The Beliefs of Politicians: Ideology, Conflict, and Democracy in Britain and Italy.* New Haven: Yale University Press.

Quirk, Paul J. 1991. "What Do We Know and How Do We Know It? Research on the Presidency." In *Political Science: Looking to the Future,* edited by William Crotty. Pp. 37–65. Evanston, IL: Northwestern University Press.

Ragsdale, Lyn. 1984. "The Politics of Presidential Speechmaking, 1949–1980." *American Political Science Review* 78:971–84.

———. 1987. "Presidential Speechmaking and the Public Audience: Individual Presidents and Group Attitudes." *Journal of Politics* 49:704–36.

Reeves, Richard. 1993. *President Kennedy: Profile of Power.* New York: Touchstone.

Reichley, A. James. 1981. *Conservatives in an Age of Change: The Nixon and Ford Administrations.* Washington, DC: Brookings.

Reiter, Howard L. 1985. *Selecting the President: The Nominating Process in Transition.* Philadelphia: University of Pennsylvania Press.

Rivers, Douglas, and Nancy L. Rose. 1985. "Passing the President's Program: Public Opinion and Presidential Influence in Congress." *American Journal of Political Science* 29:183–96.

Robinson, Michael J. 1981. "Three Faces of Congressional Media." In *The New Congress,* edited by Thomas E. Mann and Norman J. Ornstein. Pp. 55–96. Washington, DC: American Enterprise Institute.

Rockman, Bert A. 1984. *The Leadership Question: The Presidency and the American System.* New York: Praeger.

Rohde, David W. 1991. *Parties and Leaders in the Post-Reform House.* Chicago: University of Chicago Press.

Rose, Richard. 1991. *The Postmodern President.* 2d ed. Chatham, NJ: Chatham House.

Rosen, Corey M. 1973. "A Test of Presidential Leadership of Public Opinion: The Split-ballot Technique." *Polity* 6:282–90.

Russett, Bruce M. 1982. "Defense Expenditures and National Well-Being." *American Political Science Review* 76:767–77.

Sabatier, Paul A. 1991. "Public Policy: Toward Better Theories of the Policy Process." In *Political Science: Looking toward the Future,* edited by William Crotty. Vol. 2. Pp. 265–92. Evanston, IL: Northwestern University Press.

Schneider, William. 1993a. "Nafta Has the White House Spooked." *National Journal,* 21 August, p. 2112.

———. 1993b. "Why Clinton Played the Perot Card." *National Journal,* 13 November, p. 2756.

Seligman, Lester G., and Cary Covington. 1989. *The Coalitional Presidency.* Chicago: Dorsey.

Shaffer, William R. 1980a. "A Discriminant Function Analysis of Position-Taking: Carter vs. Kennedy." *Presidential Studies Quarterly* 10: 451–68.

———. 1980b. *Party and Ideology in the United States Congress.* Lanham, MD: University Press of America.

———. 1989. "Rating the Performance of the ADA in the U. S. Congress." *Western Political Quarterly* 42:33–51.

Shelley, Mack C., II. 1983. *The Permanent Majority: The Conservative Coalition in the United States Congress.* University: University of Alabama Press.

Shepsle, Kenneth A. 1972. "The Strategy of Ambiguity: Uncertainty and Electoral Competition." *American Political Science Review* 66:555–68.

Shull, Steven A. 1983. *Domestic Policy Formation: Presidential-Congressional Partnership?* Westport, CT: Greenwood.

———. 1989. *The President and Civil Rights Policy: Leadership and Change.* Westport, CT: Greenwood.

———. 1993. *A Kinder, Gentler Racism? The Reagan-Bush Civil Rights Legacy.* Armonk, NY: M. E. Sharpe.

Sigelman, Lee. 1980. "Gauging the Public Response to Presidential Leadership." *Presidential Studies Quarterly* 10:427–33.

Sigelman, Lee, and Carol K. Sigelman. 1981. "Presidential Leadership of Public Opinion: From 'Benevolent Leader' to 'Kiss of Death'?" *Experimental Study of Politics* 7:1–22.

Simon, Dennis M., and Charles W. Ostrom Jr. 1985. "The President and Public Support: A Strategic Perspective." In *The Presidency and Public Policy Making*, edited by George C. Edwards III, Steven A. Shull, Norman C. Thomas. Pp. 50–70. Pittsburgh: University of Pittsburgh Press.

———. "The Politics of Prestige: Popular Support and the Modern Presidency." *Presidential Studies Quarterly* 18:741–59.

———. 1989. "The Impact of Televised Speeches and Foreign Travel on Presidential Approval." *Public Opinion Quarterly* 53:58–82.

Skowronek, Stephen. 1982. *Building a New American State: The Expansion of National Administrative Capacities, 1877–1920.* New York: Cambridge University Press.

———. 1993. *The Politics Presidents Make: Leadership from John Adams to George Bush.* Cambridge, MA: Belknap.

Slonim, Shlomo. 1989. "Designing the Electoral College." In *Inventing the American Presidency*, edited by Thomas Cronin. Pp. 33–60. Lawrence: University Press of Kansas.

Smith, Craig Allen, and Kathy B. Smith. 1985. "Presidential Values and Public Priorities: Recurrent Patterns in Addresses to the Nation, 1963–1984." *Presidential Studies Quarterly* 15:743–53.

Smith, Eric R. A. N., Richard Herrera, and Cheryl L. Herrera. 1990. "The Measurement Characteristics of Congressional Roll-Call Indexes." *Legislative Studies Quarterly* 15:283–95.

Smith, Marshall S., Philip J. Stone, and Evelyn N. Glenn. 1966. "A Content Analysis of Twenty Presidential Nomination Acceptance Speeches." In *The General Inquirer*, edited by Philip J. Stone, Dexter C. Dunphy, Marshall S. Smith, and Daniel J. M. Ogilvie. Pp. 359–400. Cambridge, MA: MIT Press.

Smith, Steven S. 1981. "The Constituency and Ideological Structure of U. S. Senate Voting Alignments, 1957–1976." *American Journal of Political Science* 25:780–95.

Smith, Tom W. 1990. "Liberal and Conservative Trends in the United States since World War II." *Public Opinion Quarterly* 54:479–507.

Snyder, James M., Jr. 1992. "Artificial Extremism in Interest Group Ratings." *Legislative Studies Quarterly* 17:319–46.

Sorauf, Frank J., and Paul Allen Beck. 1988. *Party Politics in America.* 6th ed. New York: HarperCollins.

Sperlich, Peter W. 1969. "Bargaining and Overload: An Essay on *Presidential Power.*" In *The Presidency*, edited by Aaron Wildavsky. Pp. 168–92. Boston: Little, Brown.

Spitzer. Robert J. 1993. *President and Congress: Executive Hegemony at the Crossroads of American Government.* Philadelphia: Temple University Press.

Stanley, Harold, and Richard Niemi. 1994. *Vital Statistics on American Politics.* 4th ed. Washington, DC: Congressional Quarterly Press.

Stein, Herbert. 1972. "Tax Cut in Camelot." In *J. F. Kennedy and Presidential Power,* edited by Earl Latham. Pp. 81–94. Lexington, MA: D. C. Heath.

Stern, Mark. 1989a. "Presidential Strategies and Civil Rights: Eisenhower, the Early Years, 1952–54." *Presidential Studies Quarterly* 19:769–95.

———. 1989b. "John F. Kennedy and Civil Rights: From Congress to the Presidency." *Presidential Studies Quarterly* 19:797–823.

———. 1992. *Calculating Visions: Kennedy, Johnson, and Civil Rights.* New Brunswick, NJ: Rutgers University Press.

Stevens, Sayre. 1988. "The Star Wars Challenge." In *The Reagan Revolution?* edited by B. B. Kymlicka and Jean V. Matthews. Pp. 167–79. Chicago: Dorsey.

Stimson, James A. 1991. *Public Opinion in America: Moods, Cycles, and Swings.* Boulder, CO: Westview.

Stimson, James A., Michael B. MacKuen, and Robert S. Erikson. 1994. "Opinion and Policy: A Global View." *PS: Political Science and Politics* 27:29–34.

———. 1995. "Dynamic Representation." *American Political Science Review* 89:543–65.

Stokes, Bruce. 1993. "Mexican Roulette." *National Journal,* 15 May, pp. 1160–64.

———. 1993. "A Hard Sell." *National Journal,* 16 October, pp. 2472–76.

Stone, Deborah A. 1988. *Policy Paradox and Political Reason.* Glenview, IL: Scott, Foresman.

Stuckey, Mary E. 1991. *The President as Interpreter-in-Chief.* Chatham, NJ: Chatham House.

Sullivan, Terry. 1990. "Bargaining with the President: A Simple Game and New Evidence." *American Political Science Review* 84:1167–96.

Tetlock, Philip E. 1981. "Pre- to Postelection Shifts in Presidential Rhetoric: Impression Management or Cognitive Adjustment?" *Journal of Personality and Social Psychology* 41:207–12.

Thomas, Dan B., and Larry R. Bass. 1982. "Presidential Identification and Mass-public Compliance with Official Policy: The Case of the Carter Energy Program." *Policy Studies Journal* 10:448–64.

Thomas, Dan B., and Lee Sigelman. 1985. "Presidential Identification and Policy Leadership: Experimental Evidence on the Reagan Case." In *The Presidency and Public Policy Making,* edited by George C. Edwards III, Steven A. Shull, Norman C. Thomas. Pp. 37–49. Pittsburgh: University of Pittsburgh Press.

Thomas, Martin. 1985. "Electoral Proximity and Senatorial Roll Call Voting." *American Journal of Political Science* 29:96–111.

Thompson, Robert J., and Carmine Scavo. 1992. "The Home Front: Domestic Policy in the Bush Years." In *Leadership and the Bush Presidency: Prudence or Drift in an Era of Change?* edited by Ryan J. Barilleaux and Mary E. Stuckey. Pp. 149–64. Westport, CT: Praeger.

Tobin, James. 1988. "Reaganomics in Retrospect." In *The Reagan Revolution?* edited by B. B. Kymlicka and Jean V. Matthews. Pp. 85–103. Chicago: Dorsey.

Towell, Pat. 1992. "Roles for Women, Homosexuals among Clinton's First Tests." *Congressional Quarterly Weekly Report* 50:3679.

———. 1993a. "Campaign Promise, Social Debate Collide on Military Battlefield." *Congressional Quarterly Weekly Report* 51:226–29.

———. 1993b. "Nunn Offers a Compromise: 'Don't Ask/Don't Tell.'" *Congressional Quarterly Weekly Report* 51:1240–42.

Tribe, Laurence H. 1990. *Abortion: The Clash of Absolutes.* New York: W. W. Norton.

Tufte, Edward R. 1978. *Political Control of the Economy.* Princeton, NJ: Princeton University Press.

Tulis, Jeffrey K. 1987. *The Rhetorical Presidency.* Princeton, NJ: Princeton University Press.

Vogel, David. 1989. *Fluctuating Fortunes: The Political Power of Business in America.* New York: Basic Books.

Wahlke, John C., Heinz Eulau, William C. Buchanan, and Leroy C. Ferguson. 1962. *The Legislative System: Explorations in Legislative Behavior.* New York: John Wiley.

Walcott, Charles E., and Karen M. Hult. 1995. *Governing the White House from Hoover through LBJ.* Lawrence: University Press of Kansas.

Walker, Jack L. 1977. "Setting the Agenda in the U. S. Senate." *British Journal of Political Science* 7:423–45.

Waterman, Richard W. 1989. *Presidential Influence and the Administrative State.* Knoxville: University of Tennessee Press.

Wayne, Stephen J. 1982. "Expectations of the President." In *The President and the Public,* edited by Doris Graber. Pp. 17–38. Philadelphia: Institute for the Study of Human Affairs.

Weatherford, M. Stephen. 1987. "The Interplay of Ideology and Advice of Economic Policy-Making: The Case of Political Business Cycles." *Journal of Politics* 49:925–52.

Weatherford, M. Stephen, and Lorraine M. McDonnell. 1985. "Macroeconomic Policymaking Beyond the Electoral Constraint." In *The Presidency and Public Policy Making,* edited by George C. Edwards III, Steven A. Shull, Norman C. Thomas. Pp. 95–113. Pittsburgh: University of Pittsburgh Press.

———. 1990. "Ideology and Economic Policy." In *Looking Back on the Reagan Presidency,* edited by Larry Berman. Pp. 122–55. Baltimore: Johns Hopkins University Press.

Weaver, R. Kent. 1988. "Social Policy in the Reagan Era." In *The Reagan Revolution?* edited by B. B. Kymlicka and Jean V. Matthews. Pp. 146–61. Chicago: Dorsey.

Weber, Robert Philip. 1985. *Basic Content Analysis.* Beverly Hills, CA: Sage.

West, Darrell M. 1982. "Rhetoric and Agenda-Setting in the 1980 Presidential Campaign." *Congress and the Presidency* 9:1–21.

Wilcox, Clyde, and Robin Wolpert. 1995. "President Clinton, Public Opinion, and Gays in the Military." Paper presented at the 1995 Midwest Political Science Association Meeting.

Williams, Steven D., and Charles H. McCall. 1983. "The Presidency and Rhetorical Absolutism." Paper presented at the 1983 Southern Political Science Association Meeting.

Wilson, Woodrow. 1908. *Constitutional Government in the United States.* New York: Columbia University Press.

Wood, B. Dan. 1987. "Bureaucrats, Principals, and Responsiveness: The Case of the Clean Air Act." *American Political Science Review* 82:213–34.

Woodward, Bob. 1995. *The Agenda: Inside the White House.* New York: Pocket Books.

Wright, Gerald C., and Michael Berkman. 1986. "Candidates and Policy in United States Senate Elections." *American Political Science Review* 80:567–90.

———. 1988. "Do U. S. Senators Moderate Strategically." *American Political Science Review* 82:241–45.

Zaller, John R. 1992. *The Nature and Origins of Mass Opinion.* New York: Cambridge University Press.

Zernicke, Paul Haskell. 1990. "Presidential Roles and Rhetoric." *Political Communication and Persuasion* 7:231–45.

Zuckman, Jill. 1991a. "Congress Clears Benefits Bills, But Funding Is Unlikely." *Congressional Quarterly Weekly Report,* 3 August, 49:2164–65.

———. 1991b. "Democrats Vow to Battle Bush on Unemployment Benefits." *Congressional Quarterly Weekly Report,* 14 September, 49:2628.

———. 1991c. "Showdown Expected with Bush over Unemployment Benefits." *Congressional Quarterly Weekly Report,* 21 September, 49:2693–94.

———. 1991d. "Bush's Perfect Veto Record Faces Its Severest Test." *Congressional Quarterly Weekly Report,* 28 September, 49:2784–85.

———. 1991e. "Unemployment Bill Feels Tug of Presidential Campaign." *Congressional Quarterly Weekly Report,* 5 October, 49:2868–69.

———. 1991f. "Jobless Benefits Deal Crumbles after Bush Seeks Compromise." *Congressional Quarterly Weekly Report,* 2 November, 49:3205–6.

———. 1991g. "House Nearing a Compromise on Jobless Benefits Bill." *Congressional Quarterly Weekly Report,* 9 November, 49:3282–83.

———. 1991h. "Jobs Benefits Bill Cleared after Hard-fought Deals." *Congressional Quarterly Weekly Report,* 16 November, 49:3383–84.

———. 1991i. "Increase in Jobless Benefits Has White House Approval." *Congressional Quarterly Weekly Report,* 23 November, 49:3462.

———. 1992a. "Unemployment Benefits Debate Hinges on Financing Plan." *Congressional Quarterly Weekly Report,* 25 January, 50:175.

———. 1992b. "White House, Congress Move to Extend Jobless Benefits." *Congressional Quarterly Weekly Report,* 1 February, 50:252.

———. 1992c. "Bill to Extend Jobless Benefits Rushes to Enactment." *Congressional Quarterly Weekly Report,* 8 February, 50:312–13.

———. 1992d. "Disputes But No Direction on Jobless Benefits Bill." *Congressional Quarterly Weekly Report,* 2 May, 50:1164–65.

———. 1992e. "Jobless Benefits Reform Bill Draws Add-Ons, GOP Fire." *Congressional Quarterly Weekly Report,* 9 May, 50:1256–57.

———. 1992f. "Downsized Jobless Benefits Bill Emerges with Reforms Intact." *Congressional Quarterly Weekly Report,* 23 May, 50:1449–50.

———. 1992g. "Senate OKs Extended Benefits for Jobless; Conference Next." *Congressional Quarterly Weekly Report,* 20 June, 50:1811.

———. 1992h. "Bush Relents, Agrees to Sign Jobless Benefits Extension." *Congressional Quarterly Weekly Report,* 4 July, 50:1961–63.

Zupan, Mark A. 1992. "Measuring the Ideological Preferences of U. S. Presidents: A Proposed (Extremely Simple) Method." *Public Choice* 73:351–61.

Index